WITHDRAWN

Classic Reds

D1565488

CLASSIC SPORTS
Jonathan Knight, Series Editor

Classic Bucs: The 50 Greatest Games in Pittsburgh Pirates History
David Finoli

Classic Steelers: The 50 Greatest Games in Pittsburgh Steelers History
David Finoli

Classic Browns: The 50 Greatest Games in Cleveland Browns History
Second Edition, Revised and Updated
Jonathan Knight

Classic Cavs: The 50 Greatest Games in Cleveland Cavaliers History
Second Edition, Revised and Updated
Jonathan Knight

Classic Pens: The 50 Greatest Games in Pittsburgh Penguins History
Second Edition, Revised and Updated
David Finoli

Classic Bengals: The 50 Greatest Games in Cincinnati Bengals History
Steve Watkins and Dick Maloney

Classic 'Burgh: The 50 Greatest Collegiate Games in Pittsburgh Sports History
David Finoli

Classic Reds: The 50 Greatest Games in Cincinnati Reds History
Joe Heffron and Jack Heffron

Classic Reds

THE 50 GREATEST GAMES
IN CINCINNATI REDS HISTORY

Joe Heffron and Jack Heffron

BLACK SQUIRREL BOOKS®

Kent, Ohio

BLACK SQUIRREL BOOKS®

Frisky, industrious black squirrels are a familiar sight on the Kent State University campus and the inspiration for Black Squirrel Books®, a trade imprint of The Kent State University Press. www.KentStateUniversityPress.com.

All photos appear courtesy of the Cincinnati Reds and the Cincinnati Reds Hall of Fame and Museum.

Cataloging information is available at the Library of Congress.

23 22 21 20 19   5 4 3 2 1

For our parents and for Bob,
who enjoyed so many Reds games with us

Contents

Foreword
JEFF BRANTLEY

Growing up in Hoover, Alabama, I know the idea of being a Reds fan seems rather far-fetched. Back in the 1970s, my dad and I seemed to always find time to listen to Reds Radio and the Big Red Machine. We could pick up the games on WLW during the evening hours, but only on the car radio, and only when the car was moving. As long as the car eased up and down the driveway, we could hear Marty and Joe loud and clear. Many times, much to the dismay of my mom, my dad and I would take a plate of dinner out to the driveway so we could listen in on a Big Red Machine night. I have so many memories of learning to love baseball with my dad by my side—and all from a car radio.

This was the time in my life that not only did I listen to Reds baseball, but I also began to dream of actually being a baseball player. Most afternoons after school, I would come home and pull out my glove and a baseball to play in the driveway. We had a brick wall between the two garage doors, and I picked out a few bricks on the wall that would simulate the strike zone. I began to get pretty good at hitting those same bricks over and over and fielding the ball as it bounced back toward me. Before long I was not only Don Gullett on the mound, striking out the best in the National League, but I also pretended to be Marty Brennaman, announcing those strikeouts. I can only imagine what my mom thought about her son, not only throwing a ball against a brick wall repeatedly, but also talking to himself while doing it.

There weren't too many individual games that stuck with me over the years, but the nature by which those Reds played surely did. I'll never forget the hustle of Pete Rose, the bat pump of Joe Morgan, the slick glove of Concepcion. It always seemed as though no human could steal a base against the mighty Johnny Bench, and if the Reds ever had to have a big hit it came from Tony Perez. There was no team in baseball in my mind that could stand up to the Big Red Machine, especially in my driveway.

From Hoover, Alabama, on to Mississippi State, baseball continued to consume seemingly my every thought and action. I never lost sight of my favorite team, even as I made it to the major leagues with the San Francisco Giants.

I was quite enamored by the thought of playing in Cincinnati, even though my first game in the Queen City came in a Giants uniform. I remember my first view of the lights of the city, Riverfront Stadium, the names . . . oh, the names that had played here. My first game at Riverfront was by far the worst statistical day of my baseball playing career, including Little League. On the mound I was the 10-year-old boy in the driveway trying to strike out legends, and it was a very rough day.

Six years later, I put on my first Reds uniform, and I was in Riverfront. Putting on that uniform for the first time meant to me I had finally arrived, even though I had been a major league pitcher for six years. I was a Red, and there was a duty to uphold, a tradition, the Big Red Machine standard. And, as if that was not enough, my pitching coach with the Reds was none other than Don Gullet.

Now I sit almost every evening next to the man who was in my car every night in Alabama. No, it's not my dad; he's with the Lord now. It's Marty Brennaman, and I am privileged to be his broadcast partner, hoping to bring Reds baseball into the hearts of many as he did for me.

Every Reds fan should be able to relive memories of baseball both before and after the Big Red Machine. I believe that this book will help you relive some of those familiar moments from all eras of Reds baseball. Baseball provides timeless memories for all of us with our family and friends, and I know as you move through these pages your heart will forever be grateful.

Acknowledgments

Our series editor Jonathan Knight deserves our deepest thanks, for his vision and his patience. The Classic series is his idea, and we're grateful that he came to us to do the Reds book for the series. The structure and approach are his ideas. We simply tried our best to execute his vision.

We also owe a lot of gratitude to Chris Eckes, curator at the Cincinnati Reds Hall of Fame and Museum. As he's done on so many earlier projects, Chris took time from his demanding job to offer advice, as well as helping us round up photos. His smart, genial, generous nature always makes the work so much easier to do. Thanks, Chris!

Jeff Brantley was very kind to provide the foreword for the book. Having the viewpoint of someone who played in a couple of the 50 greatest games, and who has been a lifelong Reds fan, is invaluable.

Thanks to Jack Greiner, Reds fan extraordinaire, for his review of our game selections. Many thanks are also due to our good friends Joe Jacobs and Steve Watkins, excellent sportswriters and longtime followers of the boys in red.

As we did on our previous Reds book, we relied on Michael Heffron for technical support, and we appreciate his time. Designer and friend Steve Sullivan kindly helped improve the quality of the photos, performing the high level of magic we've come to expect. Thanks, too, to the great folks at Kent State University Press, especially editor Will Underwood, who work diligently to keep the Classics series available to sports fans.

Thanks, too, to the Society for American Baseball Research, for supporting baseball research and making available databases that ease the process of digging into the past of our national pastime.

Finally, doing a book like this one requires a lot of time for research and writing, and we are grateful to Amy Pelicano and to Mary and Anne Marie Heffron for their limitless patience throughout the process. While our heads were buried deep in the past, they kept the day-to-day wheels turning for us. Thank you.

Introduction

In the concourse surrounding Great American Ball Park, the Reds have erected bronze statues to honor some of the greatest players in team history—Frank Robinson and Johnny Bench, Big Klu and Little Joe, Tony Perez. Fans can stand next to the Old Left-hander pitching to Ernie Lombardi. And there's a bronze belly-sliding Pete Rose. These statues pay tribute not only to the players, but also to the team's history. In Reds country, the baseball roots run deep. That's why the team operates a first-class hall of fame and museum right next to the ballpark.

Cincinnatians take pride in claiming baseball's first all-professional team, which played its first game in 1869. But if fans remember recent stars such as Barry Larkin and Eric Davis, many don't know players with names like Bumpus, Bubbles, and Noodles, who had their own moments of glory in a Reds uniform.

It's easy for players and moments to disappear in a history that spans 150 years. Picking the 50 greatest games in this vast history is, we'll admit, nearly impossible. Ranking them is just as difficult—fodder for debate in bars and on blogs, no doubt, but an inexact science.

First, you have to determine what you mean by "great." We decided to define "great" as "historically significant." The first game at Redland Field in 1912 was no nail-biter and offered no heroics, but it marked the first time the Reds played in what would be their home park for more than 50 years. Thus: historically significant. Put it on the list.

For teams not named Yankees and Dodgers, every postseason game is historically significant to a major-league franchise; however, rather than fill the top 50 with all of them, we chose a single game from each postseason series to represent the whole. So, no, you won't find Game Six of the 1975 World Series—surely a great one—but for the Reds, Game Seven was far more important, giving the organization its first world championship in 35 years.

Games also make our list due to an individual player's accomplishment, even if the game itself wasn't especially important to the team or to that season's pennant race. The Reds finished last in the Central Division in 2017, and the game on June 6 with the St. Louis Cardinals was a lopsided contest, but in it Scooter Gennett hit four home runs—more than any Reds player ever hit in a game. Only 15 players in the modern era have ever accomplished this feat. Thus, the game must make the list.

We hope you enjoy the book and that it sparks a lot of debate. Arguing about Reds history is part of being a Reds fan. Call us crazy, if you want. Make a list of your own. Recall the games you attended. And enjoy what we hope is a unique way of telling the great story of the Cincinnati Reds—through the games that have mattered most.

#50

Base Ball Is Back!

Cincinnati had spent five years without a professional team by 1876. When newspapers reported that a new one would begin play in the new National League, jubilation ensued in the Queen City. The first all-professional team was formed in Cincinnati, back in 1869, a fact that still swells the city with pride today. It disbanded, however, after the 1870 season, rather than join the National Association of Professional Base Ball Players, the first all-professional league, which began play in 1871. For various reasons, all of them financial, the Cincinnati Red Stockings ceased to exist. George and Harry Wright, who had formed the team, headed for Boston to form a team there.

Despite the lack of a professional team, Cincinnati remained baseball-crazy, and many local amateur clubs took up the slack. During the summer of 1875, Cincinnatian John Joyce, who had been the official secretary of the original Red Stockings, put together a new independent professional club, gathering investors and players. In August of that year, the team started playing exhibition games, and a month later opened its home field, which became known as Avenue Grounds. When big-city teams started making plans for a new league, Cincinnati was ready to join.

Backed by wealthy meatpacker Josiah Keck, the Cincinnati Red Stockings became charter members of the new National League, along with teams from Boston, New York, Philadelphia, Hartford, Chicago, Louisville, and St. Louis. Many of the teams had played in the National Association and were further along in their development, while Cincinnati's roster was quickly assembled. The owners hired Charlie Gould, who had played on the original 1869 Red Stockings, to manage and play first base. He brought in second baseman Charles Sweasy, also a Red Stockings alum. Beyond those two, the Cincinnati players didn't have a whole lot of professional experience. How could they hope to compete against organizations that had been operating for five years?

The local newspapers, however, strongly supported the venture. The *Cincinnati Enquirer* proclaimed, "If the present club is not as strong as Harry Wright's old team, it is not far behind it." Cincinnati "base ball" fans read daily reports of the "good work" the team displayed while preparing for the first official league game, scheduled on April 25, 1876, at Avenue Grounds. The new Red Stockings would meet the St. Louis Brown Stockings and surely continue the legacy of success the previous incarnation had begun. More than 2,000 people showed up to celebrate the return of professional baseball to the Queen City, creating a tradition of Opening Day celebrations that carries on today.

Though a spring rain had blown through the day before, the *Enquirer* described the weather as "pleasant" for the first game. The field, for the most part, was dry, except for an obvious puddle in deep left field. Bursting with civic pride, the newspaper gushed that Avenue Grounds was "acknowledged to be the finest ball-field in the United States." Not only did it offer an attractive grandstand, but patrons could also pull their carriages into the outfield area to watch the game.

Following the league's rule at the time, a coin flip determined which team batted first. The Red Stockings won the honor. Shortstop Henry Kessler stepped to the plate—and professional baseball in the National League was underway in Cincinnati. Kessler struck out, an inauspicious beginning.

The Red Stockings, however, were just getting started. Third baseman Amos Booth, a native of nearby Lebanon, followed Kessler by slapping a single, as did Gould and right fielder Bobby Clark. With the bases loaded, center fielder Charley Jones, who would become the most popular star of the team, singled to bring in the first Reds run in National League history. Jones played for the team until 1878 and then returned in 1883 to play until 1887.

Behind the pitching of Cherokee Fisher, the Red Stockings held a 1–0 lead until the fourth inning, when St. Louis evened the score with a single and a triple. The game remained tied until the eighth inning, a low score, given the way baseball was played in that era. The pitcher's mound was only 45 feet from home plate, and pitchers underhanded the ball with the goal of initiating play rather than striking out hitters. Fielders didn't wear gloves, leading to frequent errors that led to more runs.

In the eighth, Kessler reached third base. Booth then knocked him in, giving the lead back to Cincinnati. During that first season, Booth was the team's second leading hitter, behind Jones; the *Enquirer* claimed that his defense during that first game was "as fine and sharp fielding as was ever seen on a ball field."

The Red Stockings tried to add to their lead in the ninth inning but failed when Jones was thrown out at the plate trying to score on a hit. In the bottom of the ninth, Fisher retired the side in order to give the new Cincinnati ball club a 2–1 victory in its first game in National League history. After winning the second game of the season two days later, the team appeared to be far better than expected, occupying first place. Cincinnati fans had gotten used to the winning ways of the original Red Stockings, who had won 81 games in a row, and their new team looked capable of carrying on that tradition.

The team's true capabilities, however, quickly revealed themselves. The Red Stockings chalked up their first loss in game three, and then lost the next one. After posting their third victory of the season, they lost the next 11 in a row. They broke the losing streak by beating Hartford, but proceeded to lose the following 13 games. Later in the season, they lost 18 in a row. The Red Stockings ended the season in the cellar with a 9–56 record. By June of the next season, the team was teetering on bankruptcy, but new investors arrived to salvage the franchise after a three-week layoff. If Cincinnati fans weren't crazy about their new team's record of wins and losses, they still were happy that professional baseball had returned to the city. And within two years, the Red Stockings would be among the top teams in the National League.

Cincinnati	1	0	0	0	0	0	0	1	0	—	2
St. Louis	0	0	0	1	0	0	0	0	0	—	1

Cincinnati Red Stockings

	AB	R	H
Kessler ss	4	1	1
Booth 3b	4	1	1
Gould 1b	4	0	1
Clack rf	4	0	1
Jones cf	4	0	2
Snyder lf	4	0	1
Sweasy 2b	4	0	1
Pierson c	4	0	0
Fisher p	3	0	0
Totals	35	2	8

St. Louis Brown Stockings

	AB	R	H
Cuthbert lf	4	0	0
Clapp c	4	0	1
McGeary 2b	4	0	0
Pike cf	4	1	1
Blong rF	4	0	0
Battin 3b	4	0	2
Bradley p	3	0	0
Dehlman 1b	3	0	0
Mack ss	3	0	0
Totals	33	1	4

Umpire: Mr. Honiz
Time of game: 2:05

#49

No Bubbly for Bubbles

As hot September winds blew across National League ball fields, three teams remained locked in fierce combat, each clawing for the pennant. The defending league champion Pittsburgh Pirates weren't letting go without a fight, and with future Hall of Famers Pie Traynor, Paul Waner, and Kiki Cuyler in their lineup and 20-game-winners Ray Kremer and Lee Meadows on the mound, they were a formidable force. The slugging St. Louis Cardinals—led by second baseman Rogers Hornsby, one of the greatest hitters of all time—along with pitchers Jesse Haines, Flint Rhem, and Grover Cleveland Alexander, also had their minds set on finishing first. Standing toe-to-toe with these teams—the Cincinnati Reds.

During the first half of the Roaring Twenties, the Reds roared plenty loud, finishing in the first division with a winning record six times. The pitching staff was strong, led by Hall of Famer Eppa Rixey, Dolf Luque, and Pete Donohue. Hall of Fame center fielder Edd Roush, one of the top hitters of the era, spearheaded an aggressive offense that included catcher Bubbles Hargrave, and outfielders Curt Walker and, in 1926, one-year wonder Cuckoo Christensen. That year, manager Jack Hendricks also relied on a deep bench, frequently calling on versatile utility player Rube Bressler and outstanding rookie prospect Ethan Allen. Red Lucas led the relief corps, which included a journeyman with the unlikely name of Pea Ridge Day. The Reds had finished third in 1925 and fought hard to take the next step the next year.

A hot streak in early May, during which they posted a 12–2 record, put them in first place. They held the top spot from May 14 until July 27, when four straight losses bumped them to second place. It took a month to grab back the top perch, and for the next month the Reds and Cardinals traded the league lead on an almost daily basis, while the Pirates sat in third place, waiting for a chance to strike. Neither the Reds nor Cardinals gave them one.

A seven-game winning streak in mid-September put the Reds back in first place. They were slogging through a long eastern road trip, with 20 games scheduled from September 8 through September 25. On September 16, the Reds met the Giants in New York. Despite the winning streak, they led the Cardinals by just a half game. This game, like every game as the season neared the end, was a must-win.

Pete Donohue took the mound for the Reds. A big Texan, he was the team's workhorse in 1926, pitching 285⅔ innings in 36 starts, while also serving in relief down the stretch when sore arms depleted the staff. The Reds jumped out to a lead in the top of the first when speedy left fielder Christensen beat out an infield hit and took second base on a bad throw.

Christensen, a 26-year-old rookie, was the talk of the league that year, finishing second in hitting with a .350 average and first with a .426 OBP. A little guy with a big sense of humor, he delighted fans with an arsenal of on-field antics, such as turning somersaults after making a catch. A poor sophomore season put him back in the minor leagues, where he spent the rest of his career.

Christiansen scored on right fielder Curt Walker's single to right. Donohue allowed a few singles, but no Giants made it to second base (and wouldn't reach scoring position the entire game). In the top of the fourth inning, Reds third baseman Chuck Dressen doubled. Giants pitcher Virgil Barnes then walked second baseman Hughie Critz and Hargrave to load the bases. Shortstop Hod Ford—a much-needed, late-season pickup—shot a base hit into left field, bringing Dressen and Critz across home plate.

Staked to a 3–0 lead, Donohue continued to dominate, retiring 15 batters in a row before surrendering a single with one out in the eighth. The Giants lineup included Hall of Famers Bill Terry and Frankie Frisch; however, Donohue, pitching on three days rest, the most he'd had in a while, retired one after the other. After giving up the base hit in the eighth, he set down the final batters with no problem. The Reds won, their third shutout in five games and their eighth straight victory during a grueling September road trip. The Cardinals, however, swept a doubleheader with the Philadelphia Phillies to move into a tie for first place.

Unfortunately, that day would be the last time the Reds would hold the top spot. The exhausted team proceeded to lose their next six games, and the Cardinals slid past them, winning the pennant by two games. The Reds did beat their rival on the last day of the season, with Donohue getting his 20th win, but—as Lee Allen described it in his book *The Cincinnati Reds*—the game, after a long season in which the Reds believed they'd proven they were the league's best team, "was a meaningless mockery."

Roush didn't even show up for the final game, heading back home to Indiana for an early start on the off-season. (Having had enough of their temperamental star, who was as famous for his annual contract squabbles as he was for hitting the ball, the Reds traded him in the off-season.) Had the Reds brought in Hod Ford sooner to fill their troubled shortstop position and had they not suffered pitching injuries in September, they likely would have won the pennant. They were a well balanced team, leading the league in batting average and finishing second in earned run average. Bubbles Hargrave won the league batting title, the first modern-era catcher to earn the award.

Baseball seasons always offer plenty of what-ifs, but this bunch was especially tough for Reds fans to swallow. Allen describes the 1926 season as one in which "the Reds had provided their full share of drama in the year that brought everything."

It would turn out to be the last time the Reds put up a serious fight for the National League pennant until 1939. Their window, as we say today, had closed. The core of stars had gotten old and soon were either traded or retired. After pitching 586⅔ innings in two seasons, Donohue suffered arm problems for the remainder of his career, never posting a winning season again.

Perhaps because the franchise waded through the worst period in its history through the late 1920s and 1930s, or perhaps just because the exploits of players named Bubbles, Cuckoo, and Pea Ridge have faded with time and now seem so alien to us, the outstanding Reds teams of this era are largely forgotten, despite being one of the most successful periods in franchise history.

Cincinnati	1	0	0		2	0	0		0	0	0	— 3	6 0
New York	0	0	0		0	0	0		0	0	0	— 0	4 2

Cincinnati Reds

	AB	R	H	RBI
Christensen lf	4	1	1	0
Walker rf	4	0	2	1
Roush cf	3	0	0	0
Pipp 1b	3	0	0	0
Dressen 3b	4	1	1	0
Critz 2b	3	1	0	0
Hargrave c	3	0	0	0
Ford ss	3	0	2	2
Donohue p	3	0	0	0
Totals	30	3	6	3

	IP	H	R	ER	BB	SO
Donohue W (19–12)	9.0	4	0	0	0	3
Totals	9.0	4	0	0	0	3

New York Giants

	AB	R	H	RBI
Mueller lf	4	0	0	0
Lindstrom 3b	4	0	0	0
Frisch 2b	3	0	1	0
Kelly 1b	3	0	0	0
Terry rf	3	0	1	0
Tyson cf	3	0	1	0
Jackson ss	2	0	0	0
Bentley ph	1	0	0	0
Florence c	0	0	0	0
McMullen c	2	0	1	0
Farrell ss	1	0	0	0
Barnes p	2	0	0	0
Moore ph	1	0	0	0
Totals	29	0	4	0

	IP	H	R	ER	BB	SO
Barnes L (8–12)	9.0	6	3	3	2	0
Totals	9.0	6	3	3	2	0

Umpires: Ernie Quigley, Barry McCormick, Monroe Sweeney.

#48

A Man Called Bumpus

The story sounds like a tall tale—one of those hayseed-makes-good-in-big-city scenarios that were popular in books and movies in the first part of the twentieth century. But a young guy named Bumpus Jones, fresh from rural Ohio, really did pitch a no-hitter in his first big-league game, and it was the first no-hitter in Reds history.

First, some background. In October 1892, the Cincinnati Reds were wrapping up a season in which the team had shown considerable improvement over the previous year's last-place finish. The National League had expanded to 12 teams in 1892 by absorbing four teams from the defunct American Association. The league also restructured its usual pennant race by splitting the season in half. The team with the best first-half record would play the team with the best second-half record in a postseason series. It would be the only time the National League used this format except for the strike-shortened 1981 season.

Under new manager Charles Comiskey, the Reds played well in the first half, finishing fourth but struggled to finish eighth in the second half. So in the closing days of the season, as the weather turned cool, they were just finishing out the schedule when, on October 12, they played an exhibition game against the semipro Wilmington Clintons. Trolling the outfield for the Clintons was 22-year-old Charles Leander Jones, commonly known as "Bumpus." After the Reds built a big lead, Jones was called in to pitch, and he held the major leaguers hitless for three innings.

Which wasn't as shocking as it might seem. A native of Cedarville, Ohio, a little town located due east of Dayton, Jones had played three seasons in the minors, in the Illinois-Iowa League, and had compiled a 24–3 record in 1892

9

before the league folded. He then jumped to Atlanta in the Southern Association, which folded a few weeks later. After he headed back home to Cedarville, the Clintons signed him to play in their much-anticipated exhibition game with the Reds.

Comiskey was impressed with the young pitcher, and the Reds signed him to pitch the final game of the season on October 15. The Pittsburgh Pirates were in town to wrap up the season, a good team that finished the year 80–73. In the postgame article, the *Cincinnati Enquirer* reported, "If Bumpus Jones was the least bit nervous or shaky, there was nothing about his external makeup to indicate it." The article describes him as "small in stature but very quick and muscular."

The newspaper account might have been a bit generous about the young pitcher's nerves. He started the game by walking the first two batters, getting out of the jam via a double play due to bad baserunning by the Pirates. In the second inning, he issued another walk, this time to left fielder Mike Smith, and was once again bailed out by a double play. Reds second baseman Bid McPhee chased down a bloop fly in shallow right field and then shot a throw to Comiskey to double up Smith.

In the bottom of the second inning, the Reds drew first blood when Comiskey doubled to score catcher Farmer Vaughn, but the Pirates came right back in the third inning to tie the score. Jones struck out right fielder Patsy Donovan, but Vaughn missed strike three, and Donovan managed to reach first base safely. He went to second on a passed ball and scored when Jones fell down trying to field a soft grounder hit by Duke Farrell and then threw wildly to Comiskey at first base. For someone who wasn't "the least bit nervous or shaky," Jones had a rough few innings to start the game.

But he regained his composure after the error. He didn't allow a Pirate to reach first for the remainder of the game. No more walks. No hits. The Reds regained the lead in the fifth inning on a two-run home run by shortstop Germany Smith. The Reds maintained the 3–1 lead until late in the game, when they piled on four more runs in the eighth.

As young Bumpus walked to the mound in the ninth inning, the 800 fans, according to the *Enquirer,* "made enough noise for ten times that many people." The first two batters, Farrell and center fielder George Van Haltren, tried to bunt their way on base and bust the no-hitter. Both failed. Jones needed just one more out. And Mike Smith complied, lining to Comiskey at first base.

Bumpus Jones had pitched the first no-hitter in Reds history. He remains the only pitcher ever to pitch a no-hitter in his first major-league game.

The Reds were quick to offer the young phenom a contract for the following season. (According to Lee Allen in his book *The Cincinnati Reds,* Jones was not paid for pitching the no-hitter. The game was viewed by the team as sort of a voluntary tryout.)

As the next season began, Cincinnati fans surely had visions of vying for a pennant behind their new ace. But in 1893, the league changed the pitching distance from 50' to 60'6", where it remains today. The longer distance seems to have not suited the diminutive Jones. He started five games for the Reds that year and surrendered 32 runs in 28.2 innings, amassing a 10.05 ERA. Control issues plagued him, as he walked 23 batters and hit five more.

On June 19, with the Reds handily beating Louisville, Jones came in to mop up. He managed to give up 12 runs but still got the victory as the Reds won 30–12. He wouldn't get another major-league win, meaning that half his career victories were no-hitters. A few weeks later, the Reds let him go to the New York Giants, where he fared no better. Appearing in just one game, he walked 10 batters in four innings.

Bumpus went on to play in the Western League—a highly competitive, big-market association that in 1900 would rename itself the American League. He eventually built a reputation as a reliable pitcher and even threw another no-hitter. After suffering some health problems, he retired in 1901, leaving his unique name and story in the record books.

Reds	0	1	0		0	2	0		4	0	x	—	7
Pittsburgh	0	0	1		0	0	0		0	0	0	—	1

Cincinnati Reds

	AB	R	H
Holiday cf	4	1	2
Latham 3b	3	1	1
McPhee 2b	4	0	0
Browning rf	4	1	1
Vaughn c	4	1	1
Hoover lf	4	1	0
Comiskey 1b	4	1	3
Smith ss	3	1	2
Jones p	2	0	0
Totals	32	7	10

Pittsburgh Pirates

	AB	R	H
Donovan rf	2	1	0
Farrell 3b	3	0	0
Van Haltren cf	4	0	0
Miller ss	3	0	0
Beckley 1b	3	0	0
Smith lf	3	0	0
Mack c	3	0	0
Bierbauer 2b	3	0	0
Baldwin p	3	0	0
Totals	27	1	0

Umpire: McQuaid.
Time of game: 1:18.

#47

A Great New Ball Park

Whenever a team plays its first game in a new home ballpark, a new era begins in the team's history. Big games are always remembered, at least in part, by where they were played. Many fans today can still recall games in Crosley Field, with its emerald sweep of grass and distinctive scoreboard featuring the iconic Longines clock. The Big Red Machine will be forever connected to saucer-shaped Riverfront Stadium, with its artificial turf and distinctive dirt cutouts around the bases. That type of multipurpose stadium was all the rage in the late 1960s, but 30 years later, major-league teams wanted their own, baseball-only ballparks. And they wanted new ballparks that looked like old ones—retro structures that evoked an earlier time.

The Baltimore Orioles set the standard in 1992 with Camden Yards, and throughout the decade more teams moved into retro ballparks. By the turn of the twenty-first century, Riverfront Stadium, by then known as Cinergy Field, was an embarrassment, an ugly reminder of an age in sports facilities that everyone wanted to forget. After the Cincinnati Bengals of the National Football League moved into Paul Brown Stadium in August 2000, the Reds had the place all to themselves, but already were planning to build a new place right next door.

By the start of the 2003 season, Great American Ball Park was ready for business. The Reds team, however, was not. The previous two seasons involved many more losses than wins. Management promised that when the new ballpark opened, it would host a winner, but fans had to wait for that wish to come true. Excitement about new Great American Ball Park, however, held their interest, at least for a while.

In 2002, the team finished a respectable third in the NL Central Division with a 78–84 record. Young outfielders Adam Dunn and Austin Kearns, both only 22 years old, showed great promise, with the former slugging 26 home runs while posting a .400 OBP and the latter producing a .315/.407/.500 slash line in 435 plate appearances. But Ken Griffey Jr. spent most of the year on the disabled list, and the team's other star, shortstop Barry Larkin, at 38, was past his prime.

The team's main problem, however, was the pitching rotation, which didn't seem likely to improve in the new smaller ballpark. Despite a mediocre 1.48 WHIP (walks plus hits per inning pitched) and a 4.12 ERA, Jimmy Haynes did win 15 games in 2002, and he was chosen as the starting pitcher on Opening Day, when the Reds played their first game in Great American Ball Park, known locally as GABP. Reflecting the city's anticipation to see the new digs, 42,343 came to the afternoon game with the Pittsburgh Pirates on Monday, March 31. Though the weather was cloudy and breezy, with temperatures in the low 50s, the beautiful ballpark—with riverboat smokestacks in center field—helped create a party atmosphere. And hopes ran high that a fresh era of success was beginning.

Those hopes lasted until the top of the second inning, when the Pirates exploded for six runs on five hits, including home runs by right fielder Reggie Sanders, center fielder Kenny Lofton, and catcher Jason Kendall. The field was clearly not big enough to keep the ball from reaching the seats, inspiring *Cincinnati Enquirer* columnist Paul Daugherty to christen it "Great American Small Park."

While plans were being made for a new home for the Reds, many fans had pushed to build it in an area on the east side of downtown, a project dubbed Broadway Commons, which offered plenty of room but a drab surrounding neighborhood. These fans pointed to similar scenarios in cities such as Cleveland, where Jacobs Field led to revitalization. Another faction wanted to keep the ballpark on the river, in a project called the Wedge. It afforded a better view, no doubt, but with the arena on one side and the not-yet-imploded Cinergy Field on the other, there wasn't enough room to build a spacious facility. Playing in one of the most hitter-friendly ballparks in the majors has made pitching an annual concern.

In the bottom of the third inning, the Reds scored a run to whittle the lead to 6–1. Haynes started the rally with a double, and the Reds loaded the bases. When Pittsburgh's Kris Benson walked Kearns, Haynes trotted across the plate. Having thrown the first pitch in Great American Ball Park, he also scored the first Reds run in the ballpark. In the top of the fourth, Haynes walked two but escaped unscathed. Still, Cincinnati manager Bob Boone had seen enough and sent pinch hitter Willy Mo Pena to bat for Haynes in the bottom of the inning.

Two walks and two singles gave the Pirates another run in the fifth, and they added two more in the seventh and another in the eighth. In their new hitter-friendly home, the Reds managed only four hits. But if the first game had not been at all great in its outcome, its historic importance cannot be denied.

The Reds lost the next two games, as the Pirates swept the opening series at Great American Ball Park. The first Reds victory was notched on Friday, April 4, with a 10–9 win over the Chicago Cubs. The Opening Day drubbing foreshadowed a bleak first year in the new ballpark, as the Reds won just 69 games, and manager Bob Boone was fired on July 28. The problem, once again, was pitching. Seventeen pitchers started at least one game for the Reds that season. Griffey missed a good chunk of the year again, as did Larkin.

But 2,355,259 people spun the turnstiles during the season, an increase of nearly 500,000 over 2002. Cincinnati had a new point of pride, and much better times lay ahead. A new generation of Reds teams would play for a new generation of fans, whose memories of favorite players and moments would be set at Great American Ball Park.

Pittsburgh	0	6	0	0	1	0	2	1	0	—	10	12	2
Cincinnati	0	0	1	0	0	0	0	0	0	—	4	0	1

Pittsburgh Pirates

	AB	R	H	RBI
Lofton cf	4	2	2	3
Kendall c	5	1	1	1
Giles lf	4	1	1	1
Ramirez 3b	5	1	2	0
Simon 1b	4	2	2	1
Young 1b	1	0	0	0
Sanders rf	5	1	3	2
Reese 2b	3	1	1	2
Wilson ss	3	0	0	0
Tavarez p	0	0	0	0
Beimel p	0	0	0	0
Benson p	1	1	0	0
Nunez ss	1	0	0	0
Totals	36	10	12	10

	IP	H	R	ER	BB	SO
Benson W (1–0)	6.1	3	1	0	3	3
Tavarez	1.2	0	0	0	0	0
Beimel	1.0	1	0	0	0	1
Totals	9.0	4	1	0	3	4

Cincinnati Reds

	AB	R	H	RBI
Larkin ss	3	0	0	0
Boone 2b	4	0	0	0
Griffey Jr. cf	4	0	1	0
Kearns rf	3	0	0	1
Dunn lf	4	0	0	0
Casey 1b	4	0	1	0
Larson 3b	4	0	0	0
LaRue c	3	0	0	0
Haynes p	1	1	1	0
Pena ph	1	0	0	0
Heredia p	0	0	0	0
Sullivan p	0	0	0	0
Riedling p	0	0	0	0
Taylor ph	1	0	1	0
White p	0	0	0	0
Williamson p	0	0	0	0
Totals	32	1	4	1

	IP	H	R	ER	BB	SO
Haynes L (0–1)	4.0	5	6	6	3	3
Heredia	0.1	1	1	1	1	0
Sullivan	1.2	1	0	0	1	2
Riedling	1.0	3	2	2	0	0
White	1.0	2	1	1	0	0
Williamson	1.0	0	0	0	0	1
Totals	9.0	12	10	10	5	6

Time of game: 3:00.
Attendance: 42,343.

REDS 19, PHILADELPHIA PHILLIES 17
AUGUST 3, 1969

What's in a Name?

The winds of change blew hard in 1969 throughout the major leagues. Both the National and American leagues expanded from 10 teams to 12, and they were divided into two divisions. For the first time—and forever after—baseball's postseason included playoffs to determine the pennant winners. To create more offense (following the "year of the pitcher" in 1968), the mound was lowered and the strike zone tightened.

Unlike most teams, the Reds had suffered no lack of offense in the year of the pitcher. They led the majors in batting average, on-base percentage, slugging, and runs scored. Right fielder Pete Rose won his first batting title, while catcher Johnny Bench won the Rookie of the Year award. In 1969, the Reds would again lead the National League in those categories, as well as in home runs. But their efforts to be the first champs of the new West Division were undermined by a sore-armed pitching staff.

Looking for help, the team, on July 7, purchased Camilo Pascual from the Washington Senators. A 20-game winner in 1962 and 1963 for the Minnesota Twins, Pascual had been a top pitcher in the American League during his prime, but by the time he arrived in Cincinnati he was 35 years old and on the downward arc of his career. The Reds hoped he had enough magic in his aging arm to help bolster the starting staff, at least until the sore arms healed.

On Sunday, August 3, Pascual made his first (and, as it turned out, his last) start for the Reds. The game was played in Philadelphia's Connie Mack Stadium, where major-league baseball had been played since 1909. The Phillies, like the Reds, would leave behind their old ballpark the next year for a new home, one designed in the "flying saucer" shape popular of that era.

Mired in fifth place in the NL East Division with a 43–61 record, the Phillies seemed like a soft opponent for Pascual to face in his first start. Despite the nagging injuries to their staff, the Reds held steady in third place in their division, only a 1½ games behind the Braves in a very tight race that included five of the division's six teams all within a few games of each other.

When Pascual took the mound in the bottom of the first inning, he already enjoyed a 1–0 lead. Facing Phillies rookie Bill Champion, Pete Rose managed a walk to lead off the game, and he scored on a single by third baseman Tony Perez. The lead would not last long. Nor would Pascual. After a ground out and a walk, he allowed three consecutive doubles, forcing manager Dave Bristol to yank him in favor of Jack Fisher. Pascual's career starting for the Reds lasted for one-third of an inning.

Not that Champion lasted a whole lot longer that afternoon. After each team crossed the plate in the second inning to make the score 4–2, Reds left fielder Alex Johnson led off the third with a single. Al Raffo replaced Champion but faired no better, giving up three runs and the lead. Fisher, and his replacement, Clay Carroll, gave it right back. When the dust cleared at the end of the third inning, the Phillies led 9–5.

But even with a four-run lead, Phillies fans surely did not feel safe when facing the league's most productive offense, which had built a reputation as a formidable force. In a July 5, 1969, article in the *Los Angeles Herald-Examiner,* sportswriter Bob Hunter referred to Bristol as "the boy manager of the Big Red Machine." Just a passing reference, a sportswriter's way of adding some color to his prose. But after this day in Philadelphia, the moniker would earn a new level of credence and popularity.

Phillies fans did not have to wait long for their fears to be realized. In the fifth inning, thanks to home runs by Rose and first baseman Lee May, along with nine hits in total, the Reds took a 16–9 lead. An inning later they widened the margin to 18–9. But there was a reason that the Reds, even with such a powerful offense, did not hold a commanding lead in the standings. Their pitching made every game, even one in which they held a nine-run lead, cause for worry.

In their half of the sixth inning, the Phillies responded with seven runs of their own, due in part to a grand slam by Tony Taylor that whittled the Reds' lead to a mere two runs. In the bottom of the seventh, after Dick Allen cut the margin to one run with a solo shot, Bristol brought in his best reliever—Wayne Granger. A tall, skinny, 25-year-old side-armer, Granger made 90 appearances in 1969 to lead the league. He was credited with 27 saves and pitched 144⅔ innings. Bristol relied heavily on Granger to bail out the sore-armed starting rotation and today would be no different.

Once again, Granger delivered, completing three innings and giving up no runs and three hits. In the top of the eighth, Tony Perez joined the home run club to stretch the lead to 19–17, where it would remain. The game ended when Rose, in right field, made a diving catch on a Ron Stone liner. Afterward, Bristol said it took a great play to finally end such a crazy game.

The following day, the game story made the front page of the *Cincinnati Enquirer*. Reporter Bob Hertzel wrote, "The Big Red Machine is what they call it and today they are also calling it something else: the No. 1 team in the Western Division of the National League." This mention of the now legendary nickname was the first to appear in a Cincinnati newspaper, and the first time many local fans had ever heard it. They quickly began using it and haven't stopped since.

The Reds' bats continued to thunder in August 1969; by the middle of the month, they held a 2½–game lead in the West Division. An article in the August 18 edition of *Sports Illustrated* made reference to the Big Red Machine, giving the nickname its first national exposure and bestowing on the franchise its identity for the next decade.

The lack of healthy pitchers finally caught up with the Reds in September that year, and they dropped back to finish third. Despite an excellent season, Bristol was replaced by Sparky Anderson. With a new manager and a new ballpark, the Reds began a new decade of baseball. The vaunted lineup was in place and ready to launch into the franchise's most successful period in its history. And thanks to a long-forgotten slugfest on a Sunday afternoon in Philadelphia, it already had a nickname.

Cincinnati	1	1	3	1	10	2	0	1	0	—	19 25 1
Philadelphia	3	1	5	0	0	7	1	0	0	—	17 21 2

Cincinnati Reds

	AB	R	H	RBI
Rose rf	4	3	3	4
Tolan cf	7	1	1	0
Johnson lf	6	3	4	4
Stewart lf	0	0	0	0
Perez 3b	5	3	4	3
May 1b	6	2	2	4
Bench c	6	2	5	1
Woodward ss	6	2	3	2
Ruiz 2b	6	2	2	1
Pascual p	0	0	0	0

	AB	R	H	RBI
Fisher p	2	0	0	0
Carroll p	2	1	1	0
Ramos p	1	0	0	0
Granger p	1	0	0	0
Totals	52	19	25	19

	IP	H	R	ER	BB	SO
Pascual	0.1	3	3	3	1	0
Fisher	1.2	5	4	4	0	3
Carroll	3.1	6	6	6	2	2
Ramos	0.2	4	4	4	0	1
Granger W (5–4)	3.0	3	0	0	1	0
Totals	9.0	21	17	17	4	6

Philadelphia Phillies

	AB	R	H	RBI
Taylor 2b	6	1	2	5
Hisle cf	3	2	1	0
Wilson p	0	0	0	0
Harmon ph	1	0	0	0
Allen 1b	6	2	2	2
Callison rf	5	3	4	1
Johnson 3b	6	2	5	2
Jackson pr	0	0	0	0
Stone lf, cf	6	2	2	1
Money ss	5	1	1	2
Ryan c	4	2	1	1
Champion p	1	0	0	0
Raffo p	0	0	0	0
Rojas ph	1	1	1	3
Boozer p	0	0	0	0
Farrell p	0	0	0	0
Palmer p	1	0	1	0
Barry ph, lf	2	1	1	0
Totals	47	17	21	17

	IP	H	R	ER	BB	SO
Champion	2.0	5	3	3	1	2
Raffo	1.0	3	2	2	0	1
Boozer	1.0	4	3	2	1	1
Farrell L (3–3)	0.1	6	6	6	0	0
Palmer	1.2	5	4	4	0	1
Wilson	3.0	2	1	1	2	0
Totals	9.0	25	19	18	4	5

Umpires: HP—Ed Sudol, 1B—Lee Weyer, 2B—Harry Wendelstedt, 3B—
Ken Burkhart.
Time of game: 3:29.
Attendance: 13,181.

Breaking Barriers

When we think back on the Reds of the mid to late 1950s, players like Frank Robinson, Vada Pinson, and Brooks Lawrence come quickly to mind. Surely some fans would add Bob Thurman, George Crowe, Joe Black, Curt Flood, and Don Newcombe to the short list.

All of these players were African American. It's strange to recall, then, that before 1954 the number of African American Cincinnati Reds amounted to exactly none. The major-league "color barrier," a gentlemen's agreement among team owners to exclude African American and Latino players, was broken in 1947 when the Brooklyn Dodgers put Jackie Robinson on the field, and the Cleveland Indians followed shortly after with Larry Doby.

With the barrier broken, other teams didn't exactly rush to sign non-Caucasian players, the Reds among them. Perhaps the delay was due, at least in part, to Cincinnati's location. Reds country included southern Ohio, Kentucky, and Tennessee, as well as southern Indiana and West Virginia, and management may have feared that the fan base wouldn't embrace an integrated team.

The delay didn't fit the team's legacy. In 1911, the Reds signed two Cuban players, Armando Marsans and Rafael Almeida, the first Latino players to log significant playing time in the major leagues. In 1918 the Reds brought in Cuban pitcher Adolfo Luque, who remained a star in Cincinnati for 12 seasons. The team—and very often the newspapers—characterized the Cuban players as "European" or "Spanish" or sometimes "Castilian," which somehow legitimized them in the eyes of the baseball world. Their presence on the team did establish a connection between the Reds and Cuba that still exists today. In the 1950s, the Reds even owned a AAA team in Cuba, the Havana Sugar Kings.

When the color barrier finally was broken, however, the Reds, like most major-league teams, took a wait-and-see attitude. In 1952, they signed African American infielder Chuck Harmon and Afro-Latino Nino Escalera, but both played in the minor league system for two years until being brought to the majors to start the 1954 season. That year the Pittsburgh Pirates, St. Louis Cardinals, and Washington Senators joined the Reds in fielding their first integrated teams.

A talented athlete who starred for the University of Toledo's basketball team, Harmon was only a few weeks from his 30th birthday when the Reds broke camp. He'd hit well in the minors and played a fine third base, but likely was held back by his race from making the majors sooner. His would be a common story during the time, as African American players waited longer than their talent warranted for a call to the Show. In 1953 Harmon hit .311 and stole 25 bases at AA Tulsa, and clearly was ready for promotion.

Nino Escalera, a native of Puerto Rico, played first base and the corner outfield spots. An excellent contact hitter with good speed, he lacked the power normally associated with corner positions. After hitting .305 at Tulsa, he had nothing left to prove in the minor leagues. He was the first dark-skinned Latino signed by the Reds and was 24 years old when he debuted in 1954.

Having placed sixth in the eight-team National League in 1954, 18 games under .500, the Reds certainly needed some help. The franchise hadn't finished with a winning record since 1944, though signs of improvement were beginning to appear. Power-hitting first baseman Ted Kluszewski, center fielder Gus Bell, and right fielder Wally Post anchored a strong offense, but the team lacked enough pitching to win consistently.

The season opened on April 13, a Tuesday, but as the third game of the season got underway four days later, neither Harmon nor Escalera had stepped onto the field and weren't in the starting lineup that day. The Reds played the Braves that Saturday afternoon at Milwaukee's County Stadium, drawing more than 20,000 people to the game.

In the first inning, the Reds scored when Kluszewski grounded out to score third baseman Bobby Adams. The Braves quickly tied the game when third baseman Eddie Mathews singled to score center fielder Bill Bruton. Having integrated in 1950, the Braves lineup included two African American players that day—Bruton and a young left fielder named Hank Aaron. Neither had broken the color barrier for the team, but both now were fixtures in the lineup.

Milwaukee scored again in the second inning, as Reds right-hander Corky Valentine walked Aaron to start the inning and shortstop Johnny Logan homered. In the sixth inning Logan clubbed his second home run of the day, again off Valentine, this one a solo shot. Valentine then walked catcher Del Crandall, who scored on a single by Bruton. Heading into the seventh inning, the Reds were losing 5–1.

To start the inning, Reds manager Birdie Tebbetts sent Escalera to the plate to bat for catcher Andy Seminick. Facing Burdette, Escalera laced a single. The team's color barrier had officially been broken. Harmon then stepped into the batter's box to pinch-hit for Valentine. He popped out to first baseman Joe Adcock. Adams then singled, moving Escalera to second base, but pinch hitter Lloyd Merriman grounded into a double play to end the inning.

Escalera and Harmon were finished for the afternoon, and the Reds lost, as neither team scored for the rest of the game, but a new day had dawned for the franchise. As a reserve infielder and outfielder, Harmon appeared in 94 games that season, batting .238/.277/.304 in 314 plate appearances. Playing the same role through the next season, he faired better at the plate and was known as a versatile defender, athletic enough to field most positions. After a slow start at the plate in 1956, he was traded to the Cardinals, where he saw little playing time. The next year the Cardinals traded him to the Philadelphia Phillies, where he made just 87 plate appearances. At 34, his major-league career was finished.

Escalera played just one year for the Reds, mostly as a pinch hitter. In 77 plate appearances, he hit .159. He was sent to the Sugar Kings, where in 1955 he hit .297/.387/.426, but those numbers weren't enough to trigger a call back to the majors. After four years with the Sugar Kings, he was traded to the Pirates organization and later to the Orioles, but he never again played in the majors.

Both players will always occupy a place in Reds history for breaking down the color barrier. Just two years after the Reds broke their barrier, the team included eight African Americans, more than any other major-league team. In 2015, the Reds unveiled a bronze statue of Harmon at the entrance to the P&G MLB Cincinnati Reds Youth Academy. At the age of 91, Harmon attended the ceremony.

Cincinnati	1	0	0	0	0	0	0	0	0	—	1	7	0
Milwaukee	1	2	0	0	0	2	0	0	x	—	5	10	0

Cincinnati Redlegs

	AB	R	H	RBI
Adams 3b	3	1	1	0
McMillan ss	3	0	1	0
Merriman ph	1	0	0	0
Fowler p	0	0	0	0
Bell cf	4	0	0	0
Kluszewski 1b	4	0	0	1
Greengrass lf	3	0	1	0
Temple 2b	4	0	2	0
Post rf	4	0	0	0
Seminick c	1	0	0	0
Escalera ph	1	0	1	0
Bailey c	1	0	1	0
Valentine p	2	0	0	0
Harmon ph	1	0	0	0
Bridges ss	0	0	0	0
Hatton ph	1	0	0	0
Totals	33	1	7	1

	IP	H	R	ER	BB	SO
Valentine L (0–1)	6.0	8	5	5	4	2
Fowler	2.0	2	0	0	0	1
Totals	8.0	10	5	5	4	3

Milwaukee Braves

	AB	R	H	RBI
Bruton cf	3	1	1	1
O'Connell 2b	4	0	2	0
Mathews 3b	4	0	3	1
Adcock 1b	4	0	1	0
Metkovich rf	4	0	0	0
Pendleton rf	0	0	0	0
Aaron lf	2	1	1	0
Logan ss	4	2	2	3
Crandall c	3	1	0	0
Burdette p	3	0	0	0
Totals	31	5	10	5

	IP	H	R	ER	BB	SO
Burdette W (1–0)	9.0	7	1	1	4	2
Totals	9.0	7	1	1	4	2

Umpires: HP—Frank Secory, 1B—Bill Jackowski, 2B—Jocko Conlan, 3B—
Artie Gore.
Time of game: 2:25.
Attendance: 20,938.

#44

Win It for Hutch

When the Reds hired Fred Hutchinson as manager in July 1959, things changed in the clubhouse. Or, more specifically, things in the clubhouse got broken—light fixtures, chairs, doors, training tables.

Hutch had a temper, and he really really liked to win. Losing put him in a bad mood, which led to stuff breaking. But he mostly took out his tirades on things, not people. He didn't abuse his players, who did, however, witness enough things being broken that they played hard to keep Hutch happy. In 1961, a Reds team no one expected to be good won the National League pennant, and posted winning records during the next two years. Players loved playing for Hutch. Fans loved his gruff yet genial old-school style.

The news released in January 1964 shocked everyone: Hutchinson, only 45 years old, had cancer. The players dedicated themselves to winning the pennant for their ailing manager and found themselves in a fierce, four-team battle that is now etched in baseball history. Many players from the pennant-winning team were still around, augmented by young stars. Frank Robinson remained the Reds' best hitter, and his supporting cast included Pete Rose, Vada Pinson, Leo Cardenas, and Deron Johnson. The rotation of Jim O'Toole, Jim Maloney, Joey Jay, and Bob Purkey remained effective, while rookie relievers Sammy Ellis and Billy McCool formed an excellent bullpen duo.

The Philadelphia Phillies set the pace through much of the summer, but the Reds, St. Louis Cardinals, and San Francisco Giants all stayed in the hunt. Reds players kept one eye on the box scores and the other on Hutchinson, whose bear-like physique seemed to grow thinner by the day. He took several leaves of absence to receive medical treatment, finally handing his duties to acting manager Dick Sisler on August 13. The Reds' pennant hunt picked up momentum through the dog days and into September, but the Phillies held onto the lead. On September 21, the Reds occupied second place, trailing by 6½ games with only 13 remaining. Fortunately, the Reds played the Phillies five more times and also played five games with the lowly New York Mets.

As the Reds prepared to play a three-game series in Philadelphia, they looked for ways to fill in for starting pitchers Jim Maloney, who was sick, and Joey Jay, who was injured. The *Cincinnati Enquirer* described the series as "what now appears an utterly hopeless pursuit of the league-leading Philadelphia Phillies." Not exactly the rah-rah sentiment the team needed in the current situation. Sweeping the series meant keeping alive their hopes of winning a pennant for Hutch.

In the first game, Sisler called on John Tsitouris to take the mound, facing Art Mahaffey. The two journeyman pitchers surprisingly kept the two powerful lineups very quiet for the first five innings. In the top of the sixth, with one out, Reds third baseman Chico Ruiz singled to right field. The consummate utility player, Ruiz had the speed and versatility to handle almost any position. He also was a switch-hitter, giving his manager a lot of flexibility. Most of all, Ruiz had the perfect attitude for a utility player. Once, while filling in for an extended period during a rash of injuries, he jokingly complained, "Bench me or trade me."

Pinson followed with a single, and the speedy Ruiz scampered to third base. Pinson, however, tried to stretch his hit into a double and was thrown out at second base. The mighty Robinson sauntered to the batter's box. He was the guy Reds fans wanted at the plate with two out and a runner on third. But Ruiz decided not to wait for Robby to be the hero. With the count no balls and one strike, Ruiz broke for home, taking the Phillies by surprise. When Mahaffey heard second baseman Tony Taylor shout, "There he goes!" he threw wildly in the direction of the plate. Ruiz slid home safely, giving the Reds a 1–0 lead. Apparently Ruiz even surprised his own team. He wasn't executing a planned squeeze play. He just saw his chance and went for it. Robinson grounded out to end the inning.

Tsitouris continued to set down the Phillies and hold the lead. In the bottom of the ninth, cleanup hitter Wes Covington led off with a double to center field and was replaced by fleet pinch runner Adolfo Phillips. Sisler thought about going to his bullpen but stayed with his starter. First baseman John Herrnstein popped out to Cardenas at shortstop. Catcher Clay Dalrymple grounded to Rose at second base for out no. 2, though Phillips ended up on third. Taylor then walked to put runners on the corners. Sisler again considered pulling

Tsitouris, but again trusted him. And again the pitcher came through, striking out Ruben Amaro to end the game.

Afterward, the Phillies couldn't decide if they were more angry or shocked about losing a critical game in such a strange way—a bench guy stealing home. "Only an idiot would try to play like that with Robby at bat," manager Gene Mauch told the press. Sisler admitted that Ruiz had run on his own and that "it wasn't a good play." But something about Ruiz's moxie, the do-or-die attitude of the play, seemed to inspire the Reds and deflate the Phillies. The Reds went on to sweep the series. They went on to New York for five games with the Mets and won them all, while the Phillies dropped four straight to the Milwaukee Braves. With five games remaining in the season, the Reds had leapt into first place, and were headed home to Cincinnati.

If only the story could end there, with the Reds giving their dying manager a pennant. But the Pittsburgh Pirates came to town and beat the Reds 2–0 and 1–0, the latter a 16-inning game. The Reds, Phillies, and Cardinals were all within a game going into the final two, which the Reds would play at home against the Phillies. In the first of the pair, the Reds blew a 3–0 lead in the eighth to lose 4–3. As the season entered its final day on October 4, the Reds and Cardinals were tied for first place, with the Phillies one game behind. Reds starting pitcher Tsitouris, who had been so masterful in the Philadelphia game, lasted just 2⅓ innings, giving up three runs, and the bullpen provided no relief. The Reds lost 10–0. The Cardinals won their game, and the pennant, and the world championship.

The bad news continued on October 19, when Fred Hutchinson resigned as manager. Less than one month later, he died. In 1965, Major League Baseball created the Hutch Award, which is given every year to one player who "best exemplifies" Hutch's "fighting spirit and competitive desire." In 1972, the Fred Hutchinson Cancer Research Center opened in Seattle.

Losing the pennant by one game obviously disappointed the Reds players, but not as much as the sting of coming so close to winning it for Hutch and falling just short of their goal.

Cincinnati	0 0 0	0 0 1	0 0 0	—	1	7	1
Philadelphia	0 0 0	0 0 0	0 0 0	—	0	6	0

Cincinnati Reds

	AB	R	H	RBI
Rose 2b	4	0	0	0
Ruiz 3b	4	1	1	0
Pinson cf	3	0	1	0
Robinson lf	4	0	2	0
Johnson 1b	4	0	0	0
Edwards c	4	0	0	0
Keough rf	4	0	2	0
Cardenas ss	3	0	0	0
Tsitouris p	2	0	1	0
Totals	32	1	7	0

	IP	H	R	ER	BB	SO
Tsitouris W (8–11)	9.0	6	0	0	2	8
Totals	9.0	6	0	0	2	8

Philadelphia Phillies

	AB	R	H	RBI
Gonzalez cf	4	0	1	0
Allen 3b	2	0	1	0
Callison rf	4	0	0	0
Covington lf	4	0	2	0
Phillips pr	0	0	0	0
Herrnstein 1b	4	0	0	0
Dalrymple c	4	0	1	0
Taylor 2b	3	0	0	0
Amaro ss	4	0	1	0
Mahaffey p	2	0	0	0
Locke p	0	0	0	0
Briggs ph	1	0	0	0
Shantz p	0	0	0	0
Totals	32	0	6	0

	IP	H	R	ER	BB	SO
Mahaffey L (12–9)	6.2	6	1	1	2	5
Locke	1.1	1	0	0	1	0
Shantz	1.0	0	0	0	0	0
Totals	9.0	7	1	1	3	5

Umpires: HP—Stan Landes, 1B—Mel Steiner, 2B—Al Barlick, 3B—Augie Donatelli.

Time of game: 2:30.

Attendance: 20,067.

#43

A Great Swat Duel

When the Reds met the Pirates for a season-ending doubleheader at the Palace of the Fans in Cincinnati on Sunday, October 8, 1905, they weren't vying for a pennant. The New York Giants had already won it, finishing nine games ahead of the pack. The Pirates had clinched a distant second place, while the Reds would finish fifth with a 79–74 record. Reds fans likely were disappointed in their team's fortunes after posting a third-place, 88-win season the year before. A National League pennant had seemed within reach. But a slow start and an early, season-ending injury to staff ace Noodles Hahn made for a mediocre year. They did get to cheer loudly and often for their spectacular center fielder—James Bentley "Cy" Seymour—who put together one of the best seasons in the Deadball Era.

As the October doubleheader with the Pirates got underway, Seymour held the lead on the National League's batting title. The only threat to catch him on this final day played for Pirates: Hall of Fame shortstop Honus Wagner, considered among the best players of his generation. The pair had been at the top of the league's list of batting leaders throughout the season, with Seymour usually in front. Wagner had won the batting crown the previous two seasons, and would win it eight times in his career. The battle for the batting title brought some drama to the season's last day. The *Sporting Life* called it "A Great Swat Duel."

Seymour, 32 years old and in his 11th season, was one of the game's best hitters, but he'd started his career as a pitcher for the New York Giants. In fact, he led the National League in strikeouts in 1897. The next season he won 25 games while posting a 3.18 ERA and won the strikout title again with a total of 239—61 Ks ahead of the runner-up. Known for a blistering fastball, he was one of the most feared pitchers in the league, earning the nickname "Cy" as in "cyclone."

Hitters mostly feared him, however, because his control was, shall we say, erratic. While twice leading the league in strikeouts, he led it three times in walks. A gifted athlete, he also could hit, and when Seymour wasn't pitching, Giants manager John McGraw put him in the outfield. By the time Seymour arrived in Cincinnati in 1902 he had converted full time to center field. The next year, his first full season with the Reds, he hit .342, the fifth-best average in the league, and he exceeded .300 seven times in his career. In his achievements as both a pitcher and hitter, Seymour ranks behind only Babe Ruth in major-league history. No other player has ever led the league in batting average and, as a pitcher, in strikeouts.

Given his amazing versatility, it's surprising that Seymour is rarely mentioned among the leading players of his era. Maybe his versatility undermines his fame, in that spending five years as a pitcher before switching to the regular lineup didn't allow him to amass enough traditional counting stats at either position. A member of the Reds Hall of Fame (inducted in 1998), Seymour has received a grand total of one vote for enshrinement in Cooperstown (back in the 1940s).

Part of his anonymity might also be due to his personality. According to many reports from the time, Seymour was a bit of an odd duck. His dandified dress and condescending attitude (he hated the nickname "Cy" and insisted on being called "J. Bentley") toward teammates and sportswriters didn't win him many friends. And he was known for behaving strangely at times. Once, while coaching third base, before teams hired full-time coaches, Seymour was outraged when a teammate ignored his shouts to hold at third and headed toward home. Seymour ran onto the field and tackled the guy. When players and managers of the era were interviewed years later, they rarely mentioned Seymour as one of the greats because, well, maybe they just didn't like him.

According to the *Sporting Life*, "ten thousand odd enthusiasts turned out" for the doubleheader with the Pirates, a huge crowd for the time, especially for meaningless October games. In its typically hyperbolic tone, the *Sporting Life* assured readers "no such autumn tribute to the national game was ever before paid in Cincinnati." The fans came to watch "the batting duel between J. Bentley Seymour and Hans Wagner." The Reds won the first game, 3–1. Seymour got two hits in four at bats and also initiated a triple play in the seventh inning, after Reds pitcher Orval Overall had walked three straight batters to load the bases. Wagner, meanwhile was hitless in three at bats.

In the second game, Wagner managed two hits in four at bats, but Seymour was not to be denied, getting two hits, including a double, in three at bats. His efforts helped the Reds to a 4–1 victory, which was pitcher Bob Ewing's 20th of the season. More importantly, Seymour ended up with a .377 batting average to Wagner's .363. Along with the batting crown, Seymour led the league in hits, doubles, triples, runs batted in, slugging, on-base plus slugging (OPS), and total bases. He finished runner-up in home runs and on-base percentage. His .377 average remains the highest in team history in the modern era and remained unsurpassed in the league until 1919.

Having hit .300 for the fifth straight season, and after putting together one of the great seasons of the era, Seymour, despite his age, looked like a player who still had productive seasons ahead of him. The Giants wanted him back, and the Reds sold his contract for $10,000—the most a team had ever paid for a player in major-league history at the time. Always the contrarian, Seymour wanted a piece of that pie for himself and threatened to quit the Giants if he didn't get a share of the money, but he was persuaded to stay. He played another few years in New York, though his skills soon eroded; by 1909 he was a part-time player. He retired the following year.

After selling Seymour, the Reds sank into the bottom half of the league for the remainder of the decade. But the fans who jammed the ballpark on that autumn day to watch him win the swat duel witnessed a piece of history.

| Cincinnati | 0 | 0 | 1 | 3 | 0 | 0 | 0 | x | — | 4 |
| Pittsburgh | 0 | 1 | 0 | 0 | 0 | 0 | 0 | 0 | — | 1 |

Cincinnati Reds

	AB	R	H
Huggins 2b	4	1	2
Barry 1b	3	0	1
Seymour cf	3	0	2
Corcoran ss	4	0	0
Odwell lf	2	0	2
Hinchman 3b	2	1	0
Siegle rf	3	1	1
Street c	2	1	0
Ewing p	3	0	1
Total	26	4	9

Pittsburgh Pirates

	AB	R	H
Clymer lf	4	0	0
Ganley rf	4	0	2
Leach cf	3	0	0
Wagner ss	4	0	2
Brain 3b	4	1	1
Howard 1b	3	0	0
Ritchey 2b	3	0	0
Pietz c	2	0	1
Kinsella p	1	0	0
Total	28	1	6

Umpire: Klem.
Time of game: 1:30.
Attendance: 10,000.

#42

REDS 11, ST. LOUIS CARDINALS 1
SEPTEMBER 29, 1923

Nuestros Queridos Rojos

The Reds franchise has a long-standing love affair with Cuba, a baseball hotbed that has produced many stars for the team, from Tony Perez and Leo Cardenas to Aroldis Chapman and Rasiel Iglesias. In the 1950s, the Reds even fielded a successful AAA minor-league affiliate in Havana known as the Sugar Kings. One of the pioneers in this ongoing legacy that began nearly 100 years ago was a short, fiery right-hander named Adolfo "Dolf" Luque (pronounced LOO-kay).

Luque pitched 12 seasons for the Reds, from 1918 through 1929. When he debuted with the Boston Braves in 1914, he was the first Latin pitcher to take the mound in a major-league game. During those years, the racist color barrier was very much in place, and it prohibited dark-skinned Latin players, along with African Americans, from competing in the major leagues. Because of his light skin, Luque managed to get a chance.

He won 10 games for the world-champion 1919 Reds, making some starts but mostly pitching in relief. The following year he joined the rotation. His 1923 season is easily among the best in team history, matched only, perhaps, by Bucky Walters in 1939 and Ewell Blackwell in 1947. Luque won 27 games that year, the most by a Reds pitcher at the time in the modern era and still tied, with Walters, for most in team history. He led the National League in wins, earned run average (1.93), shutouts (6), and other categories, including adjusted earned run average (ERA+) and fielding independent pitching (FIP). His wins above replacement (WAR) totaled 10.6, second in the majors to Babe Ruth. His 27–8 record remains the best single-season mark ever by a Latin American pitcher in the major leagues.

Luque was part of the great Reds pitching staffs in the 1920s, which included Hall of Famer Eppa Rixey and Pete Donohue. During that time, Redland

Field (later Crosley Field) was a spacious pitcher's park, rather than the hitter's paradise it became later. With their big three on the mound, the Reds enjoyed a lot of success during those years and might have won a pennant or two were John McGraw's New York Giants not seemingly always at the top of the standings. In 1923, it was no different. The Reds had finished second the year before to the Giants, and would find themselves in the same spot again, despite winning 91 games with the league's best pitching staff.

The season was winding down on September 29, with just four games remaining and the Giants already having clinched the pennant. Luque, who had originally hoped to win 30 games that season, was going for his 27th. Had he not been suspended for a week for fighting, he might have gotten a little closer to his goal. During a game in early August, Giants players had taunted him relentlessly from their dugout until he could endure no more. He plopped his glove on the mound, and beelined in their direction. Despite his small stature, Luque backed down from nobody. He punched Giants outfielder Casey Stengel and, then, while waving a bat, challenged pretty much the entire Giants team.

Only 2,000 fans showed up on September 29, a Saturday-afternoon game, to watch Luque face the St. Louis Cardinals. He didn't have his command that day and started poorly, yielding a run in the top of the first inning when left fielder Jack Smith scored on a sacrifice fly by center fielder Heinie Mueller.

The Reds quickly evened the game in the bottom of the inning against former Red Fred Toney. And after tying the score, they never looked back, adding two runs in the third inning and four in the fourth to knock Toney from the game. But they weren't finished. They piled on three more in the fifth, and a final run in the sixth, amassing 11 runs on 17 hits. Luque must have wondered where all those hits had been all season, as the Reds frequently struggled to score. Right fielder George Burns was the hitting star that day, with a single, double, triple, and a walk, scoring four times. Second baseman Wally Kimmick contributed three hits, as did left fielder Pat Duncan. Even Luque got in on the action, knocking in and scoring a run.

After the first inning, he blanked the Cardinals for the rest of the game. He surrendered only four hits but walked six, a high number for him that season, when he averaged just 2.5 per 9 innings. Maybe his mind was already focused on going home. Knowing the game would be his last of the season, Luque had already packed his bags beforehand so he could leave right after it for Havana, where he received a hero's welcome and cemented his lifelong celebrity status.

Before the next season, he became the team's second-highest-paid player, right behind Edd Roush. Luque would never win 20 again and most years would hover around the .500 mark. In 1925, he did lead the National League in ERA for a second time with a 2.63 mark. He also led the league in shutouts that year. After a rough 1929 at the age of 38, Luque was traded to Brooklyn. He went on to pitch six more seasons, ending up with the Giants, whom he had frustrated for so many years. By then he was back in the bullpen, finally calling it quits at 44.

But his legacy lives on through the relationship the Reds have been able to maintain with Cuba, one that is blossoming again as players begin to move more easily out of the country. While it's likely none of the players today have ever heard of Dolf Luque, in his time he was the first Latin star in the major leagues, and therefore revered in his homeland. His success sparked a love among fans in Cuba for the Reds. In his essay on Luque for sabr.org, Peter C. Bjarkman notes that Cuban fans for many years referred fondly to *nuestros queridos rojos*—"our beloved Reds."

St. Louis	1	0	0	0	0	0	0	0	0	—	1	4 2
Cincinnati	1	0	2	4	3	1	0	0	x	—	11	17 1

St. Louis Cardinals

	AB	R	H	RBI
Flack rf	5	0	0	0
Smith lf	3	1	1	0
Bottomley 1b	3	0	1	0
Mueller cf	4	0	0	1
Stock 3b	4	0	1	0
Toporcer 2b	3	0	0	0
McCurdy c	2	0	0	0
Bell ss	3	0	1	0
Toney p	2	0	0	0
Stuart p	0	0	0	0
Sherdel ph	1	0	0	0
North p	0	0	0	0
Douthit ph	1	0	0	0
Totals	31	1	4	1

	IP	H	R	ER	BB	SO
Toney L (11–12)	3.1	7	6	2	2	0
Stuart	2.2	8	5	5	1	0
North	2.0	2	0	0	0	0
Totals	8.0	17	11	7	3	0

Cincinnati Reds

	AB	R	H	RBI		
Burns rf	4	4	3	2		
Daubert 1b	4	0	1	0		
Kimmick 2b	4	2	3	2		
Roush cf	5	0	1	2		
Duncan lf	5	1	3	1		
Wingo c	5	0	1	1		
Pinelli 3b	4	1	2	0		
Fowler ss	4	2	2	1		
Luque p	3	1	1	1		
Totals	38	11	17	10		
	IP	H	R	ER	BB	SO
Luque W (27–8)	9.0	4	1	1	6	4
Totals	9.0	4	1	1	6	4

Umpires: Charlie Moran, Bob Hart, Frank Wilson.

#41

NEW YORK METS 5, REDS 0
OCTOBER 4, 1999

Curse You, Al Leiter

The 1999 National League season was a classic example of haves and have-nots. Only six of the 16 teams finished with winning records, but the six that did were well over .500. The Atlanta Braves and Arizona Diamondbacks broke the century mark. With an excellent 96–67 record, the Reds ended up 1½ games behind the Houston Astros in the Central Division. To determine the league's wild card entry in the postseason (there was only one wild card spot at the time), the Reds would play the New York Mets in a one-game playoff.

The Reds surprised many people that year. Experts had foreseen them finishing in the middle of the pack, following three straight years in third place in the division. But during that era of offense in the major leagues, the Reds proved to be among the best. The 1999 team still holds many modern-era Reds hitting records, among them: most runs scored (865), most runs batted in (821), highest slugging percentage (.451), most hits, and most extra-base hits. They also set single-game records for total bases (May 19), most home runs (9 on September 4), and most grand slams (2 on August 21).

The offense was led by left fielder Greg Vaughn, who was acquired in February from the San Diego Padres. Vaughn also led an effort to break the team's long-standing ban on facial hair. He wore a goatee and didn't want to shave it. Owner Marge Schott, who would sell nearly all of her stock in the team in April, and officially step down as owner in October, lifted the ban. For the first time in nearly 100 years, Cincinnati players were allowed to sport beards and moustaches.

Vaughn proved to be an inspirational leader as well as a strong hitter in his one season in Cincinnati. His 45 home runs and 118 RBIs paced the team, and he posted a .535 slugging percentage and an .881 OPS. But his hot bat wasn't alone in the lineup. First baseman Sean Casey batted .332/.399/.539, and catcher Eddie Taubensee hit .311/.354/.521. Four Reds hit more than 20 home runs, while three stole 30 or more bases, and the starting eight was well supported by a strong bench. Pete Harnisch anchored the pitching staff, which included Rookie of the Year reliever Scott Williamson. A stronger starting staff might have pushed the Reds past Houston, but Steve Parris helped out with an 11–4 record and 3.50 ERA in 128⅔ innings.

The NL Central became a two-team race, the Reds battling the Astros for the title. On the season's final day, the Astros held first place by one game, while the Reds and Mets were knotted in a tie for the wild card. Only one other time in Reds history (1964) did the last game of the regular season determine if the Reds would make it to the postseason. Playing the Milwaukee Brewers, they lost the first two games of the season's final series on Friday and Saturday, forcing a do-or-die final game on Sunday afternoon. Rain delayed the scheduled 3:05 start, but because the game would impact the postseason, the teams waited . . . and waited . . . for the rain to stop. They waited five hours and 47 minutes.

Many fans in the stands waited too. The official paid attendance was 55,992, the largest regular season crowd in Brewers history, because the game was supposed to be the last at Milwaukee County Stadium. (Construction delays on the new Miller Park, however, would postpone its opening until 2001.) When the game finally started on a soaked field, the Reds scored five runs in the third inning, thanks to four consecutive singles, followed by Vaughn's three-run homer. Harnisch won his 16th game of the year, 7–1. Unfortunately, the Astros won, too, and claimed the division title. The Mets also were victorious, forcing a one-game tiebreaker in Cincinnati the following day.

The Reds arrived back home at 3:30 in the morning. Originally scheduled to start at 2:05 in the afternoon, the game was pushed to 7:05 that evening. The Reds' box office sold 54,621 tickets between 7 A.M. and 2:30 P.M., in what must have been its busiest day ever. Reds manager Jack McKeon chose Steve Parris to start on the mound, facing Al Leiter for the Mets. Because the game was technically a tiebreaker, and not a postseason contest, statistics were counted toward the regular season.

Cincinnati Enquirer columnist Paul Daugherty described the fate-determining Monday night as a "drippy Edgar Allan Poe evening." The weather, however, didn't dampen the spirits of the packed house at Cinergy Field. The Mets' bats, however, quickly did. Left fielder Ricky Henderson led off the game with a single to left field and second baseman Edgar Alfonzo followed him with a home run to straightaway center field. With fans barely settled in their seats, the Reds were down 2–0.

With two out in the third inning, Parris walked Alfonzo, and first baseman John Olerud doubled to put runners at second and third. Parris gave catcher Mike Piazza an intentional pass to load the bases. McKeon pulled his starter, calling on Denny Neagle to get the third out. Instead, Neagle walked third baseman Robin Ventura, giving the Mets a 3–0 lead. In the fifth, they added to it on a solo shot by Henderson, and tacked on one more in the sixth when Alfonzo doubled in shortstop Rey Ordonez.

Leiter, meanwhile cruised through the Reds lineup, which apparently had left its lumber back in Milwaukee. Going into the ninth inning, Leiter had given up only one hit, a single by center fielder Jeffrey Hammonds in the second inning. In the bottom of the ninth, second baseman Pokey Reese led off with a double to left field, and shortstop Barry Larkin moved him to third with a ground out. After Sean Casey struck out, Leiter walked Vaughn, bringing up right fielder Dmitri Young. A home run would have put the Reds within two runs, but Young shot a liner to second baseman Alfonzo for the final out. The game and the season were over.

Despite the loss, the fans stood and cheered the players who had surprised everyone with an outstanding season. During the off-season, Vaughn signed a free agent deal with the Tampa Bay Devil Rays, but the Reds replaced his bat by bringing home Cincinnati native Ken Griffey Jr., raising the hopes of Reds fans for the new millennium.

New York	2	0	1		0	1	1		0	0	0	—	5	9	0
Cincinnati	0	0	0		0	0	0		0	0	0	—	0	2	0

New York Mets

	AB	R	H	RBI
Henderson lf	5	2	2	1
Mora lf	0	0	0	0
Alfonzo 2b	4	2	2	3
Olerud 1b	5	0	2	0
Piazza c	2	0	0	0
Ventura 3b	3	0	1	1
Hamilton cf	4	0	1	0
Cedeno rf	4	0	1	0
Ordonez ss	3	1	0	0
Leiter p	3	0	0	0
Totals	33	5	9	5

	IP	H	R	ER	BB	SO
Leiter W (13–12)	9.0	2	0	0	4	7
Totals	9.0	2	0	0	4	7

Cincinnati Reds

	AB	R	H	RBI
Reese 2b	3	0	1	0
Larkin ss	3	0	0	0
Casey 1b	4	0	0	0
Vaughn lf	3	0	0	0
Young rf	4	0	0	0
Hammonds cf	3	0	1	0
Taubensee c	2	0	0	0
Boone 3b	3	0	0	0
Parris p	0	0	0	0
Neagle p	1	0	0	0
Stynes ph	1	0	0	0
Graves p	0	0	0	0
Lewis ph	1	0	0	0
Reyes p	0	0	0	0
Totals	28	0	2	0

	IP	H	R	ER	BB	SO
Parris L (11–4)	2.2	3	3	3	3	1
Neagle	2.1	2	1	1	3	2
Graves	3.0	2	1	1	2	2
Reyes	1.0	2	0	0	0	0
Totals	9.0	2	0	0	0	0

Umpires: HP—Bruce Froemming, 1B—Gerry Davis, 2B—Mark Hirsch-
    beck, 3B—Ed Rapuano.
Time of game: 3:03.
Attendance: 54,621.

REDS 4, ST. LOUIS CARDINALS 0
JUNE 16, 1978

Tom's Terrific Day

When the reigning world-champion Cincinnati Reds traded for New York Mets ace Tom Seaver on June 15, 1977, many fans and baseball sages felt they'd sealed their third straight National League pennant. Seaver, after all, was one of the best pitchers in the game, a four-time 20-game winner, three-time Cy Young Award winner, a future Hall of Famer. Still just 32 years old, he'd won a Cy Young as recently as 1975. With the powerful bats of the Big Red Machine behind him, surely a pennant was as good as won.

The trade sent Reds fans into rapture. At last they had a durable and legitimate ace. And they'd given up so little to get him: reserve infielder Doug Flynn, young outfielders Steve Henderson and Dan Norman, and pitcher Pat Zachry. The core of stars remained intact.

Seaver turned out to be as good as expected, posting a 14–3 record and 2.34 ERA for the Reds that year. Unfortunately, he wasn't enough to push the team past the Dodgers; after back-to-back pennants, the Reds finished second in the West Division. They won 92 games the following year but still ended up in second place behind the Dodgers. Seaver led the staff with 16 victories and in pretty much every other statistical category. But on June 16, 1978, almost exactly a year to the day of being traded to the Reds, he did something he'd never done before and would never do again in his career.

On that warm Friday night, the Reds hosted the St. Louis Cardinals at Riverfront Stadium, facing John Denny, the top guy in their rotation that year and who would end his career nearly a decade later as a Red. With two tough pitchers throwing well, neither team managed a hit through the first four innings. Seaver had walked two batters, Denny three.

Seaver retired the Cardinals in order in the top of the fifth to keep alive his no-hitter, but the Reds spoiled Denny's bid in the bottom of the inning. Center fielder Cesar Geronimo led off with a single to center. Don Werner, who was catching for the injured Johnny Bench, singled to left. Seaver failed to sacrifice the runners, bringing up Pete Rose at the top of the order. Rose had been in a slump, but two days earlier had gotten two hits against the Cubs to start what would become his league-record 44-game hitting streak. He kept the streak alive by lacing a double to right, scoring both runners. An error by Cardinals catcher Ted Simmons allowed him to reach third base, but he didn't stay there long as second baseman Joe Morgan doubled him in.

After Seaver set down the Cardinals in order, first baseman Dan Driessen homered to lead off the bottom of the sixth. Neither team scored in the seventh; as they moved to the eighth, Reds manager Sparky Anderson replaced Rose at third with Ray Knight for added defense. The move immediately paid off. The first batter, right fielder Jerry Morales, knocked a slow roller to third. Knight charged, fielded the ball cleanly, and threw him out. Following another ground out to Knight and a fly out to left, Seaver found himself only three outs from the first no-hitter of his career. It was not an unfamiliar situation for him. He had reached this point three times before and failed in all of them to seal the deal.

Before the game, he'd even talked with Reds pitcher Bill Bonham about one of the ninth-inning failures. Their discussion was prompted by a trade on the previous day involving Cubs outfielder Joe Wallis. Seaver recalled that the closest he'd come to a no-hitter was in September 1975, facing the Cubs. Wallis had managed a single with two strikes and two outs. Seaver had thrown him a curve ball, and he told Bonham that if he ever reached the ninth inning with a no-hitter again, he wouldn't throw any curves.

No doubt that strategy was on the top of his mind as he took the mound in the final inning. The previous failures must have occurred to him too, especially after walking the first batter, pinch hitter Jerry Mumphrey. Despite yielding no hits, Seaver did not have overpowering stuff that night. He walked three and had only struck out three.

Cardinals star Lou Brock came to bat next and flied out to left. Garry Templeton followed him by grounding to shortstop, forcing out Mumphrey at second. With two out, the crowd of more than 38,000 stood cheering for Seaver. Among them was his wife, Nancy, and their daughters, Sarah and Anne. Cardinal center fielder George Hendrick stepped into the batter's box. The count ran to one ball and two strikes before he slapped a grounder to first base, where Driessen fielded it, stepped on the bag, and ran to join his teammates mobbing Seaver.

In his twelfth season, after coming so close a few times before, Tom Terrific, as he was known, had finally gotten his no-hitter.

Seaver would go on to pitch four more seasons for the Reds. In 1979 he won 11 games in a row to help the team take the division title. Two years later, he posted a 14–2 record in the strike-shortened season that saw the Reds finish with the National League's best record but be shut out of the playoffs. That year he was the runner-up for the Cy Young Award. During his time with the Reds, Seaver would reach 3,000 career strikeouts.

After the 1982 season, he was traded back to the Mets as the Reds began to rebuild. Seaver finished his career in the American League, winning 16 games at the age of 40 in 1985 before calling it quits the following year. His time with the Reds didn't produce the pennant fans had expected, but no one can complain about his performance during those six years, especially not on the night when he refused to surrender a single hit.

St. Louis	0	0	0		0	0	0		0	0	0	—	0	0	2
Cincinnati	0	0	0		0	3	1		0	0	x	—	4	7	1

St. Louis Cardinals

	AB	R	H	RBI
Brock lf	4	0	0	0
Templeton ss	4	0	0	0
Hendrick cf	4	0	0	0
Simmons c	3	0	0	0
Hernandez 1b	2	0	0	0
Morales rf	3	0	0	0
Reitz 3b	2	0	0	0
Phillips 2b	3	0	0	0
Denny p	2	0	0	0
Schultz p	0	0	0	0
Mumphrey ph	0	0	0	0
Totals	27	0	0	0

	IP	H	R	ER	BB	SO
Denny L (6–5)	6.0	6	4	4	5	3
Schultz	2.0	1	0	0	0	2
Totals	8.0	7	4	4	5	5

Cincinnati Reds

	AB	R	H	RBI		
Rose 3b	4	1	2	2		
Knight 3b	0	0	0	0		
Griffey rf	4	0	0	0		
Morgan 2b	2	0	1	1		
Foster lf	3	0	0	0		
Driessen 1b	4	1	1	1		
Concepcion ss	4	0	1	0		
Geronimo cf	3	1	1	0		
Werner c	3	1	1	0		
Seaver p	2	0	0	0		
Totals	29	4	7	4		

	IP	H	R	ER	BB	SO
Seaver W (8–4)	9.0	0	0	0	3	3
Totals	9.0	0	0	0	3	3

Umpires: HP—Terry Tata, 1B—Paul Pryor, 2B—Ed Vargo, 3B—Charlie
Williams.
Time of game: 2:09.
Attendance: 38,216.

#39

REDS 1, CHICAGO CUBS 0
AUGUST 19, 1965

Maloney Makes Sure

Talk about tough luck. On June 14, 1965, Reds ace Jim Maloney carried a no-hitter into the 11th inning against the Mets. In the game, he struck out 18 batters and walked only one. But the Reds had scored no runs. After surrendering a home run in that inning, Maloney ended up the losing pitcher.

Two months later, on August 19, on a windy afternoon in Chicago, the big right-hander might have felt a twinge of déjà vu. Once again he found himself in the ninth inning with a no-hitter and also no lead. Another scoreless tie. Surely he could have wondered if he might pitch another no-hitter and end up losing again.

During the 1960s, Maloney was the team's top pitcher. He won 134 games for the Reds, more than any other Red in the second half of the twentieth century. He was also the only member of both the 1961 and 1970 National League pennant winners. When he was pitching well, he was almost unhittable, a match for the likes of contemporaries Sandy Koufax, Juan Marichal, and Bob Gibson.

On August 19, the Reds played a doubleheader in Wrigley Field because the previous day's game had been rained out. In the first game, Maloney faced Cubs hurler Larry Jackson. The Reds occupied fourth place but were just 3½ games behind the league-leading Los Angeles Dodgers. The Cubs were in eighth place, but their lineup included three future Hall of Famers: first baseman Ernie Banks, right fielder Billy Williams, and third baseman Ron Santo.

A warm summer wind blew in from Lake Michigan that day, no doubt helping to keep long fly balls from sailing over the ivy-covered walls. Maloney had great movement on his fastball but struggled to control it. After two perfect innings, he walked the bases loaded in the third but managed to escape without giving up a hit or a run.

Larry Jackson, meanwhile, enjoyed similar mastery over Reds hitters. Reds center fielder Vada Pinson managed a single in the first inning, but Cubs catcher (and former Red) Ed Bailey picked him off. As the game moved through the middle innings, Maloney continued to struggle with his control, but refused to give up a hit. Jackson surrendered multiple singles, including one to Maloney in the third, but no runs.

In the seventh inning, with one out, Reds right fielder Frank Robinson hit a long fly ball to left field, but the strong wind prevented it from clearing the fence. He settled for a triple, but the Reds could not knock him in. When Maloney came to bat in that inning, Bailey told his former teammate, "You have been perfect, Jim, but we have somebody hiding in the weeds." Maloney was more amused than rattled by the comment, and he ignored the stillness that had settled over the Reds dugout as the possibility of a no-hitter—and another losing one—dawned on his teammates.

Visibly tired from having thrown more than 150 pitches, Maloney opened the bottom of the ninth by hitting Santo and walking Bailey. He then got two outs before walking Jackson to load the bases. But Don Landrum popped to short to end the threat.

In the top of the 10th, with one out, Reds shortstop Leo Cardenas stepped to the plate. He would win a Gold Glove for his defense that year, and had been selected to the all-star team. Though he was batting eighth in the lineup, he was a solid hitter with surprising pop in his bat—the following year he would set the team record for most home runs in a season by a shortstop. On this day, he smacked a long fly ball that caromed off the left field foul pole for a home run, giving his team, and Maloney, a 1–0 lead.

Maloney dragged himself to the mound in the bottom of the inning and walked the first batter. Slugger Billy Williams stepped into the box and on a 3–1 count proceeded to fly out—only the third fly out of the game for the Cubs, and all of them were routine. Next up: Ernie Banks. Maloney told the press after the game that he thought Banks would swing for the fences, and so would be vulnerable to pitches low and away.

And he turned out to be right. On Maloney's 187th pitch of the game, Banks grounded weakly to Cardenas, and the Reds turned a double play. The no-hitter was complete, and Maloney won it. His teammates mobbed him. It was the first time a major-league pitcher had held the opposition hitless for 10 innings twice in a season. Maloney looked exhausted as he left the field. He'd given up 10 walks and endured 13 full counts while striking out 12 batters. Compared to his no-hitter in June, this one was far less dominant. But this time he was the victor.

That year he would go on to post a 20–9 record and a career-best 2.54 ERA. Along with young Sammy Ellis, Maloney gave the Reds an outstanding one-two punch, and the offense led the National League in batting average, on-base percentage, slugging, and runs scored. But they lacked a third starting pitcher who might have put them over the top, and they wound up in fourth place. Their attempt to get that third pitcher and a pennant led them to make the most infamous trade in franchise history, sending Frank Robinson to Baltimore for right-hander Milt Pappas.

Maloney, only 25 years old, would give the Reds four more strong seasons before an injury suffered while running to first base early in 1970 cut short his career. But on that warm August afternoon in 1965, the Reds, who would lose the nightcap 5–4, must have felt pretty good about their big ace and the future.

Cincinnati	0	0	0		0	0	0		0	0	0	1	— 1	9	0
Chicago	0	0	0		0	0	0		0	0	0	0	— 0	0	1

Cincinnati Reds

	AB	R	H	RBI
Harper lf	5	0	1	0
Rose 2b	5	0	1	0
Pinson cf	3	0	2	0
Robinson rf	4	0	2	0
Coleman 1b	4	0	0	0
Keough 1b	0	0	0	0
Johnson 3b	4	0	0	0
Edwards c	4	0	0	0
Cardenas ss	4	1	1	1
Maloney p	4	0	2	0
Totals	37	1	9	1

	IP	H	R	ER	BB	SO
Maloney W (14–6)	10.0	0	0	0	10	12
Totals	10.0	0	0	0	10	12

Chicago Cubs

	AB	R	H	RBI
Landrum cf	4	0	0	0
Clemens lf	3	0	0	0
Williams rf	4	0	0	0
Banks 1b	5	0	0	0
Santo 3b	3	0	0	0
Bailey c	2	0	0	0
Beckert 2b	2	0	0	0
Kessinger ss	2	0	0	0
Stewart ph, ss	1	0	0	0
Jackson p	2	0	0	0
Totals	28	0	0	0

	IP	H	R	ER	BB	SO
Jackson L (11–15)	10.0	9	1	1	0	5
Totals	10.0	9	1	1	0	5

Umpires: HP—Mel Steiner, 1B—Al Barlick, 2B—Augie Donatelli, 3B—Stan Landes.

Time of game: 2:51.

#38

Western Avenue's Bombers

The postwar years in the Queen City were generally good ones. The economy boomed. The city expanded into new suburbs. New cars rolled off assembly lines onto new roads, and prosperity ruled the day. Life for the city's only major-league sports team, however, was cause for depression. Starting in 1945, Reds fans suffered through 11 straight losing seasons—more than a decade mired in the bottom half of the National League. Adding to their woes, in 1953 they'd even been forced to change their name to "Redlegs" to avoid association with the "Red Scare" of Communism.

Player injuries, ill-advised trades, unrealized prospect potential, and poor management combined to make one season after the next an exercise in futility and frustration. As newspaper columnist Ritter Collett noted in his book *The Cincinnati Reds,* "After World War II, West Germany was on its feet before the Reds were."

The 1956 season began with the usual hopes and the usual doubts. The previous year had offered some signs of life, as pitcher Joe Nuxhall won 17 games, and first baseman Ted Kluszewski hit 47 home runs. Second baseman Johnny Temple and shortstop Roy McMillan formed a nifty keystone combo that produced a lot of double plays. And there was talk about a very promising young rookie outfielder named Frank Robinson. Maybe this could be a season when the Reds actually competed for the National League pennant.

To bolster the sense of a new era, the team debuted a new uniform style that featured a sleeveless vest. The Cubs had worn a similar style for a few years in the early 1940s, but they were the only other team that had previously donned vests. While offering a fresh, flashy look, the uniforms also accommodated the bulging biceps of Big Klu, who had been forced to cut off his sleeves to get a full swing of the bat. The home uniform featured a wishbone "C" without the "Reds" name inside it for the first time since 1912, likely due to changing the name to "Redlegs."

With their new look, the Reds started another new trend—winning baseball games. At the All-Star break, they held first place. And they did it mostly by hitting home runs. Robinson proved to be the real deal, hitting 38 that season. He was followed by outfielder Wally Post, who hit 36, Kluszewski (35), outfielder Gus Bell (29), and catcher Ed Bailey (28). Collectively they were called the Western Avenue Bombers. (Western Avenue ran along Crosley Field's outfield fence and frequently acted as the landing zone for baseballs hit by Redleg sluggers.)

The high-water mark for the Bombers that season took place on August 18, a steamy Saturday night at Crosley Field. Locked in a fierce three-way battle for first place with the Milwaukee Braves and Brooklyn Dodgers, the Redlegs drew 21,472 patrons to the ballpark to watch their suddenly strong team take on the Braves. Right-hander Johnny Klippstein took the mound for the Reds, facing Milwaukee's Ray Crone. Filling in for injured Gus Bell, Bob Thurman played left field with Robinson shifting to center field.

The Braves scored quickly in the first inning to grab a 1–0 lead. In the bottom of the second, the Redlegs loaded the bases, and Kluszewski scored on a sacrifice fly by third baseman Alex Grammas. It wasn't until the third inning that the fireworks began, when Robinson, Kluszewski, and Post all homered. The Braves brought power of their own, sending two balls over the Crosley Field fences to tighten the score at 5–4. Thurman widened the gap again with a solo shot in the fifth inning.

Bats on both sides simmered down until the bottom of the seventh inning, when Thurman slammed a two-run homer, and Kluszewski followed with another round-tripper. Leading 9–4 in the bottom of the eighth, the Redlegs continued the slaughter, as Robinson unleashed a three-run bomb, and Thurman hit his third homer of the game. Hal Jeffcoat, who pitched the final five innings, allowing only one hit and no runs, sent the Braves down in order to seal the victory. When the dust cleared, the Redlegs had whacked eight longballs, the most in one game in National League history at the time.

The Redlegs continued to blast away for the rest of the season, tying the all-time major-league season record with 221 home runs in 154 games, held at the time by the 1947 New York Giants. Big Klu missed some games late in the season due to back problems, which might have hurt the home run output just enough to prohibit the team from setting a new record. The Reds did get contributions to the effort from bench players such as Thurman, Smoky Burgess, and George Crowe.

The 1956 Redlegs didn't, however, live by home runs alone. The powerful lineup was complemented by a solid rotation, led by 19-game-winner Brooks Lawrence, who put together a string of 13 straight wins that year. Manager Birdie Tebbetts also relied on an excellent bullpen. The Redlegs stayed in the pennant hunt for the entire season before falling short. They ended up in third place, just two games behind the Dodgers and a game behind the Braves. For the first time in its history, the team topped the one-million mark in attendance.

Going into the 1957 season, Redlegs fans, along with many sportswriters, believed the team would win the pennant, and after a strong start they did occupy first place into July, but lacked the starting rotation to hold on. They slid to fourth place with an 80–74 record. Still, there was a new spirit of optimism among the fans.

With the Reds' success in the 1960s, and the dominance of the Big Red Machine through the 1970s, the might of the Western Avenue Bombers has been largely forgotten. Even the team record of eight homers in a game was broken—on September 4, 1999. But for long-suffering Reds fans in 1956, the Bombers brought winning baseball back to town.

Milwaukee	1	0	0	3	0	0	0	0	0	—	4	9	1
Cincinnati	0	1	4	0	1	0	3	4	x	—	13	14	0

Milwaukee Braves

	AB	R	H	RBI
O'Connell 2b	5	1	1	0
Logan ss	5	0	2	0
Aaron rf	4	0	0	0
Mathews 3b	3	0	1	1
Adcock 1b	4	1	1	1
Thomson lf	3	0	1	0
Bruton cf	4	1	2	0
Atwell c	4	1	1	2
Crone p	0	0	0	0
Buhl p	1	0	0	0
Covington ph	0	0	0	0
Conley p	0	0	0	0
Jolly p	0	0	0	0
Tanner ph	1	0	0	0
Totals	34	4	9	4

	IP	H	R	ER	BB	SO
Crone L (9–8)	2.1	6	4	4	0	0
Buhl	2.2	2	2	2	0	2
Conley	2.2	5	7	3	2	1
Jolly	0.1	1	0	0	1	0
Totals	8.0	14	13	9	3	3

Cincinnati Redlegs

	AB	R	H	RBI
Temple 2b	5	0	0	0
Robinson cf	4	3	2	4
Thurman lf	5	4	4	4
Kluszewski 1b	4	3	3	3
Post rf	5	1	3	1
Bailey c	5	0	1	0
Grammas 3b	3	1	0	1
McMillan ss	3	1	1	0
Klippstein p	2	0	0	0
Jeffcoat p	1	0	0	0
Totals	37	13	14	13

	IP	H	R	ER	BB	SO
Klippstein	4.0	8	4	4	0	1
Jeffcoat W (4–2)	5.0	1	0	0	2	1
Totals	9.0	9	4	4	2	2

Umpires: HP—Frank Dascoli, 1B—Frank Secory, 2B—Bill Engeln, 3B—
   Larry Goetz.
Time of game: 2:42.
Attendance: 21,472.

#37

A Great Day in Redland

As the calendar moved into the 1910s, baseball was becoming the national pastime in America. It was also becoming big business. No longer simply the domain of rowdy "cranks" and "bugs" (popular terms for "fans" in that era), baseball's audience was expanding. Women could attend games without fear, and even families could spend an afternoon at the ballpark. The sporting crowd had become just one group within an ever-growing audience for the game.

Seeing an opportunity to pull in bigger bucks, teams—and the cities that hosted them—began to tear down their rickety (and highly flammable) wooden parks that could accommodate 5,000 to 10,000 customers, and build steel and concrete structures to hold many more. Between 1909 and 1911, Philadelphia, Pittsburgh, St. Louis, Chicago (Comiskey Park), Washington, and New York (the Polo Grounds) debuted new home fields. In 1912, Fenway Park opened in Boston and Navin Field (later Tiger Stadium) in Detroit. That same year, Cincinnati debuted Redland Field.

Since 1902, the Reds had played at the Palace of the Fans, which could seat only 6,000 people, though a few thousand more could stand in the outfield. Despite mediocre records, the Reds drew plenty of fans, and owner Garry Herrmann knew the city needed a bigger, better place to play. A consummate dealmaker, Herrmann gathered the necessary funds from stockholders and other Cincinnati business interests to fund the project. Local architectural firm Hake & Hake was commissioned to design a ballpark to be built at the same location as the old one—the corner of Western Avenue and Findlay Street in the West End. Additional ground was purchased for the larger facility, as well as to create a parking lot.

Only days after the 1911 season ended, construction crews began building the new home of the Reds. As Opening Day in 1912 drew closer, a name for the ballpark still hadn't been decided. Many local businessmen urged Herrmann to name it after himself, but he refused. He chose "Redland Field," which had been sort of a local nickname for the team's previous homes. The Reds played the Boston Red Sox in an exhibition game at the new facility on April 6, losing 13–1. According to *Redleg Journal,* by Greg Rhodes and John Snyder, workers laid down sod in deep right field during the game.

With a double-deck area stretching from first base to third and single-deckers stretching all the way to the right and left field corners, Redland Field could seat a crowd of more than 25,000 patrons. More than 26,000 showed up for the Opening Day game on April 11 against the Chicago Cubs. All could see the first scoreboard in the major leagues that tallied balls, strikes, and outs.

In the early 1910s, the Reds generally vied with Philadelphia and St. Louis for the fourth spot in the eight-team National League, hoping to finish around .500 to sneak into the top half of the league. New York, Chicago, and Pittsburgh were the elite teams, well ahead of the rest. During this Deadball Era, speed trumped power, and Reds left fielder Bob Bescher was the speediest in the league, stealing a team-record 81 bases in 1911 and leading the circuit four years in a row from 1909 through 1912. The Reds lineup also included the first two Cuban players in major-league history—outfielder Armando Marsans and reserve infielder Rafael Almeida, who debuted in July 1911. To get past the major leagues' color barrier, which would not be broken until 1947, the Reds characterized their light-skinned Cuban players as "Spanish." Marsans was the team's best hitter in 1912, posting a .317/.353/.404 line.

On opening day, the Reds took the field at three o'clock, wearing bright new uniforms. The new ballpark stretched to fit what the *Sporting Life* called "the largest crowd, without a doubt, which ever witnessed a baseball entertainment in Redland."

They scored in the first inning to take a 1–0 lead, but the fans must have felt it was the same old story as the Cubs battered around pitcher Frank Smith—who was characterized by the *Cincinnati Enquirer* as a "resourceful spit-baller"—erupting for five runs in the third inning. After second baseman Johnny Evers led off with a single, the Cubs batted around, with Evers making the third out on a fly to Bescher in left field.

In the fourth inning, the Reds' new manager, Hank O'day, replaced Smith with Bert Humphries. Losing 5–1, the Reds would seem to have little chance of pulling out a victory against Cubs right-hander King Cole, who'd led the league in ERA in 1910 and posted a combined 38–11 record during the previous two years. However, perhaps inspired by the new ballpark, new uniforms, and new manager, the Reds surprised the crowd by mounting a comeback. A one-out triple by third baseman Art Phelan scored second baseman Dick Egan, and shortstop Jimmy Esmond singled to left to score Phelan. First baseman Larry Hoblitzell drove Esmond to third. Humphries struck out, bringing up the top of the order. Bescher rifled a shot into right field, all the way into the standing room crowd. On an open field, it easily would have been a home run for speedy Bob, but it was called a ground rule triple, plating two more runs to tie the score.

Cubs manager Frank Chance replaced Cole with Charley Smith, who allowed two more runs before getting out of the inning. The Cubs scored a run in the seventh, as left fielder Jimmy Sheckard tripled and right fielder Frank Schulte doubled him in. The Reds scored two more in the bottom of the seventh. Egan tripled in Hoblitzell and Phelan knocked in Egan. Adding one more in the ninth, the Reds pulled off an exciting and convincing Opening Day win, 10–6, at their new ballpark.

They went on to win 20 of their first 25 games, holding first place into May. O'day (the only person in major-league history to serve full seasons as a player, manager, and umpire) was hailed as the inspiration behind the running Reds, who staged many a comeback that season. The lack of strong pitching, however, eventually pulled them back into the middle of the pack, where they finished in fourth place with a 75–78 record. O'day resigned at the end of the season.

Redland Field lasted far longer than the Reds' early success in 1912. It underwent several modifications through the years and even a name change, becoming Crosley Field when industrialist Powel Crosley bought the team in 1934. The ballpark would remain the home of the Reds until June 1970, when the team moved to Riverfront Stadium. After serving briefly as an impound lot for the city, an ignominious fate for a local landmark, historic Crosley Field was torn down in 1972.

Chicago Cubs	0	0	5		0	0	0		1	0	0	—	6	11	1
Cincinnati	1	0	0		6	0	0		2	1	x	—	10	14	0

WP: Bert Humphries (1–0)
LP: King Cole (0–1)

Cincinnati Reds

	AB	R	H	RBI
Bescher lf	5	3	2	2
Bates cf	4	1	3	1
Hoblitzell 1b	3	1	1	2
Marsans rf	4	0	1	1
Egan 2b	4	2	3	1
Phelan 3b	4	1	2	2
Esmond ss	4	1	1	1
McLean c	4	1	1	0
Smith p	0	0	0	0
McDonald ph	1	0	0	0
Humphries p	3	0	0	0
Totals	36	10	14	10

Chicago Cubs

	AB	R	H	RBI
Evers 2b	5	1	1	0
Sheckard lf	5	1	3	0
Schulte rf	4	1	2	2
Chance 1b	2	1	0	0
Lennox 3b	5	1	1	2
Hofman cf	3	1	0	0
Tinker ss	4	0	1	0
Archer c	4	0	1	1
Cole p	2	0	2	1
Smith p	1	0	0	0
Miller ph	1	0	0	0
Richie p	0	0	0	0
Totals	36	6	11	6

#36

REDS 23, CHICAGO CUBS 4
JULY 6, 1949

Walker to the Rescue

If asked which Reds hitter had the most productive game in team history, how many fans would say, "Walker Cooper"? How many would know that Walker Cooper had ever played for the Reds? He only appeared in 97 games for the team, arriving on June 13, 1949, in a trade that sent catcher Ray Mueller to the New York Giants. The following May the Reds dealt Cooper to the Boston Braves. During that brief stay, however, he put together a historic game.

At 34 years old, Cooper was on the downside of his career by the time he came to the Reds, but he was still considered one of the top catchers in the game. He'd been a leader for the St. Louis Cardinals during the war years, when they won three pennants and two world championships. He was a six-time all-star, and he would again be selected for the midsummer classic as a Red in 1949. Few catchers of that era, or any other, combined such a potent bat with such outstanding defense. He was also known as a crafty signal caller and a team motivator.

Mired in one of the most moribund periods in their history, the Reds needed a boost, and they hoped some of Cooper's winning ways would rub off on his teammates. That thinking didn't pan out, as the Reds finished the season with a 62–92 record, good for seventh place in the eight-team league. Cooper, however, performed well. And never better than on July 6 of that year, when the Reds met the Cubs on a hot Wednesday afternoon, temperatures reaching 99 degrees during the game. The Cubs were even worse than the Reds at the time, so the game didn't mean much. Maybe that's why only 4,036 showed up at Crosley Field to watch it.

Reds lefty Ken Raffensberger started on the mound and quickly dispatched the Cubs in the first inning, with help from Cooper. Third baseman Frankie

60

Gustine led off with a single, but his attempt to steal second was thwarted as Cooper gunned him down. Journeyman Monk Dubiel opened on the mound for the Cubs but didn't last long. After getting outs from two of the first three Reds batters, he was replaced by Warren Hacker, who entered the game to face Cooper, batting cleanup, who slashed a single, driving left fielder Peanuts Lowrey from first to third. Reds third baseman Grady Hatton and first baseman Ted Kluszewski both singled, bringing in two runs.

The score remained 2–0 when Cooper came to bat again in the next inning with two men on base. He singled to right field, knocking in both runs. He quickly crossed the plate himself, on a single by Kluszewski. When the inning ended, the Reds led by six. The suffocating Cincinnati summer heat, however, wasn't slowing down the hitters. In the third inning, the Cubs scored three to tighten up the game. If fans were hoping for a quick contest to get out of the heat, they weren't in luck that day. The Reds scored six more runs in the third inning, three of the scores coming on Cooper's home run off reliever Dewey Adkins.

With a comfy 12–3 lead, Raffensberger settled in, yielding just one more run through the remainder of the game. A crafty control artist with limited speed, Raffensberger was the Reds' top pitcher that season, winning 18 games— including five shutouts—for a bad team, while posting a 3.39 ERA. His arsenal of offspeed pitches included a deceptive forkball. Cardinal Hall of Famer Stan Musial named him the toughest pitcher he ever faced.

While Raffensberger dispatched the Cubs' batters, their pitchers were being steamrolled. Cooper clearly had awakened the Reds' bats. In the sixth inning he smacked another three-run home run as the Reds put six more across the plate.

One inning later, with his team leading 18–4, Cooper showed no mercy. With two men on base, he jacked his third home run of the game, this one off Bob Muncrief, Chicago's fifth pitcher of the day. In his final at bat of the day, Cooper grounded into a forceout that ended the eighth. But when the dust cleared on that blistering afternoon, Cooper's numbers were staggering. He was six for seven, with five runs scored and 10 knocked in, racking up 15 total bases in a single game. He remains the only catcher in major-league history to collect 10 or more RBIs in one game.

As a Red in 1949 he produced a .280/.330/.479 slash line and an .809 OPS in 331 plate appearances. He also led National League catchers in assists. There's no question that Cooper helped the Reds win some games that season, but the team's weaknesses far outweighed the contributions of an aging catcher. He returned the next season but mostly rode the bench for the first month. Catching duties had been given to Dixie Howell, who had split time with Cooper in 1949. The Reds also were excited about a young powerfully built backstop named Johnny Pramesa, who seemed to have a bright future.

On May 10, 1950, the Reds traded Cooper to the Boston Braves for light-hitting infielder Connie Ryan, one of many losing deals the team made during those years. Getting regular playing time again, Cooper hit .339 for the Braves and earned another All-Star Game appearance. He bounced around among a few more teams before ending up back in St. Louis to end his career at the age of 42. His time with the Reds had been short, but his record-setting game remains one of the greatest in team history.

Chicago	0	0	3	0	1	0	0	0	0	—	4	11	5
Cincinnati	2	4	6	0	0	6	3	2	x	—	23	26	1

Chicago Cubs

	AB	R	H	RBI
Gustine 3b	4	1	2	0
Cavarretta 1b	3	1	1	1
Baumholtz ph, rf	1	0	0	0
Pafko cf	3	1	3	0
Sauer lf	4	1	2	2
Reich rf, 1b	4	0	2	0
Smalley ss	3	0	0	0
Muncrief p	0	0	0	0
Verban ph	1	0	0	0
Kush p	0	0	0	0
Owen c	2	0	0	0
Walker c	1	0	0	0
Mauch 2b	4	0	1	0
Dubiel p	0	0	0	0
Hacker p	0	0	0	0
Adkins p	1	0	0	0
Lade p	1	0	0	0
Ramazzotti ph, ss	2	0	0	0
Totals	34	4	11	3

	IP	H	R	ER	BB	SO
Dubiel	0.2	1	1	1	0	0
Hacker L (2–4)	1.0	5	5	3	2	0
Adkins	0.2	5	5	5	1	1
Lade	3.2	9	7	7	2	1
Muncrief	1.0	3	3	3	0	0
Kush	1.0	3	2	2	1	0
Totals	8.0	26	23	21	6	2

Cincinnati Reds

	AB	R	H	RBI
Walker cf, lf	5	4	3	1
Adams 2b	5	3	3	2
Lowrey lf	5	3	2	2
Merriman cf	2	1	2	0
Cooper c	7	5	6	10
Hatton 3b	6	3	4	1
Kluszewski 1b	6	1	3	5
Wyrostek rf	3	1	2	0
Corbitt ss	6	1	1	0
Raffensberger p	4	1	0	0
Totals	49	23	26	21

	IP	H	R	ER	BB	SO
Raffensberger W (9–6)	9.0	11	4	4	2	2
Totals	9.0	11	4	4	2	2

Umpires: Lee Ballanfant, Al Barlick, George Barr.

#35

A Nice Day for Noodles

"Hey, who's the old guy?"

New Reds players would often ask this during pregame workouts in the late 1940s. A man who was close to 70 years old had a locker in the clubhouse. He wore a Reds uniform and worked out with the team, sometimes pitched batting practice. Answering the question, a teammate would say the old guy "played for the Reds a long time ago." The old man never spoke of playing in the majors, never offered advice or regaled them with tales of his glory days.

According to Reds historian Lee Allen in his classic book *The Cincinnati Reds,* sometime during World War II a player found a newspaper clipping about the mysterious old man—whose name they learned was Frank "Noodles" Hahn. They found out that almost 50 years before then he'd been one of the best in the game. But his career was cut short by arm problems, and he'd long since been forgotten.

Noodles Hahn grew up in Nashville, Tennessee, and began pitching professionally at 16. According to Daniel R. Levitt's article on Hahn for the Society for American Baseball Research, various theories exist about the nickname "Noodles"—most of them involving noodle soup. A left-hander who could throw with exceptional velocity, he drew the Reds' attention, and they signed him to a contract in 1899.

In the late 1890s, the Reds fielded strong teams. They often stood at or near the top of the National League for months at a time, but year after year they faded down the stretch. While Hahn wasn't able to get the team over the hump in his first season, he probably would have won Rookie of the Year if the award had existed at the time. He led the National League in strikeouts (145) and

Fielding Independent Pitching (2.88) while compiling a 23–8 record. Word of the flame-throwing lefty in Cincinnati quickly spread in the baseball world.

As the twentieth century began, the Reds sank into mediocrity, but no team wanted to play them when Hahn was on the mound. He led the league in strikeouts in 1900 and again in 1901. He won 20 games four times for teams that rarely finished .500; in 1901, he won 22 of the team's 52 victories. As Allen expresses it in his book, "Noodles was a life-saver."

In 1900, the Reds finished seventh in the eight-team National League, 15 games under .500 and 21½ out of first place. Other than Hall of Fame first baseman Jake Beckley and up-and-coming Sam "Wahoo" Crawford, the team lacked hitters. They didn't field the ball particularly well, either. Hahn was the ace of a pedestrian pitching staff and considered as good a left-hander as any in the majors.

He added to his bona fides on Thursday, July 12, when the Reds played the Phillies at League Park in Cincinnati. A slugging team led by three future Hall of Famers (Ed Delahanty, Elmer Flick, and Nap Lajoie), the Phillies were in fourth place at the time with a winning record, while the Reds occupied the fifth spot at 32–35. With Hahn on the mound, the Reds surely would have felt confident about a victory despite facing a lineup of good hitters. Just over 2,800 fans crowded into the grandstand, and another few hundred, according the *Cincinnati Enquirer,* paid a dime to sit on top of train cars parked at the rear of the ballpark. Other fans stood on nearby rooftops to watch, a number that grew during the game as word spread through the neighborhood that Hahn had yet to yield a hit.

In the top of the first, Hahn retired the first two batters and then walked Delahanty, the league's reigning batting champion, before striking out Flick, who batted .367 that year. The Reds then jumped on Phillies starter Bill Bernhard in the bottom of the inning to take a 1–0 lead. Hahn would need no more runs. He cruised effortlessly through the Philadelphia lineup. As he walked off the mound after each inning, cheers from the crowd grew louder. While on the mound, he took a lot of razzing from the Phillies bench, but the *Enquirer* reported, "the young southpaw was cool as could be."

After walking Delahanty in the first, he fanned him in his other two at bats. He hit Flick with a pitch and struck him out twice. He also walked catcher Ed McFarland. Other than the two walks and the hit by pitch, he didn't allow a base runner. He struck out eight. Meanwhile, the Reds scored two more runs in the third inning and another in the seventh, thanks to a triple by Beckley and a home run by Crawford. They collected seven hits on the day, including two singles by Hahn.

In the top of the ninth, Hahn needed just three more outs to pitch a no-hitter, a rare feat in that high-contact era when batters tended to slap the ball rather than swing from the heels as they do today. Shortstop Monte Cross led off with a whiff. Pearce Chiles then batted for Bernhard, but he had no better luck against Hahn, who was still going strong. Chiles also went down swinging. Center fielder Roy Thomas followed him, desperate to break up the no-hitter. A speedy runner, Thomas bunted and dashed down the baseline. Reds catcher Heinie Peitz pounced on the ball and fired it to Beckley at first base before Thomas could get there. Game over.

Noodles Hahn had thrown the first no-hitter in the twentieth century, when the modern era of the major leagues officially begins. In the exclamatory style of the era's sports reporting, the *Enquirer* called the no-hitter "the greatest pitching feat that has ever been seen on the local lot." He had made Philadelphia's renowned hitters "look like a bunch of bum amateurs." It was a great day among many great days in Hahn's short career. On May 22, 1901, he notched 16 strikeouts in a game with Boston, a record that wasn't broken until 1933—a more free-swinging era. In 1901 he set team records that still stand and likely always will: most games started (42), most complete games (31), most innings pitched (375.1). He also still holds the Reds season record for most strikeouts by a left-hander (239).

No National League pitcher in the modern era has ever won 100 games at an earlier age than Hahn. He'd won 122 games by time he was 25. But the excessive innings he pitched for six straight seasons eventually caught up with him in 1905, when arm problems ended his career. By the age of 27, when players usually reach their prime, he was gone from the game. A longer career likely would have earned him a place in Cooperstown and baseball history. But he enjoyed a successful second career as a government meat inspector, and until his late sixties he spent afternoons on the field, tossing a ball around with young players who didn't know that he'd once been among the best in the game.

About those ballpark visits, Lee Allen wrote: "Unlike some old-timers, Noodles was never one to get a rookie off in a corner and tell him how baseball used to be played or should be played. He was never a mine of misinformation about the game, and was even reluctant to discuss his own career." Having left the game too early, Noodles likely just wanted to keep playing ball.

| Philadelphia | 0 0 0 | 0 0 0 | 0 0 0 — 0 |
| Cincinnati | 1 0 2 | 0 0 0 | 1 0 x — 4 |

Cincinnati Reds

	AB	R	H
Barrett cf	2	1	1
Corcoran ss	4	1	1
Beckley 1b	3	1	1
Crawford lf	2	1	1
McBride rf	3	0	0
Quinn 2b	4	0	0
Wood 3b	4	0	1
Peitz c	4	0	0
Hahn p	4	0	2
Totals	30	4	7

Philadelphia Phillies

	AB	R	H
Thomas cf	4	0	0
Slagle lf	3	0	0
Delahanty 1b	2	0	0
Flick rf	2	0	0
McFarland c	2	0	0
Wolverton 3b	3	0	0
Dolan 2b	3	0	0
Cross ss	3	0	0
Bernhard p	2	0	0
Chiles ph	1	0	0
Totals	25	0	0

Umpire—Terry.

#34

30–30 Club

Barry Larkin was destined to play for the Reds. Born and raised in Cincinnati, he grew up in the Big Red Machine era and idolized Reds shortstop Dave Concepcion. The Reds picked Larkin out of high school in the second round of the 1982 amateur draft, but he took a football scholarship to the University of Michigan instead. In the spring of his freshman year, he decided to focus on baseball, becoming a two-time All-American and Big Ten player of the year. The Reds again chose him in the amateur draft in 1985, and this time he signed a contract.

By August of the following year, he was playing the majors and by 1988 was an all-star. Two years later, he helped lead the Reds to a world championship; throughout the 1990s, he was arguably the game's premiere shortstop.

In 1995 he was chosen as the National League's Most Valuable Player, hitting .319/.394/.492 with 15 home runs and 51 stolen bases, while leading the Reds to the National League Championship Series. He also won the second of three consecutive Gold Glove awards. Cincinnatians love their hometown players, and Larkin brought such grace and professionalism to every game that he was the team's fan favorite. They were eager to see what he would do for an encore.

Eager to take the next step and win the pennant, the Reds signed outfielder Eric Davis and catcher Joe Oliver as free agents during the off-season, bringing back two stars of the 1990 World Championship team. The 1996 season, however, got off to a terrible start. On Opening Day, home plate umpire John McSherry collapsed and died on the field seven pitches into the game. Under new manager Ray Knight, the team struggled through the early months of the season, occupying last place in the Central Division by June. The strong offense that blended speed and power eventually found itself, and the team started winning. Davis hit 26 home runs and stole 23 bases in 1996, and first baseman Hal Morris hit .313, ending the season with a 29-game hitting streak.

The brightest star, however, was Larkin once again. He led the team in home runs, runs batted in, runs scored, stolen bases, and OPS. On September 22, he was poised to achieve yet another milestone in his career. With one more home run he would become the first shortstop, and only the second infielder, in major-league history to reach the 30–30 Club, with 30 homers and 30 stolen bases in a season.

Having dug themselves out of the deep, early season hole, the Reds were a game over .500 on September 13 before losing five in a row coming into a series at Cinergy Field with the first-place St. Louis Cardinals. Occupying third-place and on the brink of being mathematically eliminated from the division race, the Reds took the first game of the series on Friday, September 20. The next day's game was rained out, and with only nine games left in the season, the teams decided to play a doubleheader on Sunday.

Right-hander Mark Portugal started the first game on the mound for the Reds, facing lefty Donovan Osborne. In the bottom of the first, Larkin launched a deep fly to left field, bringing the crowd of more than 38,000 to its feet, but the ball fell short of the wall and was caught for an out. In the top of the second inning, Portugal walked third baseman Gary Gaetti, who went to third base on a single by first baseman John Mabry and scored on catcher Tom Pagnozzi's sacrifice fly. Gaetti scored again in the fourth inning, hitting a two-run homer.

In the bottom of the inning, the Reds scored their first run of the game when Joe Oliver, pinch-hitting for Portugal, cracked a bases-loaded sacrifice fly, bringing in third baseman Eduardo Perez. The score stood at 3–1 in the bottom of the fifth when Larkin, who had walked in the third inning, came to the plate with one out. Once again he hit a long fly to deep left field, but this one cleared the fence for his 30th home run of the year. Matched with his 36 stolen bases, he was now a member of the 30–30 Club. As the home run fireworks blasted the afternoon air, fans stood and cheered. The scoreboard announced the achievement and play stopped for a few minutes while the ovation continued.

One of the first teammates to congratulate Larkin on the achievement was Eric Davis, the only other Red in history at the time who was also a member of the 30–30 Club. Davis had achieved the milestone in 1987 in only 90 games, which remains the fastest a player has ever reached 30–30. Alex Rodriguez is next on the "fastest" list, 17 games behind. Davis probably would have reached the rarified 40–40 Club that season, but missed 17 games in September with a rib injury. (On September 26, 2007, the Reds' Brandon Phillips joined the

30–30 Club with a home run against the Houston Astros. He is one of only three second basemen ever to achieve that milestone.)

When the ovation for Larkin finally subsided, the game resumed, and the Reds put four runs on the board in the bottom of the seventh inning. Second baseman Bret Boone hit a two-run triple and scored on a passed ball. Left fielder Kevin Mitchell walked and then scored on double by catcher Brook Fordyce, making the score 6–3, where it remained at the end of the game. The Reds also took the nightcap, winning 6–0 on just three hits, though none were from Larkin.

Despite finishing third in the 14-team league in slugging, home runs, and stolen bases, and second in runs scored, the Reds ended the season at 81–81. Larkin hit .298 with 33 homers and 36 stolen bases. He also walked 96 times, the most in his career and struck out just 52 times—not a bad encore to an MVP season. He retired in 2004, having played his entire 19-year career with the Reds, for whom it seemed he was always destined to play. He was enshrined in the Hall of Fame in 2012.

St. Louis	0	1	0	2	0	0	0	0	0	—	3	5 0
Cincinnati	0	0	0	1	1	0	4	0	x	—	6	10 0

St. Louis Cardinals

	AB	R	H	RBI
Smith ss	4	0	0	0
Lankford cf	4	0	0	0
Gant lf	4	1	1	0
Jordan rf	4	0	1	0
Gaetti 3b	2	2	1	2
Mabry 1b	3	0	1	0
Pagnozzi c	3	0	0	1
Gallego 2b	4	0	1	0
Osborne p	2	0	0	0
Petkovsek p	0	0	0	0
Fossas p	0	0	0	0
Young ph	0	0	0	0
Mathews p	0	0	0	0
Ludwick p	0	0	0	0
Totals	30	3	5	3

	IP	H	R	ER	BB	SO
Osborne	5.0	5	2	2	3	5
Petkovsek	0.1	2	0	0	0	0
Fossas	0.2	0	0	0	0	0
Mathews L (2–6)	1.0	3	4	4	2	1
Ludwick	1.0	0	0	0	0	1
Totals	8.0	0	0	0	0	1

Cincinnati Reds

	AB	R	H	RBI
Owens lf	5	0	0	0
Goodwin cf	0	0	0	0
Morris 1b	5	0	1	0
Larkin ss	4	1	1	1
Davis cf, lf	4	1	1	0
Perez 3b	3	1	1	0
Branson ph, 3b	0	1	0	0
Boone 2b	4	1	3	2
Mitchell rf	3	1	1	0
Fordyce c	2	0	2	1
Portugal p	1	0	0	0
Oliver ph	0	0	0	1
Salkeld p	0	0	0	0
Remlinger p	0	0	0	0
Smith p	0	0	0	0
Greene ph	0	0	0	0
Mottola ph	1	0	0	0
Shaw p	1	0	0	0
Brantley p	0	0	0	0
Totals	33	6	10	5

	IP	H	R	ER	BB	SO
Portugal	4.0	3	3	3	1	2
Salkeld	1.2	1	0	0	0	0
Remlinger	0.0	0	0	0	1	0
Smith	0.1	0	0	0	0	0
Shaw W (8–5)	2.0	1	0	0	1	1
Brantley SV (41)	1.0	0	0	0	0	2
Totals	9.0	0	0	0	0	2

Umpires: HP—Randy Marsh, 1B—Mike Winters, 2B—Brian Gorman, 3B—Angel Hernandez.

Time of game: 2:42.

#33

Who Can Dream This?

Reds fans expected the first decade of the new millennium to be a memorable one. The 1999 team had won 96 games, falling just short of the NL Central title. To put them over the hump, the Reds traded for hometown great Ken Griffey Jr. And a new ballpark was scheduled to open in 2003. Surely a National League pennant or two would fly over it before long.

That didn't happen. By the end of the decade, the Reds had slogged through nine consecutive losing seasons. They hadn't won a division title since 1995. Still, there was reason for hope as the 2010 season began. The team featured a cast of young players poised to take the next step. First baseman Joey Votto and second baseman Brandon Phillips, along with right fielder Jay Bruce, were all in their 20s and had produced on the field. To help lead them, the Reds had traded for aging All-Star third baseman Scott Rolen. Young pitchers Johnny Cueto and Homer Bailey, as well as rookie Mike Leake and veteran Bronson Arroyo, appeared ready to perform. And the Reds could bring the leather, setting a club record for fewest errors in a season. Their formula for success: keep the game close with excellent defense, solid pitching, and timely hitting. Don't beat yourself. When the opponent makes a mistake—pounce. And pounce they did, with a league-leading offense led by Votto, who was voted the league's Most Valuable Player.

Under manager Dusty Baker, the team did come together, and by late September it was on the verge of clinching the NL Central Division title. The Reds had survived a season-long dogfight with the St. Louis Cardinals—as well as an on-field fistfight with them—to stand atop the division. On Tuesday, September 28, the Reds needed one more victory to clinch the division championship. The Houston Astros were in town for a night game, and 30,751 fans (including 7,786 walk-ups) crammed into Great American Ball Park hoping to see, after a decade of futility, the Reds declared champions.

Facing Astros left-hander Wandy Rodriguez, always a tough matchup for the Reds, the home team scored quickly in the first inning. Center fielder Drew Stubs walked, stole second base, and later scored on an error by Astros third baseman Chris Johnson. Fans in the stands started buzzing—surely the long drought was ending tonight. But the Astros weren't ready to give up so early in the game. In the top of the second, with Edison Volquez on the mound for the Reds, Johnson and first baseman Brett Wallace led off with back-to-back singles. Following a force out by shortstop Angel Sanchez, catcher Jason Castro singled to score Wallace. Rodriguez then laid down a sacrifice bunt that scored Sanchez to give the Astros a 2–1 lead.

Both pitchers settled in and held the opposition scoreless until the bottom of the sixth inning. After singles by Reds shortstop Orlando Cabrera and Votto, Rolen walked to load the bases. Left fielder Jonny Gomes popped out. Phillips then managed to beat out a grounder between third and shortstop for a base hit that scored Cabrera to tie the game. With the bases still loaded and just one out, Bruce came to bat ready to break open the game. Instead he grounded into an inning-ending double play. The Reds had missed their chance to take the lead.

As he'd done throughout the season, Baker went quickly to his bullpen, which stepped up to the challenge. Reliever Arthur Rhodes shut down the Astros in order in the seventh, Nick Masset did the same in the eighth, and closer Aroldis Chapman followed their lead in the ninth. Reds hitters, however, couldn't muster a rally. Fans started getting restless in their seats. Maybe tonight would not be the night. But none of them left. Many games in the 2010 season had gone this way, and the "comeback kids" more often than not found a way to win in the end.

With left-handed hitter Bruce leading off the bottom of the ninth, the Astros put lefty Tim Byrdak on the mound. Always a streaky hitter, Bruce had been red hot in September, and surely was eager to make up for ending the rally in the sixth. If fans had to choose which player they wanted in the batter's box in the bottom of the ninth, Bruce would be the guy. And he didn't disappoint.

His bat connected with the first pitch and drove it high and long into the mild September night. As the ball cleared the center field wall, Bruce, rounding first base, shot his arm into the air—the Reds had won their first division title in 15 years, their first in Great American Ball Park. Needless to say, Bruce met a mob of teammates when he arrived at home plate after circling the bases. The fans got in on the celebration as the team took a victory lap around the playing field, shaking hands and trading high fives with the front-row faithful.

In their book *The Comeback Kids,* authors Mark Schmetzer and Joe Jacobs include a quote from Bruce at the postgame press conference. With champagne dripping down his face, Bruce said, "It's one of those things you don't know it could happen until it does. I mean, you dream about things like this, but who can dream this?" Manager Baker summed up his feelings more succinctly: "I'm as happy as a man can be."

While Reds players, wearing "division champions" T-shirts over their uniforms, jogged around the field to celebrate with fans, the futility of the previous decade disappeared. A new one had begun—with a bang that won't be forgotten by Reds' history. The Reds were headed to the playoffs to meet the powerful Philadelphia Phillies.

The high of the 2010 season ended there, as the Phillies swept the three-game National League Division Series. In the opening game, Phillies ace Roy Halladay threw a no-hitter, and the Reds were shutout in two of the three games. Even their exceptional defense fell apart. But these kids were young and talented and had already won a division championship. Surely better days lay ahead.

Houston	0	2	0	0	0	0	0	0	0	—	2	7	2
Cincinnati	1	0	0	0	0	1	0	0	1	—	3	6	0

Houston Astros

	AB	R	H	RBI
Bourgeois cf	4	0	0	0
Keppinger 2b	3	0	1	0
Pence rf	4	0	1	0
Lee lf, 1b	4	0	0	0
Johnson 3b	4	0	1	0
Wallace 1b	3	1	2	0
Michaels ph, lf	1	0	0	0
Sanchez ss	4	1	1	0
Castro c	3	0	1	1
Rodriguez p	1	0	0	1
Hernandez ph	1	0	0	0
Lopez p	0	0	0	0
Abad p	0	0	0	0
Lindstrom p	0	0	0	0
Byrdak p	0	0	0	0
Totals	32	2	7	2

	IP	H	R	ER	BB	SO
Rodriguez	6.0	3	2	1	4	8
Lopez	1.0	1	0	0	0	0
Abad	0.1	0	0	0	0	1
Lindstrom	0.2	1	0	0	0	0
Byrdak L (2–2)	0.0	1	1	1	0	0
Totals	8.0	6	3	2	4	9

Cincinnati Reds

	AB	R	H	RBI
Stubbs cf	3	1	1	0
Cabrera ss	3	1	1	0
Votto 1b	4	0	1	0
Rolen 3b	3	0	1	0
Gomes lf	4	0	0	0
Phillips 2b	2	0	1	1
Bruce rf	4	1	1	1
Hernandez c	3	0	0	0
Volquez p	2	0	0	0
Rhodes p	0	0	0	0
Alonso ph	1	0	0	0
Masset p	0	0	0	0
Chapman p	0	0	0	0
Totals	29	3	6	2

	IP	H	R	ER	BB	SO
Volquez	6.0	7	2	2	1	8
Rhodes	1.0	0	0	0	0	1
Masset	1.0	0	0	0	0	1
Chapman W (2–2)	1.0	0	0	0	0	2
Totals	9.0	7	2	2	1	12

Umpires: HP—Dan Iassogna, 1B—Scott Barry, 2B—Jerry Meals, 3B—Tim
    McClelland.

Time of game: 2:51.

Attendance: 30,151.

#32

REDS 4, LOS ANGELES DODGERS 3
JULY 1, 1973

King Hal

After winning the National League pennant in 1972, the Reds struggled with some issues in the early months of the 1973 season—even though these problems weren't reflected in their record, which for the first two months was excellent.

First of all, star pitcher Gary Nolan missed virtually the entire year with a torn ligament in his elbow; gradually the team's lack of consistent pitching began to be apparent. In June, the Reds traded outfielder Gene Locklear to the San Diego Padres for pitcher Fred Norman. Many fans didn't think much of the trade at the time, but lefty Norman would end up winning 85 games for the Reds in his career and would be seen as a reliable middle-of-the-rotation contributor on the Big Red Machine.

Another issue that year involved All-Star catcher Johnny Bench, who had undergone surgery during the off-season to remove a lesion from his lung. The lesion proved to be benign, but the Reds decided to bolster the catching corps just in case by signing Bob Barton, whom manager Sparky Anderson had talked out of retiring. Although his power numbers had dipped significantly, Bench proved capable of catching most of the games. Barton was released, and the Reds promoted a journeyman catcher from AAA Indianapolis named Hal King, who they figured would mostly serve as a pinch hitter.

On July 1, a Sunday, the much-despised (by Reds fans) Los Angeles Dodgers were in Cincinnati to play a doubleheader at Riverfront Stadium. The Reds had fallen to 10 games behind the Dodgers in the NL West race, and, despite the strong start to the year, they were now struggling to stay above .500. In the first game of the series on the previous day, the Dodgers had beaten the Reds 8–7; in the first game of the Sunday doubleheader, the Reds had to face Dodgers ace Don Sutton. Opposing him: the rather uninspiring Fred Norman.

Nevertheless, when the Dodgers came to town in that era, Reds fans came to the ballpark. Attendance for the doubleheader exceeded 46,000.

In the first inning, the Dodgers scored on a single by center fielder Willie Davis and a double by third baseman Ron Cey. Second baseman Davey Lopes hit a solo home run in the third to put the Reds down by two. The Reds scored once in the fourth inning on a single by third baseman Dan Driessen, who then stole second and crossed the plate when right fielder Larry Stahl singled him in.

Both Sutton and Norman sailed through the innings with little trouble. In the ninth inning the score remained 2–1. Willie Davis led off the top of the inning with a double to right field, and Cey singled to score him, but was thrown out trying to stretch his hit into a double. Norman retired the next two batters to end the inning. The Reds came to bat in their half of the ninth trailing 3–1. First baseman Tony Perez led off with a double. After center fielder Bobby Tolan popped out and Stahl whiffed, Bench pinch-hit for shortstop Dave Concepcion. Scheduled to catch the second game of the doubleheader, Bench had sat out the first one. Sutton walked him intentionally, defying conventional baseball strategy, which advises against putting the tying run on base and the winning run at the plate. The Dodgers, however, felt their odds of success were much better against light-hitting backup catcher Bill Plummer than the powerful Bench.

Sparky Anderson, however, had some strategic ideas of his own. He put in fleet backup infielder Darrel Chaney to run for Bench and replaced Plummer at the plate with Hal King, who had only been with the team for a couple of weeks—a somewhat surprising move in such a critical situation. While it was only the first of July, the Reds felt that losing the series to the Dodgers could be the beginning of the end. They would have to make up too much ground in the second half of the year against a team that was playing very well. The fans knew the Reds needed this game—and Sparky was leaving it up to whom? Some minor-league guy they'd never heard of?

But of such moments many great baseball memories are made, and this one has lived on in Reds history ever since. With two strikes, Sutton threw a screwball that King crushed over the right field wall to deliver an unlikely and dramatic 4–3 victory. Fans celebrated in the stands as an unlikely hero circled the bases. Everyone seemed to sense that the victory was a turning point. In the nightcap, the Reds won again, this time on a 10th-inning double by Tony Perez. From July 1 through the remainder of the season, the Reds won 60 games and lost just 26 and won their third division title in four years. Along the way, Pete Rose won his third batting title and the NL Most Valuable Player award.

The Reds went on to lose the National League Championship Series to the Mets, a stunning upset defeat after such an amazing run in the second half of the season. Hal King hit two more pinch-hit homers that year but ended up with just eight hits in in 43 official at bats. The following year, he managed just three hits in 17 plate appearances as the third-string catcher. He was sent back to Indianapolis during the season and never played in another major-league game, finishing his career in 1979 after four seasons in the Mexican League.

Reds history is packed with great plays by great players, but one of its most celebrated moments is the day that Hal was king.

Los Angeles	1	0	1		0	0	0		0	0	1	— 3	9 1
Cincinnati	0	0	0		1	0	0		0	0	3	— 4	8 0

Los Angeles Dodgers

	AB	R	H	RBI
Lopes 2b	4	1	1	1
Buckner 1b	4	0	0	0
Davis cf	4	2	4	0
Cey 3b	3	0	2	2
Mota lf	4	0	1	0
Paciorek lf	0	0	0	0
Russell ss	4	0	1	0
Crawford rf	2	0	0	0
Yeager c	3	0	0	0
Sutton p	3	0	0	0
Totals	31	3	9	3

	IP	H	R	ER	BB	SO
Sutton L (9–5)	8.2	8	4	4	2	7
Totals	8.2	8	4	4	2	7

Cincinnati Reds

	AB	R	H	RBI
Rose lf	4	0	3	0
Morgan 2b	3	0	0	0
Driessen 3b	4	1	1	0
Perez 1b	4	1	2	0
Tolan cf	4	0	0	0
Stahl rf	4	0	1	1
Concepcion ss	3	0	0	0
Bench ph	0	0	0	0

	AB	R	H	RBI
Chaney pr	0	1	0	0
Plummer c	3	0	0	0
King ph	1	1	1	3
Norman p	3	0	0	0
Totals	33	4	8	4

	IP	H	R	ER	BB	SO
Norman W (5–8)	9.0	9	3	3	2	3
Totals	9.0	9	3	3	2	3

Umpires: HP—Ed Vargo, 1B—Paul Pryor, 2B—Bruce Froemming, 3B—
Terry Tata.

Time of game: 2:24.

#31

The Clinch

After the surprising 2010 season, when the Reds won their first division title since 1995, expectations ran high for the next year. The first decade of the new millennium had been bleak for Reds fans, but a new crop of exciting young players promised good things in the years ahead. A fast start in 2011 seemed to justify the expectations, but injuries to the pitching staff, especially the rotation, and to third baseman Scott Rolen, plunged the team to a losing record and a distant, third-place finish.

To bolster the rotation, the Reds dealt four players to the San Diego Padres in exchange for rising star Mat Latos, who joined Johnny Cueto, Homer Bailey, Bronson Arroyo, and Mike Leake to form a strong rotation—if the arms could stay healthy. And the quintet did stay healthy, making every start that season except one, which was caused by a rainout. Reds' pitching placed second in the National League in 2012 with a 3.34 ERA, quite a feat when your home field is a hitter's paradise.

The season, however, was not without its share of injuries. Rolen and first baseman Joey Votto missed a significant number of games, but not at the same time, allowing reserve infielder Todd Frazier to fill in for both of them. He contributed 19 home runs and a spark that energized the team. The Reds lineup packed plenty of punch. Though he played in only 111 games, Votto hit .337/.474/.567 with 44 doubles. Before his knee injury in late June, he appeared to be on track to win another MVP award. Right fielder Jay Bruce led the team with 34 homers and 99 RBIs, and left fielder Ryan Ludwick proved to be a good addition that year, hitting 26 homers.

A six-game winning streak put the Reds atop the division on May 24, and, other than a five-day stretch around the Fourth of July, they remained there for the rest of the season. In July they put together another six-game winning streak and, then, following a couple of losses, reeled off 10 straight wins. From July 19 through August 4, they posted a record of 15–1. By September, clinching the division title seemed only a matter of time.

That time arrived on Saturday, September 22, at Great American Ball Park, when 41,117 people, hoping to witness the division clincher, gathered to watch the Reds play the Los Angeles Dodgers. With 10 games left in the season, the Reds held a 10-game lead on the St. Louis Cardinals. They needed just one more victory.

Somewhat fittingly, Latos started on the mound for the Reds, facing right-hander Stephen Fife. Latos had delivered a strong first season for the team, posting a 14–4 record in 209.1 innings. He was the rotation's no. 2 pitcher, second only to ace Johnny Cueto, who finished fourth in the voting for the Cy Young Award, winning 19 games.

Latos and Fife breezed through the first three innings, and Latos's mastery continued in his half of the fourth. In the bottom of the inning, Jay Bruce led off with a deep drive down the right field line that cleared the fence. In the fifth inning, with one out, second baseman Brandon Phillips walked. One batter later, Votto singled to left field, followed by Frazier, who did the same, scoring Phillips and staking Latos to a 2–0 lead. Frazier was thrown out at second trying to take an extra base on the hit. But Latos continued to dominate the Dodgers. Two runs seemed like plenty. Phillips, however, added one more in the seventh inning with a solo shot.

Todd Frazier led off the bottom of the eighth with a double to left field, and Bruce followed with a walk. When center fielder Chris Heisey laid down a sacrifice bunt to move the runners, reliever Jamey Wright fielded the ball but made a bad throw to first base, allowing Frazier to score. On the error, Bruce went to third base and Heisey to second. Wright then walked catcher Dioner Navarro intentionally to load the bases. Shortstop Zack Cozart lined into left field, bringing in two more runs.

Manager Dusty Baker brought in closer Aroldis Chapman in the ninth. Having Chapman and his 100-mile-per-hour fastball protect a 6–0 lead seemed like overkill to some, but the Reds wanted to take no chances in wrapping up the division title. After center fielder Matt Kemp grounded to Cozart to start the inning, Chapman walked first baseman Adrian Gonzalez. But shortstop Hanley Ramirez grounded into a double play, and the celebration began.

Much as it did in 2010, Great American Ball Park lit up—with fireworks and flashing cameras. Cincinnati fans cheered well into the night, sure that this time they'd go deeper into the playoffs than they'd gone two years earlier, when they

were swept in the first round. The Reds were no longer upstart kids. They were
an experienced team that had won 97 games, taking their division by nine games.

And maybe they would have gone deeper, but in the first inning of the first
game of the National League Division Series with the San Francisco Giants,
Johnny Cueto pulled a muscle, ending his season. He had faced just one hitter.
Baker rushed in reliever Sam LeCure, but replaced him in the third inning with
Latos, who had been scheduled to pitch the following game. The Reds won the
first two games in San Francisco, heading back to Cincinnati needing just one
win to advance. The team had overcome injuries throughout the season, but the
loss of Cueto proved to be too great. The Giants rallied to win three straight and
take the series. A tough way to end what had been a wonderful season.

```
Los Angeles    0  0  0     0  0  0     0  0  0  —  0  6  1
Cincinnati     0  0  0     1  1  0     1  3  x  —  6  8  0
```

Los Angeles Dodgers

	AB	R	H	RBI
Ellis M. 2b	4	0	1	0
Ethier rf	4	0	1	0
Kemp cf	4	0	0	0
Gonzalez 1b	3	0	1	0
Ramirez ss	4	0	0	0
Cruz 3b	3	0	2	0
Rivera lf	3	0	0	0
Guerrier p	0	0	0	0
Choate p	0	0	0	0
Wright p	0	0	0	0
Wall p	0	0	0	0
Ellis A. c	2	0	0	0
Abreu ph	1	0	0	0
Treanor c	0	0	0	0
Fife p	1	0	0	0
Gordon ph	1	0	0	0
Rodriguez p	0	0	0	0
Herrera lf	1	0	1	0
Totals	31	0	6	0

	IP	H	R	ER	BB	SO
Fife L (0–2)	5.0	5	2	2	2	4
Rodriguez	1.0	0	0	0	0	1
Guerrier	0.2	1	1	1	1	0
Choate	0.1	0	0	0	0	0
Wright	0.0	2	3	2	2	0
Wall	1.0	0	0	0	1	0
Totals	8.0	0	0	0	1	0

Cincinnati Reds

	AB	R	H	RBI
Phillips 2b	3	2	2	1
Paul lf	2	0	0	0
Stubbs pr, cf	1	0	0	0
Votto 1b	4	0	1	0
Frazier 3b	4	1	2	1
Bruce rf	3	2	1	1
Heisey cf, lf	2	1	0	0
Navarro c	3	0	0	0
Cozart ss	4	0	2	2
Latos p	3	0	0	0
Rodriguez ph	1	0	0	0
Chapman p	0	0	0	0
Totals	30	6	8	5

	IP	H	R	ER	BB	SO
Latos W (13–4)	8.0	6	0	0	0	7
Chapman	1.0	0	0	0	1	0
Totals	9.0	0	0	0	1	0

Umpires: HP—Mike Muchlinski, 1B—Sam Holbrook, 2B—Andy Fletcher, 3B—Joe West.

Time of game: 2:55.

Attendance: 41,117.

#30

Big Red Scooter

When the Reds plucked infielder Scooter Gennett from the waiver wire on March 28, 2017, the move didn't make headlines. A four-year veteran as a second baseman, Gennett had been released by the Milwaukee Brewers. While his offensive numbers weren't bad, he was viewed as a utility player, and a limited one at that. Most backup infielders can play shortstop, as well as second and third base, but Gennett had shown below-average defensive skills.

The Reds knew him well, having played against him numerous times, and thought he might be a useful addition. And picking him up didn't cost them anything. Despite his limitations, Gennett would give them a solid left-handed bat on the bench. He did have some speed and some power, hitting 14 home runs and stealing eight bases in nine attempts in 2016. Before the start of the 2017 season, the Reds had traded longtime second baseman Brandon Phillips to the Atlanta Braves, replacing him with unproven rookie Jose Peraza. Having an experienced backup who also could play the corner outfield positions and pinch-hit made sense.

Gennett also had a Cincinnati connection—he was born and spent his early childhood in the Queen City. Though his family moved to Florida when he was nine years old, he had returned during high school summers to play with a topflight amateur club that had produced many pro players, including Hall of Famers Barry Larkin and Ken Griffey Jr. The Reds have a long history of signing local players; however, since Junior's departure in 2008, the roster had not included one, the longest drought in franchise history.

In the middle of a rebuilding phase, the Reds weren't expecting to compete for the postseason or even have a winning record. They had won only 68 games the year before and just 64 the season before that. Phillips was one of the last stars of the division-winning teams in 2010 and 2012 to be replaced by the next generation. Though only 26 years old, Gennett wasn't expected to be a part of the next successful era for the team. With luck, he might make a useful reserve—but he made clear right from the start that he didn't see his role in quite the same way.

On opening day, he entered the game in the bottom of the seventh inning as a pinch hitter, lining into a double play. But he stayed in the game, replacing Peraza at second base. With two out in the bottom of the ninth and the Reds losing 4–1 to the Philadelphia Phillies, the little second baseman launched a two-run home run over the left field wall. Though the Reds lost the game, Gennett had offered a preview of what was to come.

Throughout the spring, he played second base and the corner outfield positions, displaying more versatility—and more power—than anyone expected. On Tuesday, June 6, in a game with the St. Louis Cardinals at Great American Ball Park, he started in left field. The Reds faced longtime Cardinals ace Adam Wainwright, who had beaten them many times. Despite a decimating number of injuries to their pitching rotation, the Reds came into the game near the .500 mark. That night the team paid tribute to the anniversary of D-Day by wearing camouflage uniforms. A modest crowd of 18,620 fans settled into their seats on a warm evening, not expecting to witness history.

In the bottom of the first inning, Gennett singled to score center fielder Billy Hamilton, who had singled and advanced on a ground out, giving the Reds a 1–0 lead. When Gennett stepped into the box for his next at bat in the bottom of the third, the Reds had loaded the bases via two walks and a single. Gennett shot a long fly over the right field wall for a grand-slam home run. In just three innings he had accounted for all five Reds' runs.

Obviously struggling, Wainwright gave up a single to Hamilton with two out in the fourth inning. Shortstop Zack Cozart followed with a double, and first baseman Joey Votto was walked intentionally to load the bases, bringing up third baseman Eugenio Suarez. He tripled, scoring Hamilton and Votto, and St. Louis right-handed pitcher John Gant relieved Wainwright. With Suarez on third, Gant would face Gennett, who lined a bullet over the center field fence for his second home run of the game. The Reds lead now stood at 10–0, with Gennett accounting for seven of the 10 runs.

And that's where it stood when Gennett came to the plate again in the sixth inning to face Gant again. Stunning the crowd, Gennett crushed another long drive, sending it down the left field line and over the fence. In the long history of the Reds, only six players had ever hit three home runs in a game, and the list includes players much more likely to achieve such a feat: namely Johnny

Bench, Gus Bell, Eric Davis, and Joey Votto, as well as Aaron Boone and Drew Stubbs. No backup second basemen among them.

Cardinals right fielder Stephen Piscotty opened the seventh inning with a solo shot, breaking up Tim Adelman's shutout, but with the Reds leading 11–1, the game was no longer in doubt. Most fans stayed in their seats, however, looking forward to Gennett's next at bat. Could little Scooter possibly break the team's all-time record for most homers in a game?

Gennett came to bat facing right-handed reliever John Brebbia with two outs in the eighth. Scott Schebler, who had walked, stood at first base. As Gennett settled into the batter's box, many in the crowd rose to their feet, cheering him on. Gennett, clearly swinging for no. 4, nearly rose out of his shoes on his first swing, which almost brought him to his knees. On the next pitch, he did it again, but this time connected, slashing a high fly ball to deep right field that cleared the fence. His teammates rushed to congratulate him, while the sparse crowd provided a standing ovation.

In one of the most productive games by any player in major-league history, Gennett had gone five for five, hitting four home runs, including a grand slam, knocking in 10 runs and amassing 17 total bases. Only 15 major-league hitters have ever hit four home runs in a game, a list that includes stars like Lou Gehrig, Willie Mays, Rocky Colavito, Joe Adcock, Chuck Klein, and Carlos Delgado. And only seven of them homered in four consecutive plate appearances—Mike Schmidt was the only one to do it in the National League's modern era. And only Mark Whiten had hit a grand slam among four homers in a game—interestingly, he did it as a St. Louis Cardinal in a game with the Reds, in 1993.

Despite the rousing victory and decent start, the season turned into another dismal rebuilding year for the Reds, who once again finished last in the Central Division. But Gennett went on to prove he was no one-night wonder. He took the starting job at second base by midseason; in 497 plate appearances, he batted .295/.342/.531, with 27 home runs, including four grand slams—which helped him make history once again. No player in major-league history had ever hit four home runs in a game and four grand slams in the same season.

In a well-researched article for si.com, writer Jay Jaffee concluded, "Gennett's four-homer, five-hit, 10-RBI performance belongs in the discussion of the greatest single-game performances of all time—and the most unlikely." After the game, Gennett might have summed it up even better, telling the media, "I was kind of laughing, to be honest with you. For a guy like me to do that is crazy—a little short of a miracle."

St. Louis	0	0	0	0	0	0	1	0	0	— 1	5	0
Cincinnati	1	0	4	5	0	1	0	2	x	— 13	11	0

St. Louis Cardinals

	AB	R	H	RBI
Fowler cf	2	0	0	0
Martinez lf	2	0	0	0
Carpenter 1b	4	0	0	0
Brebbia p	0	0	0	0
Piscotty rf	3	1	2	1
Gyorko 3b, 1b	4	0	2	0
Molina c	1	0	0	0
Fryer ph, c	3	0	0	0
Pham lf, cf	2	0	0	0
DeJong ss	3	0	0	0
Garcia 2b	3	0	0	0
Wainwright p	1	0	0	0
Gant p	1	0	0	0
Peralta ph, 3b	1	0	1	0
Totals	30	1	5	1

	IP	H	R	ER	BB	SO
Wainwright L (6–4)	3.2	7	9	9	3	2
Gant	3.1	3	2	2	2	3
Brebbia	1.0	1	2	2	1	1
Totals	8.0	1	2	2	1	1

Cincinnati Reds

	AB	R	H	RBI
Hamilton cf	4	2	2	0
Cozart ss	3	2	2	0
Alcantara 2b	1	0	0	0
Votto 1b	3	2	1	0
Schebler rf	0	1	0	0
Suarez 3b	3	2	1	3
Gennett lf	5	4	5	10
Kivlehan rf, 1b	4	0	0	0
Peraza 2b, ss	4	0	0	0
Barnhart c	4	0	0	0

	AB	R	H	RBI
Adleman p	3	0	0	0
Lorenzen ph	1	0	0	0
Storen p	0	0	0	0
Cingrani p	0	0	0	0
Totals	35	13	11	13

	IP	H	R	ER	BB	SO
Adleman W (4–2)	7.0	3	1	1	2	7
Storen	1.0	1	0	0	0	0
Cingrani	1.0	1	0	0	1	0
Totals	9.0	1	0	0	1	0

Umpires: HP—David Rackley, 1B—Alfonso Marquez, 2B—Bill Welke, 3B—
  Chad Fairchild.
Time of game: 2:47.
Attendance: 18,620.

#29

REDS 9, FLORIDA MARLINS 4
JUNE 9, 2008

Junior's 600

Fireworks lit the sky above downtown Cincinnati when a trade between the Reds and the Seattle Mariners was announced on February 10, 2000. Ken Griffey Jr., one of the greatest players of his generation—maybe one of the greatest of all time—was coming home to the city where he grew up. Reds fans felt sure they'd soon be buying World Series tickets. The team had won 96 games in 1999, ending a successful season with a disappointing loss in a tiebreaker game for the wild card. Would adding one of the best hitters in the majors, who was just turning 30, to their already potent lineup help them win a pennant? No doubt about it, most figured.

Junior hit 40 home runs and drove in 118, producing a .271/.387/.556 slash line. The Reds won 85 games in 2000, finishing second in the Central Division, The team's problem was pitching—or, rather, a significant lack of it. While that issue persisted in the seasons that followed, Griffey, the hometown hero, nevertheless became the fall guy for the team's lack of success. In 2001, he suffered the first of what became a series of injuries that kept him off the field more than on it for the next three years, igniting bitter fan reactions. "Junior," the fun-loving kid with the backward hat, who had delighted fans since breaking into the majors at the age of 19 in 1989, grew distant and aloof.

In the four seasons before the trade was made in 2000, Junior had hit 49, 56, 56, and 48 home runs, and many baseball experts predicted that he'd set the all-time career record. After the 2000 season, however, he would never hit 40 again. He did reach the 400 and 500 career homer milestones while playing for the Reds, and, in seasons when he was healthy, he did produce. There were simply too few of those seasons to meet the fans' enormous expectations.

By 2008, the end of his career was near. At 38, he could no longer play center field, and the team was stumbling through another losing campaign. He began the season with 593 home runs, and it seemed that the only thing he had left to do was reach 600. The countdown began on opening day and carried through April and May, with each home run bringing a roar from the crowd. The run to 600 gave positive closure on what had been a difficult relationship between Reds fans and Griffey.

On Monday, June 9, the Reds played the finale of a four-game series with the Florida Marlins at Dolphin Stadium in Miami. A huge, generic football stadium to which the Marlins drew few fans, it wasn't an ideal setting for a significant baseball milestone, but history often can't choose its stage. Once Griffey had reached 599, the national media followed him to Florida.

Only a little over 16,000 people showed up for the game. Left-hander Mark Hendrickson started on the mound for the Marlins, facing the Reds' Edinson Volquez. Cincinnati shortstop Jerry Hairston led off the game with a weak grounder to shortstop Hanley Ramirez, but beat the throw to first for an infield single. After center fielder Jay Bruce struck out, Griffey stepped to the plate. As if Hendrickson didn't have enough to worry about with history on the line, Hairston then stole second base, then stole third. With the count at 3–1, Junior unleashed the beautiful swing that had electrified baseball fans for nearly 20 years. The ball flew high into right field and sailed over the fence. In that moment, Griffey became only the sixth player in major-league history to join the 600 Club—a fraternity that included Babe Ruth, Willie Mays, Hank Aaron, Barry Bonds, and Sammy Sosa.

After the crowd rewarded Griffey with a standing ovation, play resumed. Reds catcher Paul Bako hit a three-run home run in the second inning, bringing in third baseman Edwin Encarnacion and first baseman Joey Votto. In what turned into a homer-fest, second baseman Brandon Phillips cleared the fence with a solo shot to lead off the third inning, giving the Reds a 6–0 lead. Meanwhile, Volquez, who was enjoying a great start to the season, mowed down the Marlins until the fifth inning, when he gave up three singles and two walks that put three runs on the scoreboard. In the two at bats after reaching 600, Griffey struck out and grounded out to the pitcher. In the sixth inning, he tagged a long fly to deep left field, but Luis Gonzalez made the catch.

Manager Dusty Baker replaced Volquez with Jared Burton to pitch the seventh inning; then for the eighth, he put in left-hander Bill Bray, who gave up a homer to first baseman Mike Jacobs, the first batter he faced. By the top of the ninth, the Reds had seen their six-run lead whittled down to two. After the long, strange trip of Griffey's eight years in Cincinnati, his teammates surely wanted to win the game in which he had finally reached the 600 Club.

With Renyel Pinto on the mound for the Marlins, left fielder Adam Dunn opened the ninth with a double to right field. He went to third on a wild pitch while Pinto was in the process of walking Encarnacion. Votto brought in Dunn with a sacrifice fly. Bako then clubbed his second home run of the game to push the lead to 9–4. Cincinnati closer Francisco Cordero kept it right there, sealing the victory on an historic night.

Just over a month later, the Reds traded Griffey to the Chicago White Sox for reliever Nick Masset and reserve infielder Danny Richar. The day before the trade, Griffey homered in his final game as a Red, his 15th round-tripper of the season and 210th in his Cincinnati career. The following year, he returned to Seattle, swatting 19 more home runs, but he retired in the middle of 2010.

He ranks sixth on the all-time home run list with 630. While Barry Bonds and Sammy Sosa, who rank above him, have been accused of steroid use, Junior was never accused of using performance-enhancing drugs in an era plagued by them. In 2014, he was elected to the Reds Hall of Fame, joining his dad as the hall's only father-son members. He was then inducted into the Baseball Hall of Fame in 2016, garnering the highest percentage of votes in history. While Cincinnati's celebration upon learning of the trade in 2000 had ultimately proved premature, Griffey did provide many exciting moments for his hometown team—and made some history along the way.

Cincinnati	2 3 1	0 0 0	0 0 3 — 9 11 1
Florida	0 0 0	0 3 0	0 1 0 — 4 5 3

Cincinnati Reds

	AB	R	H	RBI
Hairston ss	1	1	1	0
Janish ss	4	0	0	0
Bruce cf, rf	6	0	1	0
Griffey Jr. rf	4	1	1	2
Bray p	0	0	0	0
Weathers p	0	0	0	0
Cordero p	0	0	0	0
Phillips B. 2b	5	1	2	1
Dunn lf	5	1	1	0
Encarnacion 3b	3	2	1	0
Votto 1b	2	1	1	1

	AB	R	H	RBI
Bako c	4	2	2	5
Volquez p	3	0	0	0
Burton p	0	0	0	0
Phillips A. ph	1	0	0	0
Patterson cf	1	0	1	0
Totals	39	9	11	9

	IP	H	R	ER	BB	SO
Volquez W (9–2)	6.0	3	3	3	5	5
Burton	1.0	0	0	0	0	1
Bray	0.1	1	1	1	1	0
Weathers	0.2	0	0	0	0	1
Cordero	1.0	1	0	0	0	1
Totals	9.0	1	0	0	0	1

Florida Marlins

	AB	R	H	RBI
Ramirez ss	4	1	1	0
Hermida rf	4	0	1	2
Cantu 3b	5	0	1	1
Jacobs 1b	4	1	1	1
Uggla 2b	4	0	0	0
Gonzalez lf	2	1	1	0
Ross cf	4	0	0	0
Pinto p	0	0	0	0
Treanor c	2	0	0	0
Hendrickson p	0	0	0	0
Badenhop p	1	0	0	0
Jones ph	1	1	0	0
Lindstrom p	0	0	0	0
Helms ph	1	0	0	0
Kensing p	0	0	0	0
Amezaga cf	1	0	0	0
Totals	33	4	5	4

	IP	H	R	ER	BB	SO
Hendrickson L (7–4)	2.1	5	6	5	3	4
Badenhop	2.2	3	0	0	0	4
Lindstrom	1.0	0	0	0	0	2
Kensing	2.0	0	0	0	1	2
Pinto	1.0	3	3	3	1	1
Totals	9.0	3	3	3	1	1

Umpires: HP—Bill Hohn, 1B—Hunter Wendelstedt, 2B—Marvin Hudson, 3B—Tom Hallion.

Time of game: 3:09.

Attendance: 16,003.

#28

REDS 5, OAKLAND ATHLETICS 4
OCTOBER 20, 1972

We Go to Cincinnati

The 1972 World Series between the Reds and Oakland Athletics was one of the most competitive Fall Classics in history, with six of the seven games decided by a single run. Yet it is rarely mentioned in discussions of the greatest World Series.

In the first couple of games, the teams looked flat and uninspired. One reason might be because both teams won their league playoffs in such dramatic fashion. Both league championship series had gone to five games, with the A's downing the Detroit Tigers and the Reds beating the Pittsburgh Pirates. Heading into the World Series, the teams might have been emotionally drained. They certainly played that way. As one Cincinnati fan put it during Game Two, yelling from his seat (with the authors sitting nearby), "Guys, this is the World Series!"

The Reds lost the first two games of the series at home, just as they had in their previous trip to the Fall Classic in 1970. The Big Red Machine remained in neutral for Game Three, but eight strong innings from pitcher Jack Billingham helped deliver a 1–0 Cincinnati victory. Despite a good outing by Don Gullett in Game Four, the Reds lost again, as the A's scored two runs in the bottom of the ninth, winning 3–2. Going into Game Five in Oakland, the heavily favored Reds were one game from elimination. This was supposed to be the year the Big Red Machine redeemed the loss of the 1970 series and made it official that it was the best team in baseball.

The series was a study in contrasting styles. In their bright green-and-yellow uniforms and flashy white spikes, A's players sported long hair and mustaches, epitomizing the era. The Reds, meanwhile, forbade facial hair and flashy high-stirrup socks and required black spikes. They were seen as the conservative, midwestern team, the emotionless "Machine," playing the wild-and-wooly

West Coast rebels. In the locker room celebration following the Reds' pennant-winning victory, first baseman Tony Perez, when asked about the upcoming series, told the reporter, in his heavy Cuban accent, "We have a picnic over there." But so far the series had been no picnic.

Game Five was played on Friday, October 20, in Oakland. The start time was moved to the afternoon to allow the teams to fly back to Cincinnati that night to play Game Six the next day, should it be necessary. Perhaps hoping to wake up his teammates, left fielder Pete Rose led off the game with a home run on the first pitch from Jim "Catfish" Hunter. The lead didn't last long, however, as unlikely series hero Gene Tenace, a backup catcher, jacked a three-run home run off Reds pitcher Jim McGlothlin in the second inning.

A solo home run by Reds third baseman Denis Menke in the fourth inning tightened the A's lead to 3–2. Then, when McGlothlin walked third baseman Sal Bando to start the bottom of the inning, Reds manager Sparky Anderson brought in reliever Pedro Borbon. Anderson's decisions to pull pitchers from the mound at the first sign of trouble had inspired the nickname "Captain Hook." After center fielder George Hendrick sacrificed Bando to second base, Borbon walked the red-hot Tenace intentionally. A's manager Dick Williams then substituted Gonzalo Marquez for light-hitting second baseman Dick Green, and Marquez singled to center field, scoring Bando.

With two out in the fifth inning, Reds second baseman Joe Morgan worked a walk and scored on a single to right field by center fielder Bobby Tolan. Williams brought in relief ace Rollie Fingers to strike out Bench and end the inning. Trailing 4–3, Anderson replaced Borbon with Tom Hall, who retired six batters in a row, and then brought in Clay Carroll to pitch the seventh.

Joe Morgan led off the eighth with another walk and promptly stole second base. Tolan once again knocked him in with a base hit to tie the game, taking second on the throw home. With one out and Perez at the plate, Tolan stole third. The Reds had the go-ahead run 90 feet from home, but Fingers fanned Perez and Menke to escape the jam.

When the A's came to bat in the bottom of the inning, Carroll retired the first two hitters but then surrendered back-to-back singles. Anderson brought in left-hander Ross Grimsley, who had started Game Two, giving up two runs in five innings in a losing effort. Putting him in as a reliever at this point in the game demonstrated Anderson's desperation—the Reds needed to win this one, and he was pulling out all the stops. Grimsley delivered, retiring pinch hitter Angel Mangual to end the inning.

Reds center fielder Cesar Geronimo opened the ninth with a single to right field. Rather than pinch-hit for Grimsley, Anderson let him bat to attempt a sacrifice bunt. Grimsley popped up the bunt to the left of the plate. Racing in from third base, Bando shouted to Fingers, who was running toward the popup from the mound, to let the ball drop so they could turn a double play. Fingers followed the order but threw off the mark to first base. Though Grimsley was out at first, the poor throw left no time to make a play on Geronimo at second base. Bando then proceeded to muff a grounder by shortstop Dave Concepcion, putting runners at first and second for Pete Rose, who already had two hits on the day.

Rose settled into his crouched batting stance, looking for a pitch he could punch into the outfield to score Geronimo. He got one, lacing a single to center, and the Reds took a 5–4 lead into the bottom of the ninth.

After Grimsley walked Tenace, the first batter, second baseman Ted Kubiak popped out. Anderson brought in Billingham to pitch, and Williams replaced Tenace with pinch runner Blue Moon Odom, a pitcher with speedy wheels. When pinch hitter Dave Duncan singled down the left field line, Odom moved to third base. With the tying run at third and the winning run at first, A's short-stop Bert Campaneris stepped into the batter's box. He reached for a curveball from Billingham, popping the ball into foul territory beyond first base. Morgan ran over and caught it as he fell to his knees for the second out.

The A's had played aggressively throughout the series, seizing every oppor-tunity to get an edge on the mighty Machine. Knowing that Morgan lacked a strong arm and seeing him on his knees, Odom bolted for home. But Morgan jumped to his feet and fired a perfect throw to Bench, who applied the tag. The rail-thin Odom had no chance to knock over the Reds big-shouldered catcher, and home plate umpire Bob Engel yelled, "Out!" Reds' announcer Al Michaels, calling the game for NBC radio, exclaimed, "Odom is out, and we go to Cincinnati!"

The Reds, at last, had come to life to extend the series. In Game Six the next day, they won 8–1, ending their seven-game World Series losing streak at home—stretching all the way back to 1940. Unfortunately, the victory was their last in 1972, as they dropped Game Seven, 3–2.

It has been a bewildering series for the Big Red Machine. Oakland used excellent pitching and every trick in Dick Williams's bag to win the champi-onship. The Reds would wait until 1975 before returning to the Fall Classic, when they finally would prove they were best team in baseball.

Cincinnati	1	0	0	1	1	0	0	1	1 —	5	8	0
Oakland	0	3	0	1	0	0	0	0	0 —	4	7	2

Cincinnati Reds

	AB	R	H	RBI
Rose lf	5	1	3	2
Morgan 2b	3	2	0	0
Tolan cf	4	0	2	2
Bench c	4	0	0	0
Perez 1b	4	0	1	0
Menke 3b	3	1	1	1
Geronimo rf	4	1	1	0
Chaney ss	1	0	0	0
Hague ph	1	0	0	0
Carroll p	0	0	0	0
Grimsley p	0	0	0	0
Billingham p	0	0	0	0
McGlothlin p	1	0	0	0
Borbon p	0	0	0	0
Uhlaender ph	1	0	0	0
Hall p	0	0	0	0
Concepcion ph, ss	2	0	0	0
Totals	33	5	8	5

	IP	H	R	ER	BB	SO
McGlothlin	3.0	2	4	4	2	3
Borbon	1.0	1	0	0	1	0
Hall	2.0	0	0	0	0	1
Carroll	1.2	3	0	0	0	1
Grimsley W (1–1)	0.2	0	0	0	1	0
Billingham SV (1)	0.2	1	0	0	0	0
Totals	9.0	7	4	4	4	5

Oakland Athletics

	AB	R	H	RBI
Campaneris ss	5	0	0	0
Alou rf	4	0	0	0
Rudi lf	3	0	0	0
Epstein 1b	2	1	0	0
Hegan 1b	1	0	1	0
Bando 3b	3	1	1	0
Hendrick cf	2	1	1	0
Mincher ph	0	0	0	0
Mangual ph, cf	1	0	0	0
Tenace c	2	1	1	3
Odom pr	0	0	0	0
Green 2b	1	0	0	0
Marquez ph	1	0	1	1
Lewis pr	0	0	0	0
Kubiak 2b	2	0	1	0
Hunter p	2	0	0	0
Fingers p	0	0	0	0
Hamilton p	0	0	0	0
Duncan ph	1	0	1	0
Totals	30	4	7	4

	IP	H	R	ER	BB	SO
Hunter	4.2	5	3	3	2	2
Fingers L (1–1)	3.2	3	2	2	1	4
Hamilton	0.2	0	0	0	0	0
Totals	9.0	8	5	5	3	6

Umpires: Bob Engel (NL), Bill Haller (AL), Chris Pelekoudas (NL), Jim
   Honochick (AL), Frank Umont (AL), Mel Steiner (NL).
Time of game: 2:26.
Attendance: 49,410.

#27

Defying the Odds

The 1961 World Series shaped up to be David versus Goliath, and nobody was betting on David.

The Reds hadn't played in a postseason game in 21 years, and had spent most of that drought in the bottom half of the National League standings. Their opponent in the 1961 Fall Classic, the mighty New York Yankees, had just won their 11th American League Championship in 13 years. Experts gave the Ragamuffin Reds no chance against the Bronx Bombers. In their book *Baseball Dynasties,* sabermetricians Rob Neyer and Eddie Epstein rank that Yankee team in their all-time top 10. Baseball scribes of the day joked that the Yankees would win the series in three games.

Those experts, however, had been wrong about the Reds all season long, beginning by picking them to finish sixth in the eight-team National League. A combination of consistent pitching and timely hitting kept the Reds at (or near) the top of the standings throughout the summer, and they surprised the baseball world by winning the pennant. In *Pennant Race,* his classic book on the season, Reds pitcher and author Jim Brosnan describes the celebration when the team returned from their pennant-clinching victory in Chicago: "A noisy, cheering crowd greeted us at the airport. Fans gathered at intersections along the 10-mile route to downtown Cincinnati, waved Reds pennants and Halloween noisemakers. Children from an orphanage near the airport squealed as the bus carrying the players crawled by in a caravan of horn-honking cars."

The Yankees, meanwhile, coasted to the American League championship, winning 109 games while setting a team record with 240 home runs. Roger Maris broke Babe Ruth's iconic home run record, blasting 61 round-trippers. Although his record would include an asterisk, because this was the first year of the expanded 162-game season, there was no doubt among baseball fans that the Yankees had a terrifying lineup and would make quick work of the Reds.

The first two games of the series were played in Yankee Stadium. Yankees ace Whitey Ford pitched a two-hit shutout in Game One to beat the Reds 2–0. Reds starter Jim O'Toole pitched well, allowing the powerful Bronx Bombers just six hits in seven innings. Two of those hits, however, were solo homers, and that's all Ford needed to seal the victory.

After the Game One loss, even many Reds fans must have readied themselves for the inevitable sweep the experts had predicted. In Game Two, the Yankees started Ralph Terry, who had posted a 16–3 record that year, while the Reds countered with their ace, Joey Jay, who was the first Reds pitcher to win 20 games in a season since Ewell Blackwell in 1947.

Jay had been acquired from the Milwaukee Braves during the previous off-season in exchange for shortstop Roy McMillan. The Braves had signed him right after high school in 1953 as a bonus baby, which meant he got a large bonus but had to remain on the major-league roster for two years, an arrangement that inevitably stunted his early development. Before coming to the Reds, he'd never started more than 19 games in a season, splitting time between the rotation and relief. In the baseball world, he was known mostly for being the first Little Leaguer to make it to the majors. But when he arrived in Cincinnati, he showed he was ready to take the next step, leading the National League in wins (21) and shutouts (4).

As in Game One, pitching dominated for the first three innings. In the top of the fourth, the Reds scored their first runs of the series when Frank Robinson got on base due to an error by third baseman Clete Boyer, and Gordy Coleman followed with a home run. The lead didn't last long. In the bottom of the inning, Jay walked Roger Maris and surrendered a home run to Yogi Berra that tied the game.

The Reds, however, responded quickly. With two out in the inning, Elio Chacon dropped a single into center field. Usually a reserve, Chacon started the game at second base in place of Don Blasingame, who had jammed his finger fielding a ground ball in Game One. When Reds shortstop Eddie Kasko singled to right field, the speedy Chacon ended up on third. With Vada Pinson batting, Terry threw a pitch that eluded Yankee catcher Elston Howard. The ball only rolled roughly 10 feet from Howard, but Chacon figured he had a chance to score and darted toward the plate without a green light from his third-base coach. Chacon slid into home feet first, his helmet flying off, as Howard made a desperate—and futile—dive to tag him.

Chacon's alert, aggressive decision had given the Reds the lead, and they wouldn't give it back. With two out in the sixth inning, Wally Post doubled to left field, and Gene Freese was intentionally walked to bring up rookie catcher Johnny Edwards, who had batted just .186 in 165 plate appearances during the season. Edwards surprised Terry, and the right side of the Yankee infield, by lacing a low liner into right field for a single, scoring Post.

Jay continued to set down the Bronx Bombers, allowing just two hits after Berra's homer in the fourth. The Reds, meanwhile, widened their lead in the eighth. Following a walk by Robinson, Yankee reliever Luis Arroyo misplayed a weak grounder off the bat of Coleman, hurling the ball past first baseman Moose Skowron and into right field. Robinson came all the way around to score. Later in the inning, a double by Edwards scored Post to put the Reds ahead 6–2. In the bottom of the ninth, Jay allowed a two-out walk to Boyer, but pinch hitter Billy Gardner lined out to Kasko at short to end the game.

With the series tied and heading to Cincinnati for the next three games, many fans dared hope for a miracle. The Ragamuffin Reds had defied the experts once again by refusing to be swept, but could they actually win the series?

The answer, alas, was no. Game Two would be their only win, as the Yankees swept them at Crosley Field to win the world title. Elio Chacon, whose daring play was the highlight of the surprising Game Two victory, would be plucked from the team right after the series in the expansion draft by the New York Mets, for whom he would play just one year, his last in the majors. Though losing the 1961 World Series was a disappointment, the Reds had turned a corner that year with an amazing season, leaving behind more than a decade of frustration and beginning more than two decades of success.

| Cincinnati | 0 | 0 | 0 | 2 | 1 | 1 | 0 | 2 | 0 | — | 6 | 9 | 0 |
| New York | 0 | 0 | 0 | 2 | 0 | 0 | 0 | 0 | 0 | — | 2 | 4 | 3 |

Cincinnati Reds

	AB	R	H	RBI
Chacon 2b	4	1	1	0
Kasko ss	5	0	1	0
Pinson cf	5	0	1	0
Robinson lf	4	2	0	0
Coleman 1b	5	1	2	2
Post rf	4	2	2	0
Freese 3b	2	0	0	0
Edwards c	4	0	2	2
Jay p	4	0	0	0
Totals	37	6	9	4

	IP	H	R	ER	BB	SO
Jay W (1–0)	9.0	4	2	2	6	6
Totals	9.0	4	2	2	6	6

New York Yankees

	AB	R	H	RBI
Richardson 2b	4	0	1	0
Kubek ss	4	0	1	0
Maris cf	3	1	0	0
Berra lf	4	1	2	2
Blanchard rf	4	0	0	0
Howard c	3	0	0	0
Skowron 1b	3	0	0	0
Boyer 3b	2	0	0	0
Terry p	2	0	0	0
Lopez ph	0	0	0	0
Arroyo p	0	0	0	0
Gardner ph	1	0	0	0
Totals	30	2	4	2

	IP	H	R	ER	BB	SO
Terry L (0–1)	7.0	6	4	2	2	7
Arroyo	2.0	3	2	1	2	1
Totals	9.0	9	6	3	4	8

Umpires: Jocko Conlan (NL), Frank Umont (AL), Augie Donatelli (NL), Ed Runge (AL), Bob Stewart (AL), Shag Crawford (NL).
Time of game: 2:43.
Attendance: 63,083.

#26

Homer Strikes Twice

When the Reds drafted David "Homer" Bailey out of LaGrange High School in Texas with the seventh overall pick in 2004, MLB Draft Tracker described him as a "young RHP w/extremely high ceiling, effortless power arm w/plus pitchability." *USA Today* chose him as their High School National Player of the Year. He was billed as the next Nolan Ryan, and as a professional he has worn no. 34, Ryan's number with the Texas Rangers. The pitching-poor Reds salivated at the possibilities. This kid had "ace" written all over him.

He moved quickly through the minor leagues, maybe too quickly. His performance was inconsistent, as would be expected of a teenaged pitcher, but he showed enough dominance to continue earning promotions. Mired in yet another losing season in 2007, the team (and its fans) wanted a boost, and so they brought up Bailey, barely 21 years old, to the majors. A month later, he was sent back to Louisville, clearly not ready for the Show, but he returned at the end of the season. For the next two years, he was up and down between the majors and minors, struggling with control. By 2010, he was up for good. The results, however, were mixed. Comparisons to Nolan Ryan were rare indeed.

The knock on him has mostly been a lack of consistency. Games with an electrifying performance have too frequently been followed by ones in which he takes a beating. Some of the good days, however, have been nothing short of historic. On September 28, 2012, he threw a no-hitter against the Pirates in Pittsburgh, striking out 10 and walking only one. He won 13 games that year, his best total to date.

As he prepared for his start on July 2, 2013, his record was 4–6 while pitching for an excellent team that was 11 games over .500 and headed for the postseason. The Reds had won the NL Central the previous season and were positioned to take the next step. Played on a hot Tuesday night at Great American Ball Park, the game drew 27,509 fans, many of them hoping to enjoy a well-pitched game from "good Homer," the one who strived to emulate Nolan Ryan, the one with the "extremely high ceiling."

He retired the side in order in the top of the first inning, and the Reds quickly took an early lead. Center fielder Shin-Soo Choo led off with a double and scored on a sacrifice fly by first baseman Joey Votto. The score remained 1–0 through the top of the sixth, in which Bailey struck out the side. So far, he'd remained perfect. In the bottom of the inning, Votto opened with a single, followed by a home run off the bat of second baseman Brandon Phillips, his 12th of the year, to extend the lead to 3–0.

Bailey then walked center fielder Gregor Blanco to lead off the seventh inning, ruining his perfect game. Giants second baseman Marco Scutaro grounded weakly to Reds third baseman Todd Frazier, who had no play at second base and threw to first for the out. With Blanco now at second, catcher Buster Posey popped a blooper down the first-base line. Votto ran in but was forced to short-hop the ball while moving to his right. Bailey was slow to cover first base, and Blanco dashed toward third. Seeing the chance to get the lead runner, Votto whipped a throw to third and Frazier applied the tag. Bailey then struck out Giants third baseman Pablo Sandoval to end the inning.

Shrugging off the loss of his perfect game, Bailey set the Giants down in order in the eighth inning. Meanwhile, fans in the seats were buzzing—could Homer do it again? Could he pitch another no-hitter? He had his good stuff, and the Giants weren't making much contact. He seemed as strong now as he'd been in the early innings. After the Reds went down one-two-three in the bottom of the eighth, Bailey strode to the mound in the ninth, while the fans cheered him on.

He started with shortstop Brandon Crawford, hitting eighth in the order. Crawford managed a grounder back to Bailey for the first out. The fans were now on their feet, reacting to every pitch. Tony Abreu came into the game to pinch-hit for reliever Sandy Rosario. Abreu was no match for Bailey, who struck him out swinging. One more out to go. With fans roaring and cheering, and his teammates gathered at the dugout fence, Bailey was poised to throw the first no-hitter in the history of Great American Ball Park.

Gregor Blanco stepped into the batter's box. Blanco's walk in the seventh inning had ended the perfect game, and he appeared ready to do anything to get on base. Bailey, however, would not be denied. He coaxed a weak grounder to the left of Frazier, who snagged it and threw to Votto for the final out. Bailey's arms shot into the air as his teammates raced to the mound to mob him. Since

1974, no other pitcher had thrown the last no-hitter of one season and the first one of the next season. Who did it in 1974? Nolan Ryan.

Bailey would go on to reach career bests that season in innings pitched (209), earned run average (3.49), strikeouts (199), and wins above replacement (3.2). The team believed that its heralded prospect was on his way to achieving the greatness everyone had predicted. Before the next season, the Reds signed him to a six-year, $105 million contract. Unfortunately, he then suffered a series of injuries that kept him mostly off the field. But his two no-hitters assure him a place in team history.

San Francisco	0	0	0		0	0	0		0	0	0 — 0	0	1
Cincinnati	1	0	0		0	0	2		0	0	x — 3	7	0

San Francisco Giants

	AB	R	H	RBI
Blanco cf	3	0	0	0
Scutaro 2b	3	0	0	0
Posey c	3	0	0	0
Sandoval 3b	3	0	0	0
Pence rf	3	0	0	0
Belt 1b	3	0	0	0
Torres lf	3	0	0	0
Crawford ss	3	0	0	0
Lincecum p	2	0	0	0
Mijares p	0	0	0	0
Affeldt p	0	0	0	0
Rosario p	0	0	0	0
Abreu ph	1	0	0	0
Totals	27	0	0	0

	IP	H	R	ER	BB	SO
Lincecum L (4–9)	5.1	6	3	3	2	8
Mijares	0.2	0	0	0	1	2
Affeldt	1.0	1	0	0	1	1
Rosario	1.0	0	0	0	0	1
Totals	8.0	0	0	0	0	1

Cincinnati Reds

	AB	R	H	RBI
Choo cf	2	1	2	0
Cozart ss	3	0	0	0
Votto 1b	3	1	1	1
Phillips 2b	3	1	1	2
Bruce rf	4	0	0	0
Frazier 3b	4	0	1	0
Paul lf	3	0	0	0
Robinson lf	1	0	0	0
Hanigan c	3	0	1	0
Bailey p	3	0	1	0
Totals	29	3	7	3

	IP	H	R	ER	BB	SO
Bailey W (5–6)	9.0	0	0	0	1	9
Totals	9.0	0	0	0	1	9

Umpires: HP—Adrian Johnson, 1B—Brian O\'Nora, 2B—Fieldin Culbreth, 3B—Bill Welke.

Time of game: 2:43.

Attendance: 27,509.

#25

HOUSTON ASTROS 4, REDS 3
SEPTEMBER 17, 1983

Johnny's Big Night

A classic story about Johnny Bench—might be true, might not. He's told it many times. During a spring training game before his first full season in the majors, the 20-year-old Bench was catching Reds pitcher Gerry Arrigo. Late in the game, sensing that Arrigo's fastball had lost its spark, Bench kept calling for a curve ball. The veteran Arrigo wanted to throw a heater, but this cocky rookie wouldn't put down the sign. Finally, Bench gave him the sign for the fastball. Arrigo threw one. Bench caught it with is bare hand.

Who knows if it really happened that way. Bench stories are like that. They illustrate his supreme confidence in his extraordinary abilities. If Pete Rose was the spark plug of the Big Red Machine, Joe Morgan its fuel, and Tony Perez its engine, Bench was at the wheel, steering the team to victory. If perhaps less beloved by fans than the other three, Bench was still revered. While he might have lacked the warm personalities of Rose, Morgan, and Perez, Bench embodied the team's superior attitude. With him at the helm, fans—and even opposing players—sensed that the Reds could win on any given night.

If there was an official end to the Big Red Machine era, 1982 would be the year. After having the best record in the National League the previous season, the Reds saw their entire outfield head to New York. Left fielder George Foster was traded to the Mets and right fielder Ken Griffey Sr. to the Yankees, both trades fueled by economics—salary dumps that brought little in return. It was too expensive to keep them in Cincinnati, as was Dave Collins, who signed a free agent contract with the Yankees.

Third baseman Ray Knight was dealt to the Houston Astros, but that trade was made to open a spot for Johnny Bench. After catching an average of 127 games per season, Bench, at 34, could no longer handle the physical demands of that position. During the 1981 season he had played 38 games at first base, filling in for injured Dan Driessen, but Bench broke his ankle on May 28 and didn't return until the players strike ended. He hit .309 for the year.

With Bench at third base in 1982 and the Big Red Machine dismantled, the Reds finished last in the NL West Division, losing over 100 games for the first time in franchise history. Bench struggled at third and was clearly not the hitter he'd once been. Though the Reds improved a bit in 1983, they still finished last, losing 88 games.

On June 10 of that year, Bench announced his retirement effective at the end of the season, despite having two more years left on his contract. During his career he had been the National League's Most Valuable Player twice, had accrued 14 All-Star Game selections and 10 consecutive Gold Gloves. He'd helped win four pennants and two World Series titles. Most baseball fans and experts considered him the greatest catcher in history. With that type of legacy, he didn't want to continue playing at an inferior level just to earn a paycheck.

As the 1983 season wound down, National League teams acknowledged Bench's final visits to their cities. The Reds scheduled Johnny Bench Night for Saturday, September 17, to honor him with a pregame ceremony. Nearly 54,000 people attended the game, in which Bench would return to his old position behind the plate.

The ceremony took 45 minutes, beginning with Bench entering the field through a door in center field. He walked down a red carpet to a podium set up on a platform. The Reds gave him a new car, a two-seat bass fishing boat, and a two-week golf vacation in Scotland. Bench thanked the team and the fans, ending his speech by saying, "I'm going to try like hell to play good for you tonight."

The Reds played the Astros that night, with Houston sending left-hander Mike Madden to the mound. In the bottom of the first inning, with two out, shortstop Dave Concepcion singled. Bench, batting cleanup, followed with a walk, but third baseman Nick Esasky flied out to end the inning. The Astros put two across the plate in the second inning on a single by left fielder Jose Cruz, a double by first baseman (and former Red) Ray Knight, and a single by third baseman Phil Garner.

Down 2–0 in the bottom of the third, the Reds staged a comeback. Center fielder Paul Householder led off the inning with a single to left field. After Concepcion struck out, Bench stepped up to the plate to a standing ovation. Pretty much any move he made that night was accompanied by thunderous applause. After what happened next, the noise reached record decibels.

With the count no balls and one strike, Bench turned on a pitch and sent it into the left field seats. The crowd, needless to say, went wild. As he rounded first base he raised a "no. 1" finger in the air, holding it there to acknowledge the fans. He trotted around the bases and after reaching home plate he hopped in the air, high-fiving Householder. Radio broadcaster Joe Nuxhall exclaimed, "I'll tell you what, you can't write anything like that." It was the 389th and final home run of Bench's career, and it has become one of the iconic moments in Reds history.

Bench led off the bottom of the fifth with a single, but Esasky followed with a grounder to third for a double play. The Astros scored again in the sixth on Cruz's two-run homer, taking a 4–2 lead. No doubt trying to win one for Johnny, the Reds rallied in the bottom of the inning. Second baseman Ron Oester singled to center field, and Skeeter Barnes, pinch-hitting for starter Jeff Russell, drew a walk. Vern Ruhle replaced Madden on the mound, but the reliever walked left fielder Gary Redus to load the bases. Householder flied out to center field, scoring Oester, but the Reds could do no more damage in the inning.

In the eighth, Dann Bilardello replaced Bench behind the plate, though the future Hall of Famer took one last curtain call. For a final time, fans stood and cheered for him. The Reds lost, but fans who attended the game still talk about being there on that special night to give one of the franchise's most storied players one last hurrah.

Houston	0	2	0	0	0	2	0	0	0	— 4	6	0
Cincinnati	0	0	2	0	0	1	0	0	0	— 3	9	0

Houston Astros

	AB	R	H	RBI
Doran 2b	4	0	0	0
Puhl rf	4	0	0	0
Mumphrey cf	4	1	1	0
Cruz lf	4	2	2	2
Scott lf	0	0	0	0
Knight 1b	1	1	1	1
Walling 1b	2	0	1	0
Garner 3b	4	0	1	1
Ashby c	3	0	0	0
Reynolds ss	3	0	0	0
Madden p	1	0	0	0
Ruhle p	1	0	0	0
DiPino p	0	0	0	0
Totals	31	4	6	4

	IP	H	R	ER	BB	SO
Madden W (8–4)	5.1	8	3	3	4	4
Ruhle	3.1	1	0	0	1	2
DiPino SV (17)	0.1	0	0	0	0	1
Totals	9.0	9	3	3	5	7

Cincinnati Reds

	AB	R	H	RBI
Redus lf	4	0	0	0
Householder cf	4	1	1	1
Concepcion ss	5	0	1	0
Bench c	3	1	2	2
Bilardello c	0	0	0	0
Milner ph	0	0	0	0
Knicely ph	1	0	0	0
Esasky 3b	4	0	2	0
Driessen 1b	4	0	0	0
Cedeno rf	3	0	1	0
Oester 2b	3	1	1	0
Russell p	2	0	1	0
Barnes ph	0	0	0	0
Scherrer p	0	0	0	0
Walker ph	1	0	0	0
Hume p	0	0	0	0
Totals	34	3	9	3

	IP	H	R	ER	BB	SO
Russell L (3–3)	6.0	6	4	4	1	3
Scherrer	2.0	0	0	0	0	4
Hume	1.0	0	0	0	1	1
Totals	9.0	6	4	4	2	8

Time of game: 2:15.
Attendance: 53,790.

REDS 5, SAN FRANCISCO GIANTS 4
JUNE 24, 1970

Good-bye, Crosley

Crosley Field was the home of the Reds from 1912 until 1970—a beloved structure that provided the setting for many a baseball tale told at Cincinnati bars, picnics, and family gatherings. Generations of Cincinnatians saw their first major-league game at Crosley and recalled fondly the magical moment when they first glimpsed the magical green carpet of grass.

The Reds had played at that location in the West End since 1884, first in League Park and then, from 1902 through 1911, at the Palace of the Fans. In 1912 the park opened under the name Redland Field. When Cincinnati industrialist Powel Crosley Jr. bought the team in 1934, he changed the name. Known as a hitter's park, since the fences were moved in during the late 1930s, Crosley Field featured a terrace in deep left field and an open grandstand in right field know as the "Sundeck" (or "Moondeck" for night games).

By the 1960s, however, the ballpark had outgrown its usefulness. Hemmed in by a rundown neighborhood and undermined by inadequate parking and traffic infrastructure, Crosley Field no longer gave fans a pleasurable getaway. As Cincinnatians continued moving to distant suburbs, getting to and from a game had become more frustrating than enjoyable. The city decided to build a new multipurpose facility on the river as part of a sweeping urban redevelopment plan.

The goal was to open Riverfront Stadium for the 1970 season. Designed in the then popular (and now despised) generic saucer shape, the Reds new home would lack Crosley Field's character, but fans didn't seem to mind. Offering more than 50,000 seats, wide concourses, and up-to-date bathrooms and concession stands, along with the latest Astroturf playing surface, Riverfront Stadium seemed like a move up to the big time.

Construction delays, however, pushed the opening a few months into the season. The Reds continued to play at Crosley until June 24, when they faced the San Francisco Giants. On their way to the National League pennant, the first-place Reds had won 48 of their first 69 games, and the "Big Red Machine" nickname had come to define the team. A powerful lineup led by right fielder Pete Rose, first baseman Lee May, third baseman Tony Perez, center fielder Bobby Tolan, and that year's Most Valuable Player, catcher Johnny Bench, was balanced by a strong pitching staff led by eventual 20-game winner Jim Merritt and rookie sensation Wayne Simpson.

The Giants, while well behind the Reds in the West Division standings, fielded a good team that included three future Hall of Famers—Willie Mays, Juan Marichal, and Willie McCovey.

Pitcher Jim McGlothlin started for the Reds. An off-season acquisition from the California Angels, he pitched well in 1970, winning 14 games and posting a 3.59 ERA in 210⅔ innings. A solid, midrotation hurler, he would also start the first game in Riverfront Stadium.

More than 28,000 fans—nearly a sellout in Crosley's cozy confines—showed up for the Wednesday game to say farewell to the ballpark they'd known all their lives. The Giants scored in the first inning when Willie Mays knocked in Bobby Bonds with a single to right field. Facing Marichal, the Reds took the lead in the bottom of the second inning, scoring two runs after loading the bases. McCovey quickly evened things at 2–2 in the next inning, scoring Bonds from third base with a single; in the fourth, the Giants scored two more as McGlothlin struggled with his control.

In the bottom of the fifth inning, Pete Rose doubled, and center fielder Bobby Tolan brought him in with a single. The next day's *Cincinnati Enquirer* featured a photo of Rose emphatically stepping on home plate. Though the game mattered little in the standings, the Reds, for obvious reasons, wanted to win what they knew was a historic contest in team history. Perhaps it meant even more to Rose, a hometown boy who had attended games at Crosley Field his entire life. With the score still 4–3 in the seventh inning and only one out, Rose tripled, but Tolan and Perez couldn't bring him in.

Manager Sparky Anderson brought in relief ace Wayne Granger to start the eighth inning. A lanky right-hander with a deceptive side-arm delivery, Granger posted 35 saves that year, and his devastating sinker forced batters into easy ground ball outs. He quickly set down the Giants without a hit.

In the bottom of the inning, Johnny Bench led off, followed by first baseman Lee May. As Bench started heading for the batter's box, May said, "Let me be the hero, Johnny." Bench later said that he almost replied, "Why don't we both hit one out?" The question would have been prophetic because that's exactly what happened. Bench crushed his 25th home run of the season (he would go on to hit 45 that year). May did become the hero of the game, following Bench by crushing one of his own to give the Reds a 5–4 lead.

Granger returned to the mound in the ninth. The first two batters grounded out to shortstop Darrel Chaney. Bonds came up next. During his career, he produced five seasons in which he hit 30 or more home runs and stole 30 or more bases. On this night, as the big Longines clock on the scoreboard read 10 minutes before 11 o'clock, Bonds dribbled a grounder to Granger, who tossed it to May on first to seal the victory in the final game at Crosley Field.

The Reds players celebrated as if they had just won the World Series. Local TV star Marian Spelman then took the field to lead the crowd through a few choruses of "Auld Lang Syne." Home plate was placed on a helicopter and flown the short distance to Riverfront Stadium, where a new era in the team's—and the city's—history would begin.

Within a generation, however, teams and their fans lost interest in the saucer-shaped, multipurpose stadiums. They longed for a return to the quirky little ballparks of old. In less than 30 years, discussions would begin for a new ballpark in Cincinnati, one reminiscent of Crosley Field.

San Francisco	1	0	1		2	0	0		0	0	0	— 4	7 1
Cincinnati	0	2	0		0	1	0		0	2	x	— 5	10 2

San Francisco Giants

	AB	R	H	RBI
Bonds rf	4	2	1	0
Fuentes 2b	3	0	2	1
Mays cf	3	0	1	1
McCovey 1b	4	0	1	1
Henderson lf	4	0	0	0
Dietz c	2	1	0	0
Gallagher 3b	4	1	1	0
McMahon p	0	0	0	0
Lanier ss	3	0	0	0
Marichal p	3	0	1	1
Heise 3b	0	0	0	0
Taylor ph	1	0	0	0
Totals	31	4	7	4

	IP	H	R	ER	BB	SO
Marichal L (3–7)	7.0	10	5	5	1	4
McMahon	1.0	0	0	0	0	0
Totals	8.0	10	5	5	1	4

Cincinnati Reds

	AB	R	H	RBI
Rose rf	4	1	2	0
Tolan cf	4	0	2	1
Perez 3b	4	0	0	0
Bench c	4	2	3	1
May 1b	4	2	2	1
Carbo lf	2	0	1	0
Stewart pr, lf	0	0	0	0
Helms 2b	4	0	0	1
Woodward ss	2	0	0	1
Cline ph	1	0	0	0
Chaney ss	1	0	0	0
McGlothlin p	2	0	0	0
Bravo ph	1	0	0	0
Granger p	0	0	0	0
Totals	33	5	10	5

	IP	H	R	ER	BB	SO
McGlothlin	7.0	7	4	4	5	5
Granger W (3–1)	2.0	0	0	0	0	0
Totals	9.0	7	4	4	5	5

Umpires: HP—Satch Davidson, 1B—Augie Donatelli, 2B—Chris Pelekoudas, 3B—John Kibler.

Time of game: 2:38.

Attendance: 28,027.

#23

REDS 3, ATLANTA BRAVES 2
JULY 31, 1978

The Hit Streak

Most baseball fans know about Joe DiMaggio's 56-game hitting streak in 1941. It's one of those legendary records in the history of the game, a number that needs no explanation. Far fewer fans today know who holds the modern era's all-time consecutive-game hitting record in the National League. That would be Pete Rose of the Cincinnati Reds.

Technically, he shares the record with Willie Keeler, who set the single-season mark in 1897. The pre-1900 game, of course, was considerably different. "Wee Willie" frequently bunted foul numerous times during an at bat while waiting for a pitch he could hit, sparking the rule change calling batters out when bunting foul with two strikes. Keeler also patented what became known as the Baltimore Chop, slapping straight down on the ball to create a high bounce that gave him time to reach first. In an era when every pitcher throws 90 miles per hour, that approach would be tough to execute on a regular basis.

In 1978, the Reds fielded another good team, but the Big Red Machine was showing signs of age. The oldest member, Rose, turned 37 in April of that year. His contract expired at the end of the season, and rumors circulated that this might be his last one with the Reds. Some fans scoffed at such lunacy. Pete Rose playing for a different team? He'd been the face of the franchise for a decade, the hometown hero. Ridiculous.

But with high-priced stars such as Joe Morgan, Johnny Bench, and Tom Seaver, as well as younger stars including George Foster and Ken Griffey, the team couldn't afford to pay them all. Someone had to go. When Rose got off to a slow start in 1978, he appeared to be the likely candidate. While he drew national attention on May 5 by getting his 3,000th career hit, he looked like he was past his prime. On June 14, in a game with the Chicago Cubs, he got two hits to break a 5-for-44 slump; he was hitting just .267 on the season. Fans hoped that the hits signaled he was heading toward the .300 mark, where he'd finished 12 out of the past 13 years.

No one realized that those two hits started a record-breaking hitting streak that still stands as the National League's modern record. In the early weeks of the streak, the media outside of Cincinnati paid little attention, but the number kept rising. By July 11, when Rose led off for the National League in the All-Star Game, the national buzz had begun to build. (Even though it didn't affect his streak, he did get a hit in the All-Star Game, a double in the seventh inning.)

Four days later, he reached 28 consecutive games, setting a new modern Reds record. At this point, every major sports page in the country offered daily updates on the streak. While some players might have buckled under such scrutiny, Rose seemed to relish it. On July 19, in a game in Philadelphia, it appeared the streak would end at 31, six shy of the modern National League record set in 1945 by outfielder Tommy Holmes of the Boston Braves. Rose failed to get a hit through eight innings, walking in the eighth and not likely to bat again. But the Reds put together a long rally, capped by a George Foster grand slam, and Rose was able to get one more shot. He bunted for a hit in the ninth.

In New York on July 25 he broke Holmes's modern National League record with a single in the third inning in a game with the Mets. Holmes attended the game and walked onto the field to congratulate Rose. The next milestone: Keeler's premodern record of 44 games. On July 31, the Reds played the Braves in Atlanta, and Rose needed a hit in just one more game to tie the record. In that game, however, he would face Hall of Famer Phil Niekro, whose knuckleball befuddled even the heavy hitters of the Big Red Machine.

In his first at bat, Rose walked to begin the game. Catcher Johnny Bench put the first score on the board with a solo home run in the second inning. Rose came to the plate again in the third inning but lined out to shortstop Jerry Royster. The Braves tied the score in the fourth, as the Reds' starting pitcher, Mike LaCoss, loaded the bases and Braves catcher Biff Pocoroba brought in a run with a sacrifice fly. Niekro set down the Reds in order in the fourth and fifth innings, so Rose didn't get another chance to bat until the sixth.

Leading off the inning, he shot a ground ball through the infield and into right field to extend the streak to 44 games. The Atlanta crowd of more than 44,000 stood and cheered for several minutes, and fireworks exploded in the air above Atlanta–Fulton County Stadium. As he stood on first base, he received a bouquet of 44 roses. Rose raised his helmet to acknowledge the tribute. After 182 plate appearances and nearly that many media interviews, he had reached another pinnacle.

When the game continued, Griffey doubled to right field, sending Rose to third, but Niekro managed to escape without giving up a run. With the score still tied 1–1, Rose grounded out to first base in his next plate appearance. The Reds finally broke through in the top of the ninth, when center fielder Cesar Geronimo singled to center field, scoring shortstop Dave Concepcion. Morgan knocked in Geronimo later in the inning. Rose ended the inning by grounding out again to first base. The Braves mounted a rally in the bottom of the inning, but fell short by a final score of 3–2.

Thirty thousand people attended the next game, but the good feelings in Atlanta would end there, as did the streak. Facing rookie left-hander Larry McWilliams, Rose walked in his first plate appearance and scored later in the inning. He lined out to McWilliams in the second inning and grounded out to Royster in the fifth. In the seventh, with reliever Gene Garber on the mound, Rose lined a shot right at third baseman Bob Horner.

Leading 11–4, Garber set down the Reds in order in the eighth, and the Braves scored five more in their half of the inning. In the ninth, Rose would bat third. Garber, who threw with a submarine delivery, struck out the first two batters, and Rose came to the plate, eager for any pitch he could hit. Garber admitted later in an interview with the *Savannah Morning News*, "I was scared to death I might walk him. I'd be a horse's rear end and never live it down if I walked him to end the streak." With one strike on Rose, Garber threw back-to-back changeups, which came in right down the middle of the plate and then dipped low. Rose swatted over both of them, striking out. The hit streak was over.

After the game, a frustrated Rose told the media, "I was a little surprised that in a game that was 16–4, he pitched me like it was the seventh game of the World Series. I guess he thought it was Joe DiMaggio up there."

Never one to stay down for long, Rose collected four hits, including a home run, in the next day's game. During the streak, he batted .385 (70–182), exceeding DiMaggio's average in his first 44 games, and he struck out only five times.

Despite his slow start to the season, Rose batted .302 and led the National League in doubles (51) for the fourth time in five years. Nevertheless, his contract negotiations with the team were unsuccessful, and on December 5 he signed as a free agent with the Phillies. Charlie Hustle had left Cincinnati; given Rose's age, Reds fans assumed he was gone for good. In 1984, however, he would return to a hero's welcome.

| Cincinnati | 0 | 1 | 0 | 0 | 0 | 0 | 0 | 0 | 2 | — | 3 | 9 | 1 |
| Atlanta | 0 | 0 | 0 | 1 | 0 | 0 | 0 | 0 | 1 | — | 2 | 11 | 0 |

Cincinnati Reds

	AB	R	H	RBI
Rose 3b	4	0	1	0
Griffey rf	4	0	2	0
Driessen 1b	4	0	1	0
Foster lf	3	0	0	0
Bench c	4	1	1	1
Concepcion ss	4	1	1	0
Geronimo cf	4	1	1	1
Kennedy 2b	4	0	1	0
LaCoss p	3	0	0	0
Morgan ph	1	0	1	1
Knight pr	0	0	0	0
Bair p	0	0	0	0
Totals	35	3	9	3

	IP	H	R	ER	BB	SO
LaCoss W (2–1)	8.0	8	1	1	4	1
Bair SV (20)	1.0	3	1	1	0	1
Totals	9.0	11	2	2	4	2

Atlanta Braves

	AB	R	H	RBI
Royster ss	5	0	1	0
Office cf	5	0	2	0
Matthews rf	5	1	3	0
Burroughs lf	3	0	2	1
Horner 3b	4	0	0	0
Pocoroba c	3	0	0	1
Murphy 1b	3	0	0	0
Gilbreath 2b	4	0	1	0
Niekro p	3	0	1	0
Beall ph	1	1	1	0
Totals	36	2	11	2

	IP	H	R	ER	BB	SO
Niekro L (12–11)	9.0	9	3	3	2	10
Totals	9.0	9	3	3	2	10

Umpires: HP—Andy Olsen, 1B—Jim Quick, 2B—Jerry Crawford, 3B—
   Doug Harvey.

Time of game: 2:29.

Attendance: 45,007.

#22

REDS 4, BROOKLYN DODGERS 0
JUNE 22, 1947

The Whip

In Reds history, there have been a number of pitchers who produced outstanding seasons. Few (okay, none) have displayed the utter dominance of Ewell Blackwell in 1947.

That year, he led the National League in wins (22), strikeouts (193), and complete games (23). From May 10 to July 25, he won 16 games in a row, including a no-hitter against the Boston Braves on June 18. Choosing a game to commemorate this spectacular year isn't easy, but we'll go with the one after his no-hitter, when he came within two outs of matching Johnny Vander Meer's incomparable back-to-back no-hitters.

Blackwell stood 6'6", but weighed right around 200 pounds—a long and lanky guy, all arms and legs. Standing on the mound—in an era when he was taller than pretty much everybody in the majors—he looked very intimidating. And he *was*. He said that he "pitched mean," and no hitters of the time ever doubted the claim. With his sweeping, sidearm motion, he earned the nickname the "Whip," and he was known to enjoy brushing back hitters who showed enough moxie to dig in on him. It wasn't unusual for right-handed batters to bail out of the box or even hit the dirt—only to hear the umpire call a strike. At just 24, with one full season under his belt, Blackwell became, in 1947, the most feared pitcher in the game.

Unfortunately, the Reds didn't have much beyond Blackwell that year. Most of the players from the 1940 world championship were either gone or in the declining phase of their careers. After two lackluster postwar seasons, the team brought in new manager Johnny Neun to guide them back to the league's upper echelon; however, Reds fans wound up waiting 10 years for their next winning team. In the meantime, they would have a reason to cheer every fourth game—for Ewell Blackwell.

The game in which he nearly repeated what was thought to be impossible—Vander Meer's two straight no-hitters—was played on a Sunday afternoon at Crosley Field: the first game of a doubleheader with the Brooklyn Dodgers, who would win the National League pennant that year. For a while it seemed as though neither team would get a hit. Blackwell breezed through the Dodgers lineup, and Brooklyn's Joe Hatten had little trouble retiring the Reds. Then, in the bottom of the fifth inning, Reds shortstop Eddie Miller broke through with the first hit of the game, a two-out double to center field. Hatten walked catcher Ray Lamanno to get to Blackwell, who flied out.

The Whip set down the Dodgers in order in the sixth, having given up no hits in the game with two walks. Hatten, however, lost his control in the bottom of the inning, giving up a run on four walks. With a rare lead, Blackwell breezed through another one-two-three inning. He walked Brooklyn right fielder Dixie Walker to open the eighth, but then retired the next three Dodgers.

Reds third baseman Grady Hatton singled with one out in the bottom of the eighth, and center fielder Bert Haas followed with a single of his own. First baseman Babe Young flied to deep center field, but Carl Furillo chased it down for the second out. Miller then cracked his second double of the game, clearing the bases and giving the Reds a 4–0 lead.

As Blackwell ambled from the dugout to the mound with his long strides, the fans packed into Crosley Field buzzed with excitement, hoping they would see a history-making final inning. Announced attendance for the doubleheader was 31,204, and it's a fair bet most fans had shown up for the first game to see the Whip pitch. And they were happy they did. At the start of the ninth, he had pitched 18 hitless innings, going back to a single by Johnny Mize of the Giants in the eighth inning of a game on June 14. On the top step of the Reds dugout stood teammate Vander Meer, eager to see if the amazing Blackwell would equal his record.

Gene Hermanski led off the inning, pinch-hitting for reliever Hank Behrmann. He lofted a lazy fly ball to Haas in center field for the first out. Next up: second baseman Eddie Stanky, who so far that day had taken two called third strikes and grounded out. A fiery little competitor, Stanky lived up to his nickname—the "Brat." Dodgers general manager Branch Rickey had said Stanky couldn't hit, field, run, or throw. All he could do is beat you. And on that day, he managed to beat Blackwell. He slapped a ground ball to the mound, where it shot between Blackwell's long legs and past the outstretched glove of Miller, rolling into center field for a base hit. The no-hitter was broken.

Vander Meer sat back down in the dugout, the sellout crowd booed mightily that such a cheap little squib of a hit had ended the Whip's date with destiny.

Blackwell was even angrier. He cursed at the next batter, Al Gionfriddo, who flied out, and apparently yelled racial slurs at first baseman Jackie Robinson, who came up next and singled to right field. Furillo then tapped an easy grounder to Young at first base, who tagged the bag and ended the game.

Afterward, Blackwell posed with Vander Meer and former Reds pitcher Noodles Hahn, who had thrown the team's first no-hitter in the modern era. The Whip would continue his winning streak until losing to the Giants more than a month later, on July 30. During the streak, he threw 151 innings, during which he gave up just 110 hits and 32 runs. Although victories aren't necessarily a good yardstick for a pitcher's effectiveness, while Blackwell was posting a 16–0 record, the Reds went 35–37. Over the course of the season, he won 22 of the team's 70 victories.

That year, he started the All-Star Game for the National League and was runner-up for the Most Valuable Player Award. In the spring of 1948, however, Blackwell's enormously promising career was sidetracked by shoulder problems. He managed to make 20 starts that season, mostly in severe pain, and the next year he made only four. He bounced back in 1950, posting 17 wins and a 2.97 ERA, regaining his old form and his reputation for pitching mean. The following year he performed almost as well, though his fastball had lost some of its zip.

Shoulder problems returned in 1952, and the Reds traded him to the Yankees. He was never effective again. Had he avoided injury, he likely would be the greatest pitcher in Reds history. Instead, he has to settle for pitching the greatest season.

Brooklyn	0	0	0	0	0	0	0	0	0	—	0	2	0
Cincinnati	0	0	0	0	0	1	0	3	x	—	4	4	0

Brooklyn Dodgers

	AB	R	H	RBI
Stanky 2b	4	0	1	0
Gionfriddo lf	4	0	0	0
Robinson 1b	4	0	1	0
Furillo cf	3	0	0	0
Walker rf	1	0	0	0
Jorgensen 3b	3	0	0	0
Reese ss	2	0	0	0
Vaughan ph	1	0	0	0
Rojek ss	0	0	0	0

	AB	R	H	RBI
Hodges c	2	0	0	0
Snider ph	1	0	0	0
Bragan c	0	0	0	0
Hatten p	2	0	0	0
Behrman p	0	0	0	0
Hermanski ph	1	0	0	0
Totals	28	0	2	0

	IP	H	R	ER	BB	SO
Hatten L (7–5)	5.2	1	1	1	6	2
Behrman	2.1	3	3	3	3	1
Totals	8.0	4	4	4	9	3

Cincinnati Reds

	AB	R	H	RBI
Baumholtz rf	2	0	0	0
Zientara 2b	4	0	0	0
Hatton 3b	4	2	1	0
Haas cf	3	1	1	0
Young 1b	2	0	0	0
Galan lf	2	1	0	1
Miller ss	4	0	2	3
Lamanno c	2	0	0	0
Blackwell p	4	0	0	0
Totals	27	4	4	4

	IP	H	R	ER	BB	SO
Blackwell W (11–2)	9.0	2	0	0	3	6
Totals	9.0	2	0	0	3	6

Umpires: Larry Goetz, Jocko Conlan, Beans Reardon.

#21

One-in-a-Million Feeling

Player strikes are never good for the game, at least from a fan perspective. And seasons interrupted by strikes have been particularly tough on the Reds.

In 1981, the Reds posted the best record in the major leagues and would have won the NL West Division by four games, except that a strike lasting nearly two months interrupted the season. When play resumed, Major League Baseball determined that the teams with the best first-half and second-half records, rather than the ones with the best overall records, would play in the postseason. The Reds didn't finish first in either half and were left out.

A strike ended the 1994 season on August 11, with the Reds leading the NL Central. No postseason games were played. Would an extra National League pennant or two hang today at Great American Ball Park if the seasons had played out normally? We'll never know.

Continuing negotiations to resolve the strike delayed the start of the 1995 season until April 25, and MLB declared that the season would be shortened to 144 games. Fans who felt angry and betrayed stayed away from ballparks throughout the majors, leading to a 20 percent drop in attendance.

Hoping to break their back luck in strike years, the Reds made the most of the shortened season. Outfielders Reggie Sanders (.306/.397/.579) and Ron Gant (.276/.386/.554) powered the offense, which also featured shortstop Barry Larkin, who won the National League Most Valuable Player Award. Pete Schourek posted an 18–7 record and 3.22 ERA as the unlikely star of the rotation, while closer Jeff Brantley saved 28 games.

In his third (and final) season as manager, Davey Johnson kept his players fighting for every victory. In an effort to bolster the rotation, general manager Jim Bowden made trades during the season, bringing in Dave Burba and Mark

Portugal from the San Francisco Giants in an eight-player trade on July 21 and David Wells in a four-player swap 10 days later. Burba was particularly effective in the stretch run, posting a 3.27 ERA in 63.1 innings, while winning six games.

The Reds won the NL Central title, nine games ahead of the Houston Astros. Their 85–59 record was second best in the league (behind the Atlanta Braves) and fourth best in the majors. In a new extended playoff format, the Braves, with the best record, would play a three-game series with the second-place team with the best record, the Colorado Rockies. As champs of the Central Division, the Reds played the winners of the West Division, the Los Angeles Dodgers. In this new format, the first two games of the series were played at the home of the team with the lesser record, the final three played at the home of the team with the better record.

The series opened, therefore, in Los Angeles. The Reds took the first game 7–2, with Schourek throwing seven strong innings and getting the win. Larkin, first baseman Hal Morris, and catcher Benito Santiago were the hitting stars. The next evening the Reds won Game Two. Taking a 5–2 lead into the bottom of the ninth inning, the Reds gave fans a scare when Brantley surrendered a two-run homer to first baseman Eric Karros. But Brantley retired the next two batters, ending the Dodgers' potential comeback. As the teams traveled to Cincinnati for Game Three, the spirits of Cincinnati players and fans soared higher than the Reds' plane, though they all knew the next game would be a battle.

Dodgers starter Hideo Nomo was the sensation of the season, winning Rookie of the Year while leading the National League in strikeouts (236 in 191.1 innings) and shutouts (3) and posting a 13–6 record and 2.54 ERA. The first player to permanently jump from Japan to the major leagues, Nomo confused batters with a whirling-dervish delivery and a devastating forkball. The Reds countered with David Wells, who had won six games since coming to the team on July 31.

While attendance was down during the season, Reds fans apparently were in a forgiving mood for the playoffs, as more than 53,000 of them filled Riverfront Stadium for Game Three. With one out in the first inning, Larkin gave them something to cheer about when he laced a single into right field, stole second base, and then stole third. Gant and Sanders failed to bring him home, but Gant didn't fail, however, in his next opportunity.

In the bottom of the third inning, Larkin singled again; this time Gant shot a liner over the fence for a two-run homer. It was a rarity to hit one off Nomo, who had only given up only 14 home runs during the season. With three stolen bases already in the game, the Reds had been prepared to play small ball, but Gant clearly had other ideas.

The Dodgers scored once in the fourth, when Karros reached second on an error by Sanders and right fielder Raul Mondesi knocked him in. But in the bottom of the inning, the Reds once again played long ball when second baseman Bret Boone cleared the fences with a solo shot. A big, bull-like competitor, Wells handled one Dodgers hitter after the next, maintaining the 3–1 lead into the bottom of the sixth inning. Then Morris led off with an infield single and went to second base on a wild pitch. Nomo clearly was struggling. When Santiago singled, moving Morris to third, Dodgers manager Tommy Lasorda had seen enough, bringing in right-hander Kevin Tapani to face Boone, who proceeded to walk, loading the bases. With lefty-swinging third baseman Jeff Branson coming to the plate, Lasorda went to left-hander Mark Guthrie; Johnson countered by replacing Branson with pinch hitter Mark Lewis.

A native of Hamilton, Ohio, in the Greater Cincinnati area, Lewis had been a high school phenom. The Cleveland Indians made him the second overall pick in the 1988 draft, but he struggled as a big leaguer. The Reds acquired him in December 1994, and used him mostly as a reserve infielder and pinch hitter. Now he had a chance to break open the game. In an interview for our book *The Local Boys: Hometown Players for the Cincinnati Reds,* Lewis said he came to the plate focused on hitting a sacrifice fly to score Morris from third. His fly ball, however, flew farther than expected, sailing over the left field fence for a grand slam. Lewis raced around the bases, nearly passing Boone along the way. He said it was a "one-in-a-million feeling."

The Reds piled on in the seventh. With the bases loaded and two outs, Johnson let reliever Michael Jackson bat for himself, and he lined a three-run double into left field, making the score 10–1. When Brantley retired Piazza to end the game, the players stormed the field, while fans cheered the series sweep, which tasted especially sweet to longtime fans, who remembered the great Reds-Dodgers rivalries of the 1970s.

The Reds went on to be swept in the National League Championship Series by the Braves, ending the season on a sour note, but Cincinnati fans had little to complain about. The strike was over, baseball was back, and their team had earned some bragging rights with a division title and a postseason series sweep of the Dodgers. Ill feelings about the strike seemed a million miles away.

Los Angeles	0	0	0	1	0	0	0	0	0 — 1	9	0
Cincinnati	0	0	2	1	0	4	3	0	x — 10	11	2

Los Angeles Dodgers

	AB	R	H	RBI
Butler cf	5	0	0	0
Fonville ss	4	0	1	0
Gwynn ph	1	0	0	0
Piazza c	5	0	1	0
Karros 1b	4	1	2	0
Wallach 3b	4	0	0	0
DeShields 2b	4	0	1	0
Mondesi rf	2	0	1	1
Hollandsworth ph, rf	1	0	0	0
Kelly lf	3	0	2	0
Nomo p	2	0	0	0
Tapani p	0	0	0	0
Guthrie p	0	0	0	0
Astacio p	0	0	0	0
Webster ph	1	0	0	0
Cummings p	0	0	0	0
Osuna p	0	0	0	0
Hansen ph	1	0	1	0
Totals	37	1	9	1

	IP	H	R	ER	BB	SO
Nomo L (0–1)	5.0	7	5	5	2	6
Tapani	0.0	0	1	1	1	0
Guthrie	0.0	2	1	1	0	0
Astacio	1.0	0	0	0	0	1
Cummings	0.2	2	3	3	2	2
Osuna	1.1	0	0	0	0	2
Totals	8.0	0	0	0	0	2

The 1869 Cincinnati Red Stockings were the first all-professional baseball team. Playing teams throughout the United States, they posted a 65–0 record.

Champions of the American Association, the 1882 Red Stockings played in the first postseason series of major league champions.

Frank "Noodles" Hahn
pitched the first major
league no-hitter of the
twentieth century. An
undersized left-hander,
Hahn won 127 games
for the Reds in seven
years with the team.

Hall-of-Fame center fielder
Edd Roush played 12 years
for the Reds, twice leading
the National League in batting average.

Johnny Vander Meer pitched back-to-back no-hitters in June 1938, a feat that has never been repeated in the major leagues.

Pitchers (*left to right*)]
Reds win the 1961 Nat
led to the team's succe

Mound aces Bucky Walters (*left*) and Paul Derringer (*right*) led the Reds to the National League pennant in 1939 and World Series title in 1940, combining to win 94 games in those two seasons.

Hall-of-Fame catcher Erni[e]
on a home run. The pair le[d]
seasons.

One of the most dominant Reds pitchers in the postwar era, Jim Maloney threw two no-hitters (in 1965 and 1969) and a third nine-inning no-hitter that he lost in the 10th inning.

In 1978, Tom Seaver threw the first no-hitter of his Hall-of-Fame career after being traded from the New York Mets the year before. It was the first no-hitter thrown by a Red at Riverfront Stadium.

Frank Robinson (*left*) and manager Fred Hutchinson (*right*) led the Reds to the 1961 National League pennant. From 1956 through 1965, Robinson was one of the greatest sluggers in team history.

Pitchers (*left to right*) Jim O'Toole, Bob Purkey, and Joey Jay helped the Reds win the 1961 National League pennant and formed a tough trio that led to the team's success in the early 1960s.

One of the most dominant Reds pitchers in the postwar era, Jim Maloney threw two no-hitters (in 1965 and 1969) and a third nine-inning no-hitter that he lost in the 10th inning.

In 1978, Tom Seaver threw the first no-hitter of his Hall-of-Fame career after being traded from the New York Mets the year before. It was the first no-hitter thrown by a Red at Riverfront Stadium.

Clockwise from top left: Joe Morgan, Pete Rose, Tony Perez, and Johnny Bench formed the core of the Big Red Machine in the 1970s, one of the greatest teams in major league history.

The Reds celebrate their three-game sweep of the Los Angeles Dodgers in the 1995 National League Division Series.

Jay Bruce declares the Reds "No. 1" while circling the bases after hitting a home run to clinch the National League Central Division title in 2010.

The 2012 Reds gather around the trophy signifying their National League Central Division title. The Reds won 97 games that season.

Cincinnati Reds

	AB	R	H	RBI
Howard cf	3	0	0	0
Lewis D. ph, cf	2	0	0	0
Larkin ss	5	1	2	0
Gant lf	4	1	2	2
Walton lf	1	0	0	0
Sanders rf	5	0	0	0
Morris 1b	3	2	1	0
Santiago c	3	1	1	0
Boone 2b	3	3	2	1
Branson 3b	1	0	0	0
Lewis M. ph, 3b	1	2	1	4
Wells p	3	0	1	0
Jackson p	1	0	1	3
Brantley p	0	0	0	0
Totals	35	10	11	10

	IP	H	R	ER	BB	SO
Wells W (1–0)	6.1	6	1	0	1	8
Jackson	1.2	1	0	0	0	1
Brantley	1.0	2	0	0	0	1
Totals	9.0	2	0	0	0	1

Umpires: Joe West, Terry Tata, Harry Wendelstedt, Charlie Reliford, Jerry Layne, John McSherry.
Time of game: 3:27.
Attendance: 53,276.

REDS 2, PHILADELPHIA PHILLIES 1
MAY 24, 1935

And Then There Was Light

During the Great Depression, people didn't have extra money to spend on ballgames. In small-market Cincinnati at that time, when some of the worst teams in franchise history regularly took the field, attendance was particularly bad. In 1934, only 206,773 paying customers came to Crosley Field to watch a game. But new general manager Larry MacPhail had some ideas for attracting more fans. The one idea he particularly liked was playing games at night.

The idea for night baseball in Cincinnati actually began in 1908. Reds president Garry Herrmann, along with a handful of other local businessmen, invested $50,000 and formed the Night Baseball Development Company to investigate the idea. On June 18, 1909, they staged an amateur game at the Palace of the Fans, erecting temporary light poles to try out the idea. Emil Haberer, who had played for the Reds, took part in the game. A second game under the lights was played on June 30. The lighting system, however, didn't effectively illuminate the field, and the idea was discarded.

A handful of minor league teams started trying out the idea in the early 1930s, including the Columbus, Ohio, franchise run by MacPhail. The Reds even played an exhibition game lit up by a temporary system on September 12, 1931. But despite struggling to draw fans, most owners opposed the idea. The national pastime, after all, wasn't some circus sideshow. But MacPhail was a persuasive guy, and he convinced the Reds' new owner, Powel Crosley Jr., that the idea had merit. People who worked during the day, and had money in their pockets, could pay to watch the Reds play in the evening. Together they made a formal proposal to the National League to play seven night games in 1935, one against each of their league rivals. Given that all the teams were hard up for attendance, the owners voted 4–3 to allow it. The richer teams also wanted to help the poorest franchises survive, and the Reds surely were among the needy.

The first major-league game in which man would defy nature and play in the dark of night was, fittingly, rained out. Nature apparently wasn't giving up quite so easily. The game was rescheduled for the following night, May 24, with the Reds playing the Philadelphia Phillies. Though the skies were clear, it was a cool evening for late May in Cincinnati, with temperatures creeping down into the upper 50s. The *Cincinnati Enquirer* observed, "There were enough overcoats and blankets in evidence to supply a football crowd."

At 8:30, a half hour before the first pitch, President Franklin Roosevelt, seated in a chair in Washington, DC, flipped a switch, and the dark field exploded in a burst of bright, white light, as the electric lamps switched on. The crowd of 20,442 burst into cheers. Average attendance at Reds games was around 3,000, so the size of the crowd made the evening a success before the players even took the field. Each team was allotted 15 minutes for infield practice to get acclimated to the lights. National League president Ford Frick threw the first ceremonial pitch. Finally, Reds right-hander Paul Derringer threw the first pitch that counted, and the game got underway.

A clash of titans the game definitely was not. More like a battle of bottom feeders. The Phillies had won only eight games in a season more than a month old, and the Reds weren't a whole lot better. But the appeal of watching a major-league game at night was undeniable.

After Derringer retired the Phillies in order, Reds shortstop Billy Myers led off the bottom of the inning with the first hit in a night game in major-league history—a double to left field. Third baseman Lew Riggs then grounded out to Phillies second baseman Lou Chiozza, moving Myers to third. Right fielder Ival Goodman followed with a ground out down the first base line that scored Myers, who also became the first player to score a run in a major-league night game.

The game remained 1–0 until the bottom of the fourth inning, when Phillies starter Joe Bowman gave up back-to-back singles to first baseman Billy Sullivan and left fielder Harlin Pool. With runners on the corners, catcher Gilly Campbell grounded to Chiozza, scoring Sullivan, who filled in that night for ailing first baseman Jim Bottomley. By this point in the game, it seemed clear that the players could function in the artificial light. The game progressed just as it would during the day.

The Phillies finally scored in the fifth inning, when Bowman grounded to Alex Kampouris at second base, scoring catcher Al Todd from third base. In the sixth, Philadelphia's slugging first baseman Dolph Camilli hit a long, high fly ball to deep center field, sending Sammy Byrd to the wall, where he made the catch. If there had been doubts about players being able to locate the ball in the night sky, those doubts were put to rest. If neither team hit much in the first night game, the lights likely weren't to blame.

The Phillies' inability to hit Derringer was hardly uncommon. He would win 22 games that season for a team that won only 68. Though the Reds finished sixth in 1935, the seeds of future success were already being sown. Derringer, Myers, and Goodman, along with catcher Ernie Lombardi, who sat out the first night game, formed a core of players that four years later won the National League pennant.

In the ninth inning, holding onto a 2–1 lead, Derringer faced Phillies right fielder Johnny Moore, who shot a long drive to center field, where, once again, Byrd made a fine catch. Camilli then popped out to Campbell, and third baseman Johnny Vergez flied to Goodman in right field for the final out. The Reds had won the first major-league night game, which lasted just an hour and 35 minutes. Everyone declared the experiment a success.

The *Enquirer* reported that neither the fans nor the players had trouble following the ball. In the seven night games the Reds played in 1935, attendance was four times larger than the average for day games. Night baseball was here to stay. With most major-league games today played at night, it's hard to imagine a time when night baseball was a radical idea.

Philadelphia	0	0	0		0	1	0		0	0	0 — 1	6 0
Cincinnati	1	0	0		1	0	0		0	0	x — 2	4 0

Philadelphia Phillies

	AB	R	H	RBI
Chiozza 2b	4	0	0	0
Allen cf	4	0	1	0
Moore rf	4	0	1	0
Camilli 1b	4	0	1	0
Vergez 3b	4	0	1	0
Todd c	3	1	1	0
Watkins lf	3	0	0	0
Haslin ss	3	0	1	0
Bowman p	2	0	0	1
Wilson ph	1	0	0	0
Bivin p	0	0	0	0
Totals	32	1	6	1

	IP	H	R	ER	BB	SO
Bowman L (0–3)	7.0	4	2	2	1	1
Bivin	1.0	0	0	0	0	1
Totals	8.0	4	2	2	1	2

Cincinnati Reds

	AB	R	H	RBI
Myers ss	3	1	1	0
Riggs 3b	4	0	0	0
Goodman rf	3	0	0	1
Sullivan 1b	3	1	2	0
Pool lf	3	0	1	0
Campbell c	3	0	0	1
Byrd cf	3	0	0	0
Kampouris 2b	3	0	0	0
Derringer p	3	0	0	0
Totals	28	2	4	2

	IP	H	R	ER	BB	SO
Derringer W (5–2)	9.0	6	1	1	0	3
Totals	9.0	6	1	1	0	3

Umpires: Bill Klem, Ziggy Sears, Babe Pinelli.
Time of game: 1:35.
Attendance: 20,422.

#19

REDS 8, LOS ANGELES DODGERS 0
AUGUST 16, 1961

Ragamuffins to Riches

The Reds began the 1960s as they'd begun the 1950s—finishing sixth in the eight-team National League. They had finished fifth or sixth eight times between 1950 and 1960. Fans hoping that a new decade would be a new beginning must have felt very disappointed. But if results on the field were the same, things were changing in the front office. On October 25, 1960, general manager Gabe Paul resigned to take the same job for the new Houston franchise. Paul had been in the organization since 1936, and his departure stunned fans and the local media. A week later, the Reds hired Paul's replacement, Bill DeWitt, who quickly started making deals.

The Reds sold second baseman Billy Martin to the Milwaukee Braves, and then traded shortstop Roy McMillan to the Braves for pitchers Joey Jay and Juan Pizarro, the latter being immediately dealt to the Chicago White Sox, along with pitcher Cal McLish, for third baseman Gene Freese. Jay and Freese would play critical roles during the 1961 season, as would the replacements for Martin and McMillan. In a few deft strokes, DeWitt addressed team needs and set up the possibility for success. While baseball experts weren't impressed (most of them picking the Reds to finish sixth again), DeWitt would have the last laugh.

The team had talent. Frank Robinson, Vada Pinson, Wally Post, and Gus Bell made up an excellent outfield, and Bob Purkey led a pitching staff with promising youngsters Jim O'Toole and Jay Hook, as well as an effective bullpen tandem of Bill Henry and Jim Brosnan. Adding Jay and Freese to the mix, while promoting first baseman Gordy Coleman to the starting lineup, gave manager Fred Hutchinson a competitive cast in the well-balanced league. The Los Angeles Dodgers and San Francisco Giants were considered the top teams, but neither had performed particularly well in 1960.

Still, the baseball world was surprised when the Reds jumped out to a good start. After a 20–6 record in May, they occupied first place. In *Pennant Race,* Brosnan's classic memoir of the season, he mentions that throughout the year many people asked him when the Reds would reveal their true colors and sink to the bottom half of the standings. Surely neither he nor his teammates expected to remain in the thick of the pennant race much longer, right? Bronson's chronicle does make clear the ups and downs of the season; however, in the heat of Cincinnati summer, the team didn't wilt. Jay and Freese proved to be excellent additions, while youngsters O'Toole, Pinson, and shortstop Leo Cardenas came of age.

After surviving a six-game losing streak in the second half of July, the Ragamuffin Reds, as they were called, did start to sputter a bit, and the Dodgers and Giants pounced. The three teams battled into the dog days of August. A trip to California for three games in San Francisco and three more in Los Angeles shaped up to be a watershed for the season. Sportswriters felt that it spelled doom for the upstarts. When the Reds lost the first two games in San Francisco, the experts appeared to be right, but the Reds bounced back to win the getaway game and headed to Los Angeles, two games behind the Dodgers.

Before Dodger Stadium opened in 1962, the Dodgers played in the expansive Los Angeles Memorial Coliseum, which was not built for baseball. One of its eccentricities was the left field fence, which stood a laughable 251 feet from home plate. A 42-foot screen was hung to make hitting a homer to left more difficult. The one advantage offered by the coliseum was seating capacity, and more than 72,000 paying customers grabbed that advantage to attend a twi-night doubleheader on Wednesday, August 16. It was the largest crowd to ever attend a Reds game.

The Reds had downed the Dodgers in the series opener the day before, beating ace Sandy Koufax to move within a game of first place. In the first game of the doubleheader, the Reds won 6–0 as Purkey pitched a four-hit, complete game shutout. The Reds scored four runs in the first inning and two more in the third to coast to a victory that tied the teams at the top of the league. Lefty Jim O'Toole manned the mound for the nightcap, facing Dodgers veteran Johnny Podres. This game proved tougher than the first, as neither team scored until the fourth inning, when Freese launched a solo shot down the left field line, barely clearing the screen.

The game remained 1–0 until the seventh, when catcher Darrell Johnson, getting a rare start, hit a surprising home run, one of two he hit in his entire career. Then in the eighth, Freese struck again, clearing the left field screen with a three-run blast that put the Reds ahead 5–0. Meanwhile, O'Toole was cruising. For *Before the Machine,* his book about the 1961 Reds, author Mark Schmetzer talked to O'Toole, who recalled, "I was in such a groove when I pitched against them that day that I had complete confidence. I was throwing everything . . . for strikes. When that happens, it's Katy bar the door for the other team."

O'Toole retired the Dodgers in order in the eighth, before the Reds piled on again. With two out, reliever Turk Farrell surrendered four straight singles—to second baseman Elio Chacon, shortstop Eddie Kasko, Pinson, and Robinson. He also threw two wild pitches and walked Freese. When the dust settled, three more Reds runs had crossed the plate. O'Toole then closed out the game, aided by a double play.

The California games that experts predicted would be the end of the Ragamuffin Reds proved to be just the opposite. Starters Purkey and O'Toole surrendered only six hits combined in the two games, while the Reds won by a combined score of 14–0. In *Pennant Race,* Brosnan writes, "We all had something to celebrate. By sweeping the series we'd regained first place, a full game ahead of LA. The Reds were for real."

The Reds have never again swept a doubleheader with two shutouts. Having recaptured first place, they didn't give it back. They held the top spot for the remainder of the season, finishing four games in front of the Dodgers to win the National League pennant. After the flight from Los Angeles back to Cincinnati the next day, several hundred fans met the Reds' plane at the airport, many of them believing for the first time that their team was really going to go all the way.

Cincinnati	0	0	0		1	0	0		1	3	3	— 8	12 0
Los Angeles	0	0	0		0	0	0		0	0	0	— 0	2 0

Cincinnati Reds

	AB	R	H	RBI
Chacon 2b	4	1	1	0
Kasko ss	5	2	2	0
Bell rf	4	0	0	0
Pinson cf	1	1	1	1
Robinson cf, rf	3	1	2	2
Freese 3b	4	2	2	4
Post lf	5	0	2	0
Coleman 1b	3	0	0	0
Johnson c	4	1	1	1
O'Toole p	4	0	1	0
Totals	37	8	12	8

	IP	H	R	ER	BB	SO
O'Toole W (12–9)	9.0	2	0	0	4	7
Totals	9.0	2	0	0	4	7

Los Angeles Dodgers

	AB	R	H	RBI
Wills ss	4	0	0	0
Gilliam lf	1	0	0	0
Davis cf	4	0	1	0
Howard rf	4	0	0	0
Hodges 1b	2	0	0	0
Spencer 3b	3	0	0	0
Neal 2b	3	0	1	0
Sherry c	3	0	0	0
Podres p	1	0	0	0
Perranoski p	0	0	0	0
Aspromonte ph	1	0	0	0
Farrell p	0	0	0	0
Totals	26	0	2	0

	IP	H	R	ER	BB	SO
Podres L (15–4)	7.1	8	5	5	4	7
Perranoski	0.2	0	0	0	0	0
Farrell	1.0	4	3	3	1	0
Totals	9.0	12	8	8	5	7

Umpires: HP—Ken Burkhart, 1B—Mel Steiner, 2B—Chris Pelekoudas,
  3B—Jocko Conlan.
Time of game: 2:21.
Attendance: 72,140.

Double No-No

When a major-league pitcher tosses a no-hitter, it's a big deal. When two pitchers throw a no-hitter in a single major-league game, it's, well, almost impossible to believe. But it did happen. Once.

On May 2, 1917, the Reds played the Cubs in Chicago's Weeghman Park, later renamed Wrigley Field. On an unseasonably cold Wednesday afternoon, only 3,500 fans came to see a game between two teams playing roughly .500 baseball. But the pitching matchup looked promising. The Cubs started James "Hippo" Vaughn, a big Texan large enough to live up to his nickname. One of the top left-handers in the game at the time, 29-year-old Vaughn was Chicago's ace and would win 23 games in 1917. The Reds countered with Fred Toney, a strapping guy himself, who would win 24 games that year, second in the National League.

Facing such a devastating left-hander, the Reds started an all-righty lineup, which meant that Edd Roush, the team's best hitter and winner of the National League batting title in 1917, would ride the bench. Manager Christy Mathewson hoped that loading up on right-handed hitters would neutralize the Cubs' ace.

For three innings, Vaughn didn't allow a base runner. Toney allowed only one, walking center fielder Cy Williams in the second inning. After three innings—no runs and no hits (and probably no feeling among the shivering fans that they were about to witness baseball history).

Reds third baseman Heinie Groh led off the fourth inning with a walk, but shortstop Larry Kopf hit into a double play. Greasy Neale then reached first on an error by shortstop Rollie Zeider, but Neale's attempt to steal second base failed, ending the inning. Despite the two runners, Vaughn had still faced just 12 batters in the game as he walked off the mound.

In the fifth inning, Vaughn struck out the side. Then he struck out the leadoff hitter in the next inning. The Reds clearly weren't able to touch him. Fortunately, the Cubs were having no luck with Toney, who yielded his second runner in the fifth by walking Williams again. Cubs catcher Art Wilson forced Williams at second, and Toney quickly got out of the inning.

In the final three innings, the pitchers ruled. Neither surrendered a hit or walk; by then the faithful in the stands must have realized they were witnessing a special game—a duel for the ages. When the Cubs went down in order in the bottom of the ninth, the fans had seen the first—and only—double no-hit game in major-league history.

But there was more baseball to be played. The game moved to extra innings with both starting pitchers remaining on the mound. The Reds came to bat, hoping to finally break through against the masterful Hippo. After Gus Getz (who had replaced Groh at third base) popped out to the catcher Wilson, Larry Kopf laced a single into right field for the first hit of the game. Neale then flied out to center field, and it looked like the Reds might come up empty again. Star first baseman and cleanup hitter Hal Chase had other thoughts, however, and shot another liner to center. Williams missed this one, which allowed Kopf to reach third base.

With runners on the corners, right fielder Jim Thorpe entered the batter's box. Thorpe was a world-famous runner, winning gold medals in the 1912 Olympics. A solid but unspectacular baseball player, he did still possess blazing speed, which made him dangerous. He knocked a bouncer between third and pitcher's mound. As Vaughn raced to field it, Kopf sprinted toward the plate. Perhaps thinking he had no chance to get the speedy Thorpe at first, Vaughn threw home—surprising Wilson. The ball plunked off Wilson's shoulder and dribbled away as Kopf crossed the plate for the first run.

Meanwhile, Chase rounded the bases. Wilson chased the ball, grabbed it, and raced to the plate as Chase sped toward the same destination. When they met, Chase was tagged out a little short of his goal, and the inning ended.

Toney took a 1–0 lead into the bottom of the 10th inning. He struck out second baseman Larry Doyle for out no. 1. The second out arrived when first baseman Fred Merkel flied to deep left field, driving Manuel Cueto all the way to the fence to haul it in. Toney then faced Williams, whom he had been pitching around that day, walking him twice.

The first two pitches were wide of the plate. Toney clearly was giving Williams nothing to hit. He followed with two pitches close enough for called strikes. Williams then fouled off the next two offerings. The tension continued to build. Toney then missed the strike zone with his next pitch. Full count.

On the following pitch, Toney threw a sweeping, sidearm curve that fooled Williams. He swung valiantly but to no avail. Strike three. Game over.

A tough loss for Vaughn, who had struck out 10 batters to Toney's three and obviously had pitched well enough to win. But Toney, if less dominating, bested him. The Reds would go on to a fourth-place finish that year, with a 78–76 record. The Cubs finished fifth.

Toney and Vaughn, sad to say, are largely forgotten, despite good major-league careers. Starting in 1917, Vaughn reeled off three exceptional seasons. In 1918 he led the league in wins, earned run average, innings pitched, shutouts, and strikeouts. If there had been a Cy Young Award that year, he surely would have won it.

While not enjoying quite as much success as Vaughn, Toney did pitch well in the years that followed, though not for the Reds, who traded him in 1918. He went to the New York Giants, where he posted seasons of 21 and 18 wins.

Neither reached the Hall of Fame. Today, when they're mentioned at all, they are mentioned together—forever linked by one chilly afternoon in 1917, when for nine innings, neither gave up a hit.

Cincinnati	0	0	0	0	0	0	0	0	0	1 —	1	2	0
Chicago	0	0	0	0	0	0	0	0	0	0 —	0	0	2

Cincinnati Reds

	AB	R	H	RBI
Groh 3b	1	0	0	0
Getz ph, 3b	1	0	0	0
Kopf ss	4	1	1	0
Neale cf	4	0	0	0
Chase 1b	4	0	0	0
Thorpe rf	4	0	1	1
Shean 2b	3	0	0	0
Cueto lf	3	0	0	0
Huhn c	3	0	0	0
Toney p	3	0	0	0
Totals	30	1	2	1

	IP	H	R	ER	BB	SO
Toney W (5–1)	10.0	0	0	0	2	3
Totals	10.0	0	0	0	2	3

Chicago Cubs

	AB	R	H	RBI
Zeider ss	4	0	0	0
Wolter rf	4	0	0	0
Doyle 2b	4	0	0	0
Merkle 1b	4	0	0	0
Williams cf	2	0	0	0
Mann lf	3	0	0	0
Wilson c	3	0	0	0
Deal 3b	3	0	0	0
Vaughn p	3	0	0	0
Totals	30	0	0	0

	IP	H	R	ER	BB	SO
Vaughn L (3–2)	10.0	2	1	0	2	10
Totals	10.0	2	1	0	2	10

Umpires: Al Orth, Cy Rigler.
Time of game: 1:50.
Attendance: 350.

#17

REDS 4, PHILADELPHIA PHILLIES 3
SEPTEMBER 18, 1940

Respect

The pennant-winning 1939 season ended on a sour note for the Reds, as they were swept mercilessly in the World Series by the New York Yankees, who fielded one of the greatest teams of all time.

The reigning National League champions still had something to prove as they prepared for the next season, and some weaknesses to address. While Bucky Walters and Paul Derringer gave the rotation a league-leading one-two punch, 36-year-old Jim Turner was brought in to join young starters Gene Thompson and Johnny Vander Meer behind the dynamic duo. Mike McCormick (no relation to star first baseman Frank McCormick) helped stabilize the outfield, where light-hitting center fielder Harry Craft and a revolving door in left didn't bode well for another pennant run. Reliever Joe Beggs seemed like a minor add-on when he came aboard, but ended up playing a vital role.

The Reds won 15 of their first 19 games to start the year, but the Brooklyn Dodgers stayed right with them. The two teams traded the top spot more than a half-dozen times through the first three months of the season. Walters, Derringer, and Thompson provided exceptional pitching, which helped prohibit losing streaks, and the Reds played excellent defense. The McCormicks, along with catcher Ernie Lombardi and third baseman Billy Werber, contributed just enough offense, but left field remained an issue, and Vander Meer struggled so much he was sent down to AAA Indianapolis to regain his form.

In early July, the Reds caught fire, reeling off an 18–2 record that put the Dodgers behind them for good. As August opened, they were a happy bunch, except for backup catcher Wally Hershberger. A popular, dedicated, hustling player, Hershberger sank into an emotional funk in late July, claiming responsibility for a couple of tough losses. His bat had gone cold, and he began to brood. During an early August game in Boston, a Braves player laid down a bunt in front of the plate and rather than pounce on it, Hershberger just stood and stared at the ball. Reds manager Bill McKechnie took the sullen catcher to dinner, where Hershberger confessed suicidal feelings. McKechnie comforted him and felt the issue had been resolved. When Hershberger didn't show up for the next day's game, McKechnie sent someone to the team's hotel, where the catcher was found dead in his bathroom, having slit his throat.

His teammates, loose and confident in their pennant run, were stunned. The mood in the clubhouse suddenly changed. Black armbands appeared on their uniforms, and a dark cloud settled over the team. The pall led to a short slump, but the Reds held on to first place. They continued to win more than they lost. Vander Meer returned and was pitching well again, while Jimmy Ripple, a late-August pickup, solidified left field, hitting .307/.397/.525 in 119 plate appearances.

On September 15, Lombardi sprained his ankle in Brooklyn. The injury threatened to keep him off the field for the rest of the year. And with the loss of Hershberger, McKechnie needed help behind the plate. He turned to one of his coaches, 40-year-old Jimmie Wilson, to put on the mask and chest protector.

Three days later, the Reds played the Philadelphia Phillies in Shibe Park on a Wednesday afternoon, with a chance to clinch the National League pennant. The Phillies were terrible that year, winning just 50 games, and only 2,093 people bothered to show up. Vander Meer took the mound for the Reds, facing Hugh Mulcahy.

The Phillies scored first, in the bottom of the second inning, putting up two runs on a double and two singles. The Reds didn't get on the scoreboard until the fifth inning, when left fielder Ripple led off with a single to center field. Catcher Bill Baker, subbing for the injured Lombardi, doubled to left field, scoring Ripple. In the seventh inning, the Reds tied the score. Frank McCormick led off with a single, and Baker singled to put runners on first and second. Second baseman Lonnie Frey then shot a single into center field, scoring McCormick.

The score remained 2–2 through nine innings. Both starting pitchers stayed on the mound. Frey led off the top of the 10th with a single to left field, and with two out Mike McCormick singled him in. The Reds looked ready to celebrate winning the pennant, but the hapless Phillies still had a little bit of hap left in them. Vander Meer walked the first batter, pinch hitter Neb Stewart, who would make all of 32 major-league plate appearances in his one-year career. Center fielder Joe Marty doubled him in with a long drive to right field, tying the score again. The game proceeded to the 11th inning, in which Mulcahy and Vander Meer faced three batters each. And they would do the same in the 12th. If the pitchers were tiring, they showed no signs of it yet.

Demonstrating confidence in his pitcher's stamina, McKechnie sent Vander Meer to the plate to start the 13th inning, and the move paid off with a double to left field. Eddie Joost executed a sacrifice bunt to move Vander Meer to third base. Right fielder Ival Goodman then launched a long fly ball to left field, deep enough to put the run across and regain the lead.

McKechnie apparently felt comfortable with pitching Vander Meer for 12 innings, but assumed his guy would be too tired after running the bases. So he called on Joe Beggs to pitch the bottom of the 13th. Beggs posted a 12–3 record and a 2.00 ERA that year, pitching 76⅔ innings, nearly all in relief. Like a modern closer, his job was to hold leads or keep scores close enough for late-inning comebacks. McKechnie relied heavily on Beggs, who usually proved up to the task. On this day, he retired the Phillies in order, coaxing a fly ball from Hall of Famer Chuck Klein for the final out.

The Reds had won back-to-back pennants, which the franchise has done only one other time in its history. A champagne-soaked clubhouse bacchanal had followed the previous year's pennant-clinching game, but the 1940 team hadn't yet achieved its goal—winning the World Series. In his book *The Under-rated Reds,* Leo Bradley writes, "After the game, McKechnie climbed up on a stool in the clubhouse and requested, 'no celebrating.'"

The Reds finished the regular season with 100 wins, 12 games ahead of Brooklyn and 20 ahead of third-place New York—10 more victories than any other major-league team. For the third year in a row, a Red was chosen as the league's Most Valuable Player, this time Frank McCormick taking the honor. But they had one more mission to accomplish before breaking out the champagne. They still had to prove to the world that they were the best. A few weeks later, they would do just that.

Cincinnati	0	0	0	0	1	0	1	0	0	1	0	0	1 —	4	13 0
Philadelphia	0	2	0	0	0	0	0	0	0	1	0	0	0 —	3	8 2

Cincinnati Reds

	AB	R	H	RBI
Werber 3b	1	0	0	0
Joost 3b	3	0	1	1
McCormick M. cf	6	0	2	0
Goodman rf	6	0	0	1
McCormick F. 1b	6	1	3	0
Ripple lf	5	1	1	0
Baker c	5	0	2	0
Frey 2b	5	1	2	1
Myers ss	5	0	1	0
Vander Meer p	5	1	1	0
Beggs p	0	0	0	0
Totals	47	4	13	3

	IP	H	R	ER	BB	SO
Vander Meer W (2–0)	12.0	8	3	3	5	11
Beggs SV (7)	1.0	0	0	0	0	0
Totals	13.0	8	3	3	5	11

Philadelphia Phillies

	AB	R	H	RBI
May 3b	5	0	0	0
Mahan 1b	4	0	1	0
Stewart ph	0	1	0	0
Mazzera 1b	1	0	0	0
Litwhiler rf	6	0	1	0
Rizzo lf	5	0	0	0
Marty cf	6	1	3	1
Warren c	3	1	1	0
Bragan ss	5	0	0	0
Klein ph	1	0	0	0
Schulte 2b	5	0	0	1
Mulcahy p	5	0	2	1
Totals	46	3	8	3

	IP	H	R	ER	BB	SO
Mulcahy L (12–21)	13.0	13	4	3	1	7
Totals	13.0	13	4	3	1	7

Umpires: HP—Al Barlick, 1B—Bick Campbell, 2B—Bill Klem, 3B—Lee Ballanfant.

Time of game: 2:51.

Attendance: 2,093.

#16

REDS 7, PHILADELPHIA PHILLIES 6
OCTOBER 12, 1976

The Machine Rolls On

The Big Red Machine cruised through the 1976 season, winning 102 games and repeating as NL West Division champs. They led the league in home runs, stolen bases, runs scored, and batting average, among other offensive categories. Second baseman Joe Morgan won the Most Valuable Player award, and pitcher Pat Zachry won the Rookie of the Year award. Five members of the Great Eight hit over .300. As defending world champions, they looked ready to take on the East Division champion Philadelphia Phillies in the National League Championship Series.

But victory was far from assumed. The Phillies won 101 games that year with a lineup loaded with stars coming of age, including third baseman Mike Schmidt, who was 26, and left fielder Greg Luzinski, who was 25. First baseman Dick Allen was their only starting position player over 30. The Reds lineup included three starters in their mid-30s. Some baseball writers, and fans, thought the series might signal a changing of the guard.

In the first two games, however, the Reds continued to cruise, beating the Phillies in Philadelphia 6–3 and 6–2. For Game Three in the best-of-five series, the teams traveled to Cincinnati, where Reds starter Gary Nolan faced the Phillies' Jim Kaat on Tuesday, October 12. More than 55,000 fans jammed into Riverfront Stadium, the Reds faithful hoping to celebrate winning another pennant, which would be the Big Red Machine's fourth of the 1970s.

Through the first three innings, both Nolan and Kaat were in complete command. Nolan, the Reds' top starter in 1976, surrendered two singles, while Kaat allowed a single and a walk. In the top of the fourth, back-to-back doubles by Schmidt and Luzinski gave the Phillies a 1–0 lead. Nolan retired the next three to end the inning, and by the sixth inning had allowed no more runs. But after giving up a single and two walks to load the bases in the sixth, he was replaced by Manny Sarmiento, who put out the rally. Sarmiento was less effective in the next inning. He walked shortstop Larry Bowa and allowed back-to-back doubles by center fielder Garry Maddox and Schmidt.

Trailing by three runs in the bottom of the seventh, the Reds finally came alive. Right fielder Ken Griffey led off with a base hit. Joe Morgan walked. After six quiet innings, the ballpark started rumbling. Ron Reed replaced Kaat on the mound, but he wasn't able to stop the rally. First baseman Tony Perez banged a base hit to score Griffey and drive Morgan to third base. Left fielder George Foster lofted a sacrifice fly to right field to bring in Morgan. Reed then walked Johnny Bench. After shortstop Dave Concepcion popped out, center fielder Cesar Geronimo tripled in Perez and Bench, giving the Reds a 4–3 lead. Reds fans smelled a sweep—and a pennant.

The heralded new guard, however, wasn't ready to be swept quite so easily. To pitch the eighth, manager Sparky Anderson brought in his best reliever, young right-hander Rawley Eastwick, who had saved 26 games in 1976 and won 11, while posting a stingy 2.09 ERA in 107⅔ innings. Eastwick whiffed Dick Allen to start the inning, but right fielder Jay Johnstone then doubled and went to third on a wild pitch. Eastwick's trouble continued when he walked catcher Bob Boone. Speedy Terry Harmon replaced Boone as a pinch runner. Bowa promptly doubled, scoring Johnstone and moving Harmon to third base. After Eastwick walked Bobby Tolan intentionally, second baseman Dave Cash sent a sacrifice fly to right field to score Harmon and give the Phillies a 5–4 lead.

Third baseman Pete Rose led off the Reds' half of the eighth with a single, but Griffey, Morgan, and Perez couldn't move him along. In the top of the ninth, Eastwick retired the first two Philadelphia batters, but a Rose error and a Johnstone triple put the Phillies two runs ahead going into the bottom of the final inning.

Left fielder George Foster strode to the plate to lead off. During the season, he'd hit a team-leading 29 home runs and driven in 121 runs. Once again he stepped up, clearing the left field fence with a solo shot. Bench, who had struggled at the plate through much of the year, settled into the batter's box. Four years earlier, he had hit a game-tying, ninth-inning home run in the 1972 National League Championship Series, and Reds fans prayed that he'd once more rise to the occasion.

And he did—clubbing the ball over the wall in left-center to tie the score. Gene Garber replaced Reed, but the Reds were rolling now. Concepcion singled to continue the rally and end Garber's night. Twenty-two-year-old lefty Tom Underwood took the mound next. He had started 25 games during the season and posted a 10–5 record. Manager Danny Ozark was pulling out all the stops to keep his team alive. Underwood walked Geronimo, who made a couple of bunt attempts before taking a base on balls. Pinch hitter Ed Armbrister laid down a sacrifice bunt, moving Concepcion to third and Geronimo to second.

Underwood now faced the top of the Reds order, beginning with Pete Rose. Wanting no part of Rose, the Phillies walked him intentionally, loading the bases for Griffey. Trusting his young pitcher, Ozark kept Underwood on the mound. Meanwhile, a collective full-throated roar filled the stadium as Reds fans bounced on their feet, cheering and screaming in the chilly October air for their beloved Machine. Griffey didn't get good wood on the ball, but he did hit a roller down the first-base line, and Tolan was unable to field it. Concepcion raced in from third base and crossed the plate.

Pandemonium, of course, ensued. Players rushed the field to celebrate, while fans danced and hugged each other in the stands. The Reds had won back-to-back National League pennants.

The Reds were still the league's best team. Actually, the world's best, as they would prove in the World Series. They swept the Yankees in four straight, becoming the only team to sweep a league championship series and the World Series during the years of the two-tiered postseason format. While the Phillies would go on to success in the future, and the Reds would not capture another flag until 1990, in 1976 the guard had yet to change.

Philadelphia	0	0	0		1	0	0		2	2	1	—	6	11	0
Cincinnati	0	0	0		0	0	0		4	0	3	—	7	10	2

Philadelphia Phillies

	AB	R	H	RBI
Cash 2b	4	0	1	1
Maddox cf	5	1	1	1
Schmidt 3b	5	1	3	1
Luzinski lf	4	0	1	1
Reed p	1	0	0	0
Garber p	0	0	0	0
Underwood p	0	0	0	0
Allen 1b	3	0	0	0
Martin lf	1	1	0	0
Johnstone rf	4	1	3	1
Boone c	3	0	0	0
Harmon pr	0	1	0	0

	AB	R	H	RBI
Oates c	1	0	0	0
Bowa ss	3	1	1	1
Kaat p	2	0	1	0
Tolan lf, 1b	0	0	0	0
Totals	36	6	11	6

	IP	H	R	ER	BB	SO
Kaat	6.0	3	2	2	1	1
Reed	2.0	5	4	4	1	1
Garber L (0–1)	0.0	1	1	1	0	0
Underwood	0.1	1	0	0	2	0
Totals	8.1	10	7	7	4	2

Cincinnati Reds

	AB	R	H	RBI
Rose 3b	4	0	1	0
Griffey rf	5	1	2	1
Morgan 2b	3	1	0	0
Perez 1b	4	1	2	1
Foster lf	3	1	1	2
Bench c	3	2	1	1
Concepcion ss	4	1	1	0
Geronimo cf	3	0	1	2
Nolan p	1	0	1	0
Sarmiento p	1	0	0	0
Borbon p	0	0	0	0
Lum ph	1	0	0	0
Eastwick p	0	0	0	0
Armbrister ph	0	0	0	0
Totals	32	7	10	7

	IP	H	R	ER	BB	SO
Nolan	5.2	6	1	1	2	1
Sarmiento	1.0	2	2	2	1	0
Borbon	0.1	0	0	0	0	0
Eastwick W (1–0)	2.0	3	3	2	2	1
Totals	9.0	11	6	5	5	2

Umpires: Dick Stello, Ed Vargo, Doug Harvey, Terry Tata, Jerry Dale, Ed
    Sudol.

Time of game: 2:43.

Attendance: 55,047.

#15

Sort of a World Series

Cincinnati has been a beer town for most of its history. So it's no wonder that Cincinnatians didn't like the National League's rule about not selling beer on Sundays. The league didn't even schedule games on Sundays during the 1880 season—so no big deal, right? Well, the Reds had the audacity to rent their Bank Street Grounds to amateur teams and allowed them to sell suds.

National League bigwigs felt that renting the ballpark violated the spirit of the rule and amended it to forbid such shenanigans. The Reds objected, stating that they needed the rental revenue to remain solvent and that Cincinnati fans would demand that beer be served whenever baseball was played. Officials briefly considered this argument before booting the team from the league. The following season, Cincinnati sportswriter Oliver Perry Caylor (known as O.P.) organized a local team to play exhibition games against teams from other large cities that lacked National League franchises. In November 1881, six of those cities formed a major league of their own. Baltimore, Louisville, Philadelphia, Pittsburgh, and St. Louis joined with Cincinnati in the new American Association.

The new league set lower ticket prices, opening the game to working-class fans. Teams were allowed to schedule games on Sundays, and beer flowed freely at those games. The midwestern river cities that made up much of the league offered a rougher, rowdier atmosphere on the field and in the stands than had been seen in the National League. The American Association quickly earned the nickname the "Beer and Whiskey League."

While there was no great love lost between the leagues, they did respect each other's contracts and territories, and they played by the same rules. They acted as separate but (relatively) equal major leagues, though the senior circuit felt their teams were superior to the unruly upstarts.

The Red Stockings fielded an excellent team in the inaugural season. Its star that year was slugging third baseman Hick Carpenter, who batted .342 and led the league in hits and runs batted in. Joe Sommer, 23 years old and a native of Greater Cincinnati, played left field and led the league in plate appearances while scoring 82 runs during the 80-game season. The team's other big star was pitcher Will White, who had been the Reds' ace during the National League era. At 27, he looked more like 57, a small, bespectacled character who nonetheless was master of the mound. He led the league in wins (40), winning percentage (.769), complete games (52), shutouts (8), and innings pitched (480.0).

With a 55–25 record, the Red Stockings won the first American Association pennant by 11½ games. Not ones to leave well enough alone, the team challenged the National League champion Chicago White Stockings to a playoff series, a de facto World Series, of sorts. It would be the first ever postseason baseball series between two major-league champions. The National Leaguers accepted the challenge, eager to demonstrate their superiority, but AA officials forbade it. American Association teams were strictly forbidden from playing games against National League teams. So the Red Stockings decided to disband the AA team—for a day—and then form a new, temporarily independent team made up of the same players and funded by an "anonymous donor."

A crowd of 2,700 fans showed up at the Bank Street Grounds in Cincinnati to watch Game One of the series, which didn't have a defined number of planned games. Will White kept the mighty Chicago bats quiet through the first five innings, but White Stockings pitcher Fred Goldsmith kept Cincinnati hitters equally silent until the sixth inning. With one out, Carpenter singled to center field, and first baseman Ecky Stearns followed with another single. Shortstop Chick Fulmer then singled to center, scoring Carpenter and giving the Reds the lead.

They would quickly add to it when rookie second baseman Bid McPhee, who would go on to a Hall of Fame career with the Red Stockings, slashed a triple, scoring Stearns and Fulmer. Facing the next batter, Goldsmith, who would later claim to have invented the curveball, launched a wild pitch that allowed McPhee to race home.

White continued to blank the White Stockings, and the Red Stockings held a 4–0 lead into the ninth inning. During the season, the White Stockings had averaged seven runs per game. They had won three consecutive National League pennants. Were they going to lose a shutout to these upstart beer leaguers? Not without a fight.

Chicago left fielder Abner Dalrymple led off the inning with a single. After getting the next out, White yielded a double to third baseman Ned Williamson, but Dalrymple stopped at third. Next up—Hall of Famer Adrian "Cap" Anson, arguably the greatest player of the era. Anson shot a liner to center field, but Jimmy Macullar was waiting for it. He caught it for the second out. Perhaps sizing up the diminutive Macullar (who was known as "Little Mac"), Dalrymple bolted for home. Macullar launched a great throw to catcher Phil Powers, who slapped the tag on the surprised Dalrymple, ending the game.

Red Stockings fans went crazy. Not only had they won the first postseason game between league champions, they had beaten the powerful White Stockings and, best of all, had avenged themselves against the league that had booted them out two years before. They also had validated the credibility of their own league. No doubt much beer and whiskey was drunk that night in Cincinnati.

In the second game of the series, the Reds made two errors in the first inning, giving up two runs. White was masterful again, but the White Stockings held on for a 2–0 victory. Oddly, no further games were scheduled. For their efforts to bring respectability to the new league the Red Stockings were fined $100—a small price to pay after proving the American Association could beat the National League's best.

From 1884 through 1890, the two leagues played an annual postseason series of varying lengths. When the Reds moved back to the National League in 1890, beer sales on Sundays were no longer forbidden, no doubt making Cincinnati fans very happy.

Cincinnati	0	0	0		0	0	4		0	0	0 — 4
Chicago	0	0	0		0	0	0		0	0	0 — 0

Cincinnati Red Stockings

	AB	R	H
Sommer lf	4	0	0
Wheeler rf	4	0	0
Carpenter 3b	4	1	2
Stearns 1b	4	1	1
Fulmer ss	4	1	1
McPhee 2b	4	1	3
Macullar cf	3	0	1
Powers c	3	0	0
White p	3	0	2
Totals	33	4	10

Chicago White Stockings

	AB	R	H
Dalrymple lf	4	0	2
Gore cf	4	0	1
Williamson 3b	4	0	2
Anson 1b	4	0	1
Burns 2b	3	0	0
Goldsmith p	3	0	0
Corcoran ss	3	0	0
Nicol rf	3	0	0
Flint c	3	0	1
Totals	31	0	7

Time of Game: 1:40.
Umpire—C. M. Smith.

#14

REDS 5, ST. LOUIS CARDINALS 3
SEPTEMBER 28, 1939

Reds Take Flag

The 1930s were difficult years for America, as the country struggled through the Great Depression. The decade wasn't much better for the Cincinnati Reds. In one of the lowest points in franchise history, the Reds finished last five times, including four seasons in a row. But just like the national economy, fortunes began to brighten a bit by the end of the decade.

In 1934, Cincinnati industrialist Powel Crosley Jr., purchased the team from cash-strapped Sidney Weil, signaling the start of the franchise's turnaround. Four years later, future Hall of Famer Bill McKechnie took over as manager, and he led the Reds to their first winning season of the decade, kindling hope in the hearts of fans as the 1939 season began.

With a strong, balanced attack, the team started well, riding the arms of Bucky Walters and Paul Derringer, while first baseman Frank McCormick, catcher Ernie Lombardi, and right fielder Ival Goodman supplied plenty of punch. Walters won the National League's Most Valuable Player Award that year. Derringer finished third in the voting; McCormick placing fourth.

On May 26, the Reds moved into first place by beating the Cardinals, their top competitor that year. After that victory, their 11th in a row, the Reds held the top spot throughout the summer.

On September 28, the Cardinals were in town and determined to make a final surge at the pennant. They stood just 2½ games behind the Reds, with three games remaining after this series. The Reds had dropped the previous two games to the Redbirds 6–0 and 4–0. More than 17,000 fans settled into their seats on a sunny Thursday to see for themselves if this Reds team could clinch the pennant, their first since 1919, by beating the Cardinals, who had refused to go away all season long.

156

Many of the Reds' rooters must have had faith that big Paul Derringer, going for his 25th win against only seven losses, would rise to the occasion. Derringer came to the Reds in 1933 in a swap with the Cardinals that sent shortstop Leo Durocher to St. Louis. After years of pitching well for bad teams, Derringer surely felt ready to taste success.

After being shut out in back-to-back games, the Reds scored in the first inning. Third baseman Billy Werber walked, went to second on a ground out, and scored on a single by McCormick. Cardinals pitcher Max Lanier, just 23 years old, might have been rattled by giving up a run so quickly. He proceeded to walk Lombardi and hit center fielder Harry Craft. Taking no chances, Cardinals manager Ray Blades brought in 22-game winner Curt Davis, who then walked left fielder Wally Berger, allowing McCormick to score.

The Cardinals had dogged the Reds all year, and they weren't going to stop now. In the next inning, St. Louis slugger Johnny Mize reached first on an error by shortstop Billy Myers, and Terry Moore cleared the fence with a shot that tied the score at two apiece.

Mize returned the favor, however, with an error of his own in the next inning that allowed Billy Werber to score and the Reds to take back the lead and hold it—until the top of the fifth inning. The usually sure-handed Myers made his second error of the game, putting Don Gutteridge on first base. A double and a sacrifice fly brought him in; once again the two best teams in the National League were tied up.

In the bottom of the sixth, Berger led off with a double, moving to third when Myers singled. Derringer then helped his own cause with a sacrifice fly to right field, bringing in the run. The Cardinals came charging back. With one out, Joe Medwick banged a long fly over Goodman's head in right field, but was thrown out trying to stretch his double into a triple. The Cardinals followed with three straight singles, but left the bases loaded.

The light-hitting Craft provided an insurance run in the bottom of the eighth with a solo homer. In the ninth, Derringer faced three Hall of Famers: Enos Slaughter, Medwick, and Mize. Surely no one in the stands was heading to the exits. These two teams had tussled all season long and neither was going to give up. Slaughter led off by popping out to Myers at short. Medwick, perhaps hoping to redeem his earlier baserunning blunder, dug into the batter's box. But Derringer had plenty left in his arm. Medwick took a called strike three, leaving the season's fortunes to Mize, the league's leader in home runs, batting, slugging, and total bases.

Could the moment have been any more dramatic?

For the Reds: no. When Mize's mighty final swing met nothing but Cincinnati air, Crosley Field erupted. The Reds had won the pennant. They would represent the National League in the World Series against a powerful Yankees team. Before then, they took two of three from the Pirates to finish 97–57, a record that had seemed inconceivable just a few years before. The city celebrated for days afterward, while preparing for a World Series against the Yankees.

Which didn't go well, unfortunately. Still considered one of the greatest teams of all time, the 1939 Yankees won 106 games, finishing 17 games ahead of second-place Boston. Experts gave the Reds little chance for success, and their predictions proved accurate, as they were swept in four games. The most memorable moment occurred in Game Four, when Lombardi, dazed from a home plate collision with Charlie Keller, lay prone, the ball close by, while Joe DiMaggio scampered in to score. Now known as "Lombardi's snooze," the play haunted the big catcher for the rest of his life.

Despite the series loss, the Reds had proven themselves the National League's best and were ready for a new decade and a new season, which would see them become world champions.

St. Louis	0	2	0	0	1	0	0	0	0	—	3	14	2
Cincinnati	2	1	0	0	0	1	0	1	x	—	5	8	3

St. Louis Cardinals

	AB	R	H	RBI
Brown ss	5	0	3	0
Gutteridge 3b	5	1	0	0
Slaughter rf	5	0	1	0
Medwick lf	5	0	2	0
Mize 1b	4	1	1	0
Padgett c	3	0	1	1
Myers pr	0	0	0	0
Owen c	0	0	0	0
Moore cf	4	1	2	2
Martin 2b	4	0	2	0
Lanier p	0	0	0	0
Davis p	3	0	1	0
Hopp ph	1	0	1	0
Bowman p	0	0	0	0
Totals	39	3	14	3

	IP	H	R	ER	BB	SO
Lanier	0.2	1	2	2	2	0
Davis L (22–16)	6.1	6	2	1	2	1
Bowman	1.0	1	1	1	0	0
Totals	8.0	8	5	4	4	1

Cincinnati Reds

	AB	R	H	RBI
Werber 3b	3	2	1	0
Frey 2b	4	0	0	0
Goodman rf	4	0	1	0
McCormick 1b	3	1	2	1
Lombardi c	3	0	0	0
Craft cf	3	1	1	1
Berger lf	2	1	1	1
DiMaggio lf	1	0	0	0
Myers ss	4	0	2	0
Derringer p	3	0	0	1
Totals	30	5	8	4

Cincinnati Reds	IP	H	R	ER	BB	SO
Derringer W (25–7)	9.0	14	3	1	1	4
Totals	9.0	14	3	1	1	4

Umpires: HP—Larry Goetz, 1B—Babe Pinelli, 2B—Bick Campbell, 3B—
   Beans Reardon.
Time of game: 1:52.
Attendance: 17,421.

Lou's Boys

When the Reds hired manager Lou Piniella in November 1989, the team, and the city, hoped for a fresh start. After four years of second-place finishes, the Reds sank to fifth in the NL West Division in what proved to be a tumultuous season due to the Pete Rose gambling investigation, which ultimately led to Rose's banishment from the game in August 1989. Despite talented rosters, Rose's Reds never reached the postseason, and many fans had wondered aloud for some time about Rose's ability to push his teams hard enough. He seemed to act more like a teammate than a manager.

Piniella came into the job sporting a reputation as a tough, fiery guy who was more than willing to crack the managerial whip. He lived up to that reputation from the start, creating a new intensity that pervaded the spring training camp in Florida. He wanted a fast, aggressive team that used every opportunity to beat an opponent. The Reds made a couple of crucial trades before the season, sending closer John Franco to the New York Mets in exchange for reliever Randy Myers in early December. A week later, they acquired young first baseman Hal Morris in a trade with the Yankees. And less than a week before the start of the season, they brought in speedy outfielder Billy Hatcher from the Pittsburgh Pirates.

Piniella's runnin' Reds shot out of the gate, winning their first nine games despite a slow start by star outfielder Eric Davis. On June 3, they stood at the top of the division with a record of 33–12. Pennant fever already consumed Cincinnati fans, who loved the opportunistic style of play, as well as the three-headed monster in the bullpen known as the Nasty Boys. Myers, Rob Dibble, and Norm Charlton pretty much assured that a lead in the seventh inning meant a "W" in the standings.

In *The Wire-to-Wire Reds*, the definitive book on the 1990 team, authors John

Erardi and Joel Luckhaupt write, "No team in recent Reds history embodied their manager more than the 1990 Reds." Piniella's competitive nature—never more apparent than on August 21, when he yanked first base out of the ground and tossed it into right field—infected his players. Sustaining that level of intensity, however, is difficult to do in a long season, and the Reds started to sputter. Injuries to key starting pitchers Jack Armstrong and Danny Jackson also slowed the team's success. The gap between the Reds and the rest of the division was wide enough that by playing little more than .500 ball they maintained their lead and won the NL West title.

The mighty Pirates, however, awaited them in the best-of-seven National League Championship Series, and the majority of sportswriters and baseball fans didn't give the Reds much of a chance. Outfielders Barry Bonds, the league's Most Valuable Player; Bobby Bonilla; and Andy Van Slyke powered the Pirates lineup, while Cy Young Award–winner Doug Drabek was the ace of a solid pitching staff.

As expected, the Reds lost the series opener, but they recaptured some of their early season intensity and reeled off three straight wins to come within one game of the pennant. Drabek kept his team alive with a masterful performance in Game Five. For Game Six, the teams returned to Cincinnati. More than 56,000 people filled Riverfront Stadium on a cool Friday night to watch the league's two best teams battle it out with the ferocity that made this entire series special. A Reds' victory would mean Cincinnati's first pennant since 1976, while the Pirates were looking to force a Game Seven that would give them a shot to win their first since 1979.

Left-hander Danny Jackson took the mound for the Reds. After winning 23 games in an outstanding 1988 season, in which he threw 260⅔ innings, Jackson had suffered arm injuries that limited both his starts and his success. After he cruised through a one-two-three top of the first, the Reds faced right-hander (and former Red) Ted Power, a surprising move by manager Jim Leyland, in that Power was normally a reliever and left-hander Zane Smith had been scheduled to start. But Leyland wanted to force Piniella to juggle his lineup with a right-hander on the mound.

Didn't work. The Reds lineup remained the same, and it scored the first run right away. Shortstop Barry Larkin led off with a single, stole second base, and went to third on a bad throw, finally scoring when Davis grounded out. The lead lasted until the top of the fifth, when Bonds walked and then scored on a double by first baseman Carmelo Martinez, leveling the score at 1–1. Martinez's double was the only hit Jackson surrendered in six innings. He walked four and struck out just as many.

After replacing Power in the third inning, lefty Smith kept the Reds at bay. He escaped a bases-loaded jam in the sixth inning, but the Reds were right back in his face in the seventh. Second baseman Ron Oester led off with a single to right field. Hoping to move Oester to second base, Larkin bunted but fouled out. Hatcher then shot a liner into center field, and Oester scampered to third. Piniella replaced right fielder (and lefty hitting) Paul O'Neill, one of the team's best hitters, at the plate with Luis Quinones, who had been productive on the bench throughout the season. Quinones delivered, cracking a single into right field that brought Oester across the plate. Leyland brought in right-hander Stan Belinda to face righties Davis and third baseman Chris Sabo.

To protect the one-run lead, Randy Myers took the mound in the eighth and retired the Pirates, giving up a one-out walk to R. J. Reynolds, who was stranded, but did move along the lineup. In the ninth, Myers would have to face the heart of the order—Bonilla, Bonds, and Martinez. The Reds failed to generate an insurance run in the bottom of the inning, and the one-run lead looked pretty flimsy as big Bobby Bonilla settled into the batter's box. He hit 32 home runs that season and 39 doubles. But Myers fooled him, and Bonilla popped up harmlessly to Larkin.

The Reds gave Bonds little to hit throughout the series, and Myers walked him again, the sixth free pass Bonds was given in six games. With a runner, and a very fast one, on first base, Myers faced Martinez, whose double off the wall in the fifth inning was the Pirates' only hit in the game. Pitcher and batter dueled to a full count. Then Martinez launched a rocket to right field. Playing deep, Glenn Braggs raced all the way to the wall, and, in one of the most memorable moments in a season full of them, he leapt into the air and snagged the ball just as it was clearing the wall. Braggs crashed back-first into the wall, as more than 50,000 enormously relieved Reds fans roared their delight. The catch robbed what surely would have been a two-run homer that would have put the Pirates ahead.

Bonds stayed at first, and, with two outs, catcher Don Slaught swung at strike three to end the game. Following a season riddled with scandal and shame, the Reds had gone wire to wire all the way to the pennant, finishing off the Pirates in dramatic fashion. And Lou's boys weren't done yet.

| Pittsburgh | 0 0 0 | 0 1 0 | 0 0 0 — 1 1 3 |
| Cincinnati | 1 0 0 | 0 0 0 | 1 0 x — 2 9 0 |

Pittsburgh Pirates

	AB	R	H	RBI
King 3b	2	0	0	0
Reynolds ph, rf	1	0	0	0
Bell ss	3	0	0	0
Van Slyke cf	4	0	0	0
Bonilla rf, 3b	3	0	0	0
Bonds lf	1	1	0	0
Martinez 1b	4	0	1	1
Slaught c	4	0	0	0
Lind 2b	3	0	0	0
Power p	1	0	0	0
Smith p	1	0	0	0
Belinda p	0	0	0	0
Redus ph	1	0	0	0
Landrum p	0	0	0	0
Totals	28	1	1	1

	IP	H	R	ER	BB	SO
Power	2.1	3	1	1	1	0
Smith L (0–2)	4.0	6	1	1	1	3
Belinda	0.2	0	0	0	0	0
Landrum	1.0	0	0	0	0	0
Totals	8.0	0	0	0	0	0

Cincinnati Reds

	AB	R	H	RBI
Larkin ss	4	1	2	0
Hatcher cf	4	0	2	0
O'Neill rf	2	0	1	0
Quinones ph	1	0	1	1
Myers p	0	0	0	0
Davis lf	4	0	1	1
Sabo 3b	4	0	0	0
Benzinger 1b	3	0	0	0
Duncan 2b	3	0	1	0
Charlton p	0	0	0	0
Braggs rf	1	0	0	0
Oliver c	4	0	0	0

	AB	R	H	RBI
Jackson p	2	0	0	0
Oester 2b	1	1	1	0
Totals	33	2	9	2

	IP	H	R	ER	BB	SO
Jackson	6.0	1	1	1	4	4
Charlton W (1–1)	1.0	0	0	0	0	0
Myers SV (3)	2.0	0	0	0	2	3
Totals	9.0	0	0	0	2	3

Umpires: Gerry Davis, Harry Wendelstedt, John McSherry, Paul Runge, Jerry Crawford, Dutch Rennert.

Time of game: 2:57.

Attendance: 56,079.

A Grand Feeling

Where was Christy Mathewson?

Reds management asked that question throughout January 1919. The Reds manager, and former Hall of Fame pitcher for the New York Giants, had gone to Europe in August of the previous season to help with the war effort. Expecting him to return to the team for the next season, Reds management attempted, without success, to reach him. They didn't know he'd been injured during a training exercise involving poison gas (which would lead to his early death in 1925). With spring training quickly approaching, they needed a manager and signed Pat Moran. A former major-league catcher, Moran had led an unlikely Philadelphia Phillies team to the pennant in 1915, but had been fired in 1918 when they sank to sixth place.

Switching managers at the last minute wasn't a great way to start the season, especially since Mathewson was popular with the fans and had done a great job of turning around the franchise. Taking the reins during the dismal 1916 season, when the Reds finished next to last, Mathewson helped engineer savvy trades and develop the young pitching staff. Perennial also-rans, the Reds finished fourth under "Matty" in 1917 and moved up to third in 1918. They appeared ready to take the next step.

The team's exciting young core was entering its prime, led by Hall of Famer Edd Roush, one of the league's top hitters and an exceptional center fielder. Heinie Groh at third base, catcher Ivey Wingo, and corner outfielder Greasy Neale formed a solid group behind Roush. Pitchers Hod Eller, Jimmy Ring, and Dutch Ruether provided talented young arms. Moran helped swing deals to bring in some proven veterans—first baseman Jake Daubert, catcher Bill Rariden, and pitchers Slim Sallee and Ray Fisher.

The mixture worked from the start, as the Reds won their first seven games—though after the early weeks of the season, they slumped, giving way to the Giants. But in early June, Moran's boys got hot, and the pennant race narrowed to two teams. Led by cantankerous but innovative manager John McGraw, the Giants had won the pennant in 1917 and boasted excellent pitching and a solid lineup with no weak links. Despite posting a 60–18 record from June 6 to August 26, the Reds couldn't quite break away. In July, the Reds won 22 of 29 games, setting up a showdown with the Giants as August opened.

The Reds took two out of three in a home series that drew large crowds to Redland Field and pushed them into first place. With the Reds leading by 4½ games, the teams met again in mid-August to play three straight doubleheaders in New York. The Giants could retake first place or at least narrow the Reds' lead. On August 13, the Reds swept the first doubleheader, building their lead to 6½ games. The Giants returned the favor the next day with a sweep of their own. On the final day, the Reds won 4–3 and 4–0. In the crucial six-game series, the Giants had gained no ground, sparking hope among the Cincinnati faithful that their team might actually take the National League flag. After losing the next day to Brooklyn, the Reds won 10 straight to pretty much bury their rival.

When the Giants arrived in Cincinnati for a two-game series on September 15, Reds fans eagerly awaited the chance to celebrate. A 3–0 victory in the first game set up a sweet scenario: clinching the National League pennant in Redland Field by whipping the Giants. The Reds were tough at home that season, compiling a 52–19 record.

More than 18,000 fans came to watch on a Tuesday afternoon. Dutch Ruether took the mound for the Reds. Released from the army right before the season opened, young Ruether had missed nearly the entire previous season due to military service and had minimal major-league experience. In 1919, he produced his best season in the majors, posting a 19–6 record with a 1.82 ERA in 242⅔ innings.

The Giants didn't wait long, however, to show him they weren't impressed. Ruether walked the leadoff hitter, left fielder George Burns. Center fielder Benny Kauff followed with a long single to right field, sending Burns to third. On the throw, Kauff scooted into second base. After Ruether whiffed future Hall of Famer Frankie Frisch, Giants second baseman Larry Doyle bounced to Reds shortstop Larry Kopf, who whipped the ball to the plate to cut down the lead runner. Burns beat the tag, giving the Giants an early lead. Giants shortstop Art Fletcher then stepped into the batter's box and smashed a grounder right back to Ruether, who threw home, where Rariden tagged Kauff. Giants right fielder Jigger Statz then laced a single to left field, scoring Doyle.

Down by two runs and facing Giants pitcher Fred Toney, the Reds replied in the bottom of the first. Second baseman Morrie Rath led off with a grounder to shortstop Fletcher, who threw wildly to first base. Daubert then forced Rath at second, before Roush singled to center field. Daubert reached third, and Roush took second on the throw. Kopf singled to center field to bring in both runners, tying the score. After Kopf stole second base, Neale drove him in with a single to center field. With one inning in the books, the Reds led 3–2.

Ruether didn't have his best stuff that day (eventually allowing 12 hits and 4 walks), but the Reds played great defense to keep the Giants from scoring again until the fourth. Burns and Kauff singled and Frisch drove in Burns with a single to center field, tying the score. Kauff tried to score from second on the hit, but Roush gunned him down at the plate with a great throw.

Ruether settled down but gave up at least one hit in every inning except the eighth. As the game progressed with a tie score, fans surely wondered if the hated Giants would escape town without giving up the pennant. Third baseman Hank Schreiber, starting in place of Heinie Groh, opened the bottom of the seventh with a double over the outstretched glove of first baseman George "High Pockets" Kelly. Rariden then popped up a bunt, but Kelly, racing in, muffed it. He quickly threw to third base to get Schreiber—too late. The Reds had the go-ahead run 90 feet from home plate.

McGraw replaced Fred Toney with reliever Art Nehf. Ruether grounded to Doyle at short, who fielded the ball, made sure Schreiber wasn't running, and threw to second base for the force out on Rariden. But his throw pulled Fletcher off the bag, and Schreiber raced home to score. The Reds had retaken the lead.

In the ninth, the laboring Ruether gave up a long single to Doyle, who tried to stretch it, galloping to second where Roush, with another great throw, ended his hopes. Fletcher then grounded to Rath for out no. 2. The crowd was on its collective feet now, waiting for just one more out before celebrating the Reds' first National League pennant. McGraw sent pinch hitter Lew McCarty to the plate, replacing Statz. McCarty hit a bouncer to third, Schreilber handled it and threw to Daubert at first.

End of game. End of the long pennant race. The Reds had won it. Summing up the thoughts of Cincinnati fans, the *Cincinnati Enquirer*'s Jake Ryder wrote, "What a grand feeling it is to be with a regular winner."

The city relished that grand feeling for the rest of the season, holding parades and hosting banquets for the team, while making plans for the upcoming World Series with the Chicago White Sox. There was unanimous praise for Pat Moran, the last-minute fill-in for the great Mathewson. Groh summed up the team's grand feeling: "Moran is the greatest manager in the country, and

I am glad to work under such a fine leader. I think all the boys feel the same way. About the world series, well, we ought to give the Sox a hard tussle."

| New York | 2 0 0 | 1 0 0 | 0 0 0 | — 3 12 2 |
| Cincinnati | 3 0 0 | 0 0 0 | 1 0 x | — 4 8 0 |

New York Giants

	AB	R	H	RBI
Burns lf	4	2	2	0
Kauff cf	4	0	3	0
Frisch 3b	4	0	1	1
Doyle 2b	5	1	1	1
Fletcher ss	5	0	1	0
Statz rf	4	0	3	1
McCarty ph	1	0	0	0
Kelly 1b	3	0	0	0
Gonzalez c	3	0	0	0
Toney p	4	0	1	0
Nehf p	0	0	0	0
Totals	37	3	12	3

	IP	H	R	ER	BB	SO
Toney L (13–6)	6.0	8	4	0	0	0
Nehf	2.0	0	0	0	0	0
Totals	8.0	8	4	0	0	0

Cincinnati Reds

	AB	R	H	RBI
Rath 2b	3	0	1	0
Daubert 1b	3	1	1	0
Roush cf	4	1	1	0
Duncan lf	4	0	0	1
Kopf ss	4	1	2	1
Neale rf	3	0	1	1
Schreiber 3b	3	1	1	0
Rariden c	3	0	1	0
Ruether p	3	0	0	1
Totals	30	4	8	4

	IP	H	R	ER	BB	SO
Ruether W (19–6)	9.0	12	3	3	4	4
Totals	9.0	12	3	3	4	4

Umpires: Ernie Quigley, Hank O'day.
Time of game: 1:53.
Attendance: 18,000.

Mr. Perfect

For a lot of Reds fans, the mid to late 1980s are a vague blob of second-place finishes. One season sort of blends into the next, with the Reds an annual runner-up for the NL West Division title. But in 1988, there was a changing of the guard. Star right fielder Dave Parker had been traded to the Oakland A's for pitchers Jose Rijo and Tim Birtsas in the off-season. Chris Sabo replaced Buddy Bell at third base and won the Rookie of the Year Award. In his second full season, shortstop Barry Larkin played in the All-Star Game—held that year in Cincinnati—as did Sabo.

Reds pitching, seemingly a perennial issue, was pretty good that year too, as lefty Danny Jackson led the league with 23 wins. In the Cy Young voting he was, naturally, runner-up. On May 2, Ron Robinson came within a strike of pitching a perfect game against the Montreal Expos. With two out in the ninth inning, pinch hitter Wallace Johnson hit a single on a 2–2 count. On June 6, Tom Browning came within two outs of a no-hitter against the San Diego Padres, when Tony Gwynn dropped in a single. Gwynn had been the Padres' only base runner when he walked earlier in the game. It seemed that the Reds' pitchers suffered from the same bridesmaid syndrome that inflicted the team—always close but never quite there.

The Reds were scheduled to play the first-place Los Angeles Dodgers on September 16 at Riverfront Stadium, but rain fell steadily that evening. Given that the Reds were 7½ games behind with only 15 games left, the outcome likely wouldn't affect the divisional race; however, the Dodgers were finished in Cincinnati after this series, and, rather than try to reschedule, the teams decided to wait for the rain to stop. After they waited almost two hours, Browning, the Reds starter, assumed the game would be cancelled and started to peel off his

uniform. Then a member of the grounds crew entered the clubhouse announcing that the game would start at 10 o'clock. Browning slid back into his uniform
and headed for the bullpen.

As he walked onto the field, he noticed the distinct lack of sound. The stadium was eerily quiet. Though official paid attendance that night was 16,591,
probably only a few thousand people waited through the long rain delay. (Surely
10 times that many have since claimed that they attended what turned out to
be a historic game.)

That night Browning faced Tim Belcher, who would pitch for the Reds later
in his career. Five days earlier, the pair had matched up in Los Angeles, and
Belcher homered off Browning, who had thrown the gopher ball on an 0–2
count. Manager Pete Rose was still upset with him about the gaff.

When the game finally got underway on the wet field, both pitchers appeared to have weathered the wait far better than the hitters, as neither team
managed to get a hit through the first five innings. Only Reds center fielder
Eric Davis, who walked in the second inning, had reached first base. For the
hardy fans who stayed, at least the game was moving right along.

With two out in the bottom of the sixth, Larkin broke up the double no-hitter
with a double down the right field line. Sabo followed him with a ground ball
to third baseman Jeff Hamilton. The ball took a high hop off the edge of the
Astroturf, forcing Hamilton to hurry his throw, which skittered into the dirt in
front of first base. When Mickey Hatcher tried to scoop it, the ball flipped into
the air and bounced away from him, allowing Larkin to score from second base.

As he took the mound in the seventh inning, Browning said to himself,
"Well, there's your lead." He calculated that he needed to get each hitter out one
more time. After he got the first two, Browning faced left fielder Kirk Gibson,
a hypercompetitive player who would win the league's Most Valuable Player
Award that year. When he looked at a called strike three, Gibson blew up in a
rage, screaming at home plate umpire Jim Quick, who was quick in ejecting
him from the game.

Browning was cruising right along. He produced strong numbers in 1988,
with an 18–5 record and 3.41 ERA in 250⅔ innings. Although he lacked
overpowering stuff, he worked fast, delivering the ball in a compact motion
that kept batters off balance. And his pitching arsenal included a screwball
with erratic movement that was tough to hit.

After the Dodgers went down in order in the eighth, Browning sat in the
dugout, trying not to feel the pressure of knowing that if he could retire the
next three batters, he would achieve a very rare feat. Catcher Jeff Reed sat
beside him, doing his best to calm and encourage him. Rose knew Browning

was a quick worker and told him not to rush his pitches in the final inning. Browning nodded and headed to the on deck circle. When second baseman Ron Oester hit a two-out single into center field, Browning walked to the plate. He received as much of an ovation as a few thousand soaking-wet fans could muster, but struck out to end the inning.

Going into the ninth, he wanted to preserve the perfect game, of course, but he also just wanted to win. One run would tie the score. To start the inning, he faced catcher Rick Dempsey, who flied out to Paul O'Neill in right field. Second baseman Steve Sax came to the plate next and grounded harmlessly to Larkin. Browning took a deep breath—one more to go. Would the bridesmaid curse strike the Reds again? Tracy Woodson stepped into the batter's box, pinch-hitting for Belcher.

Rushing his pace, Browning quickly threw two pitches outside the strike zone. (No Dodger batter had gone to three balls in a count the entire game.) Woodson took the next pitch for a strike and fouled off the one after, evening the count. Like his teammate Robinson back in May, Browning was one strike from a perfect game.

He threw high on the next one, but Woodson chased it—and missed. Tom Browning had pitched the first perfect game in Reds history, the twelfth in major-league history, and still the only one ever against a team that wound up winning the World Series. Of the 100 pitches he threw, 72 had been strikes.

Ecstatic Reds players rushed the mound, hugging their pitcher and finally burying him in a pile. He emerged with a cut lip but didn't care. In his book *Tales from the Reds Dugout,* Browning recalls that the moments after getting the final out "felt like an out-of-body experience." More than 20 years later, he is still known by Reds fans as "Mr. Perfect."

Los Angeles 0 0 0   0 0 0   0 0 0 — 0 0 1
Cincinnati   0 0 0   0 0 1   0 0 x — 1 3 0

Los Angeles Dodgers

	AB	R	H	RBI
Griffin ss	3	0	0	0
Hatcher 1b	3	0	0	0
Gibson lf	3	0	0	0
Gonzalez lf	0	0	0	0
Marshall rf	3	0	0	0
Shelby cf	3	0	0	0
Hamilton 3b	3	0	0	0
Dempsey c	3	0	0	0
Sax 2b	3	0	0	0
Belcher p	2	0	0	0
Woodson ph	1	0	0	0
Totals	27	0	0	0

	IP	H	R	ER	BB	SO
Belcher L (10–5)	8.0	3	1	0	1	7
Totals	8.0	3	1	0	1	7

Cincinnati Reds

	AB	R	H	RBI
Larkin ss	3	1	1	0
Sabo 3b	3	0	1	0
Daniels lf	3	0	0	0
Davis cf	2	0	0	0
O'Neill rf	3	0	0	0
Esasky 1b	3	0	0	0
Reed c	3	0	0	0
Oester 2b	3	0	1	0
Browning p	3	0	0	0
Totals	26	1	3	0

	IP	H	R	ER	BB	SO
Browning W (16–5)	9.0	0	0	0	0	7
Totals	9.0	0	0	0	0	7

Umpires: HP—Jim Quick, 1B—Mark Hirschbeck, 2B—John Kibler, 3B—
Eric Gregg.

Time of game: 1:51.

Attendance: 16,591.

#10

REDS 6, BROOKLYN DODGERS 0
JUNE 15, 1938

Vandy's Dandies

Turning points are turning points only in retrospect; however, even at the time, Reds fans could feel the winds of change blowing in 1938.

The team had a new manager with a proven record of success—Bill McKechnie. After 10 years of losing, the Reds were winning—and would end the season 14 games over .500. And by moving home plate 20 feet closer to the outfield fences at Crosley Field, the Reds hit more than 100 home runs for the first time in team history, led by right fielder Ival Goodman, who hit 30, the most ever by a Reds player at the time.

There was a lot for McKechnie to like about his team, including that kid Vander Meer, a lefty who could really bring the gas. He just needed to harness his control. On days when he could locate the fastball, the 23-year-old Vander Meer was almost unhittable. One of those days occurred on Saturday, June 11, when the Reds played the Boston Bees (later called the Braves) at Crosley Field. Through nine innings, Vander Meer *was* unhittable. He walked four, struck out three, and surrendered not a single hit. It was the first no-hitter thrown by a Reds pitcher since Hod Eller's in 1919.

He made his next start in Brooklyn, facing the Dodgers in the first night game at Ebbets Field—and the first night game in major-league history outside of Cincinnati. The Reds had introduced night baseball to the majors in 1935 at the urging of their general manager, Larry MacPhail, who had become the general manager for the Dodgers. Coincidentally, MacPhail also had signed Vander Meer while still with the Reds. The special event drew a crowd of 38,748, which included Vander Meer's parents and around 500 people from his hometown of Midland Park, New Jersey.

Most people at the ballpark had never seen a night game before, as the concept was slow to catch on. Three Reds players—Lew Riggs, Billy Myers, and Ival Goodman—had played in the first one back in 1935, as did Dodgers first baseman Dolph Camilli, who had been with the Phillies for the inaugural event in Cincinnati.

After a good bit of fuss, fireworks, and festivities, the game finally got underway at 9:20. Reds second baseman Lonnie Frey led off with a base hit, but Dodgers pitcher Max Butcher escaped unscathed. Vander Meer then took the mound and retired three Dodgers. With two out in the second inning, he allowed his first base runner, walking Camilli, and in the third walked right fielder Kiki Cuyler.

By that point his teammates had booted Butcher from the game with a four-run outburst. Left fielder Wally Berger, acquired in a trade just 10 days earlier, had reached base with an infield single and took second on third baseman Cookie Lavagetto's wild throw to first. Goodman followed with a walk, and first baseman Frank McCormick cleared the bases with a three-run homer. After catcher Ernie Lombardi walked, singles by center fielder Harry Craft and third baseman Riggs brought him in.

Vander Meer breezed through the fourth and fifth innings. He retired every batter between the walk to Cuyler and then another walk to Cuyler again in the sixth. The Reds added a run in the seventh inning when Ival Goodman walked, stole second base, and scored on a single by Craft. With a five-run lead, Vander Meer could have relaxed a bit. But he didn't. Instead, he started speeding up his pace and losing his command. In the bottom of the seventh, he walked Lavagetto and then Camilli before getting two outs to end the inning.

Myers led off the eighth with a grounder to third base, and once again Lavagetto threw wildly to first. Vander Meer grounded into a fielder's choice that forced Myers at second base. Frey struck out, leaving Vander Meer still at first base before Berger tripled, bringing the tired pitcher around the bases and across the plate. Despite all the running, Vander Meer faced only three batters in the next inning, striking out two of them. After the Reds went down in order in the top of the ninth, the stage was set for what seemed like an impossible feat—back-to-back no-hitters.

With the game pretty much out of reach, Dodgers fans started cheering for Vander Meer. Though they wouldn't see a Brooklyn victory, they just might see history. But first Vander Meer had to get through the heart of the Brooklyn order one more time. Left fielder Buddy Hassett led off with a weak roller toward first that Vander Meer fielded. Rather than risk a bad throw, he tagged the base himself. He proceeded to walk catcher Babe Phelps and then walked Lavagetto. For the first time in the game, the Dodgers had put a runner past first base. Feeling the pressure, Vander Meer faced Camilli—and walked him.

McKechnie hustled to the mound to settle down his young pitcher. The infielders joined them, offering encouragement. Vander Meer later said he was pressing too hard to throw strikes. McKechnie said, "Take your time, Johnny. Quit pitching so fast and pitch the way you know how to pitch." After a few deep breaths, Vander Meer was ready to face center fielder Ernie Koy, who hit a grounder to third base. Riggs fielded the ball and threw home to force out the lead runner. Two gone.

The crowd cheered even louder. Into the batter's box stepped shortstop Leo Durocher, the type of pesky hitter that has ruined many a no-hitter with a slap through the infield. But this time, Durocher hit a lazy fly to center field, where Craft made the catch for the final out.

Vander Meer had achieved what the *Cincinnati Post* called the "top feat in 100 years of ball." Then, as the *Cincinnati Enquirer* reported, "frenzied fans streamed through the exits and vaulted over the railings in tribute to baseball's newest No. 1 hero." Vander Meer rushed to the dugout to avoid the mob, but he remained the talk of the baseball world for the rest of the season. He started for the National League in the All-Star Game played at Crosley Field, pitching three scoreless innings.

After his achievement, however, he posted only an 8–8 record, and the following season he continued to struggle with control. He spent much of the 1940 world championship season in the minor leagues. But the next year things seemed to come together for Vander Meer, who went on to lead the National League in strikeouts three consecutive seasons, posting sub-3.0 ERAs in all of them. Following two years in the military, he pitched for the Reds until 1949 and later managed in their farm system. The control issues never fully disappeared, as he led the league in walks in 1943 and 1948, but he became a dependable starter and what we now call the "face of the franchise." In 1969, the team named its Pitcher of the Year award after him.

When asked about his record of back-to-back no-hitters in later years, Vander Meer often said, "Somebody might tie it, but I don't think anybody will break it."

| Cincinnati | 0 0 4 | 0 0 1 | 1 0 0 — 6 11 0 |
| Brooklyn | 0 0 0 | 0 0 0 | 0 0 0 — 0 0 2 |

Cincinnati Reds

	AB	R	H	RBI
Frey 2b	5	0	1	0
Berger lf	5	1	3	1
Goodman rf	3	2	1	0
McCormick 1b	5	1	1	3
Lombardi c	3	1	0	0
Craft cf	5	0	3	1
Riggs 3b	4	0	1	1
Myers ss	4	0	0	0
Vander Meer p	4	1	1	0
Totals	38	6	11	6

	IP	H	R	ER	BB	SO
Vander Meer W (7–2)	9.0	0	0	0	8	7
Totals	9.0	0	0	0	8	7

Brooklyn Dodgers

	AB	R	H	RBI
Cuyler rf	2	0	0	0
Coscarart 2b	2	0	0	0
Brack ph	1	0	0	0
Hudson 2b	1	0	0	0
Hassett lf	4	0	0	0
Phelps c	3	0	0	0
Rosen pr	0	0	0	0
Lavagetto 3b	2	0	0	0
Camilli 1b	1	0	0	0
Koy cf	4	0	0	0
Durocher ss	4	0	0	0
Butcher p	0	0	0	0
Pressnell p	2	0	0	0
Hamlin p	0	0	0	0
English ph	1	0	0	0
Tamulis p	0	0	0	0
Totals	27	0	0	0

	IP	H	R	ER	BB	SO
Butcher L (4–3)	2.2	5	4	4	3	1
Pressnell	3.2	4	1	1	0	3
Hamlin	1.2	2	1	0	1	3
Tamulis	1.0	0	0	0	0	1
Totals	9.0	11	6	5	4	8

Umpires: Bill Stewart, Dolly Stark, George Barr.
Time of game: 2:22.
Attendance: 38,748.

REDS 2, SAN DIEGO PADRES 0
SEPTEMBER 11, 1985

4,192

Dismantling the Big Red Machine, the most dominant major-league team in the 1970s, was an odious task that sank the franchise to the depths of the league by 1982.

As if to make amends, on August 15, 1984, while mired in a third consecutive terrible season, the team stunned the baseball world by trading for 43-year-old Pete Rose, bringing him back to his hometown as player-manager. No longer the superstar leadoff man who sparked the Machine, Rose was hitting .259 for the Montreal Expos at the time, a slow-footed first baseman with little power. The move was seen by many experts as mostly a way to rekindle the interest of a disillusioned Cincinnati fan base rather than to improve the team.

Rose tried to prove them wrong, hitting .365/.430/.458 in 107 plate appearance for the rest of the season. He later said that his goal was to stay on the field so he could break Ty Cobb's all-time hit record. He wasn't ready to settle for just the manager's job, which seemed to be management's preference. General Manager Bob Howsam always referred to him as "manager-player," and told the media that Rose's top priority was running the team, not breaking records.

The next season Rose continued to play, and the Reds surprised everyone by winning more games than they lost. Right fielder Dave Parker belted 34 home runs and drove in 125 runs, hitting .312/.365/.551. Pitcher Tom Browning won 20 games, becoming the first rookie to reach that mark since New York Yankee Bob Grimm in 1954. With Rose at the helm, baseball in Cincinnati was exciting again. Compiling an 89–72 record, the Reds finished second in the West Division. But his chase to surpass Cobb's 4,191 hits overshadowed the team's startling success and turned the season into a countdown to the big event.

At the start of the season, Rose needed only 95 hits to break the record that had stood since 1928 and had been thought to be unreachable. In spring training, a reporter asked him how many at bats it would take to reach his goal. Rose replied, "Ninety-five." When the reporter scoffed, saying surely he wouldn't get a hit every time, Rose said "No, but that's the attitude I have to have." (Despite much searching, we couldn't locate the published source of this story.) In many interviews through the years, Rose has said that even when he got three hits in a game, he focused on getting the fourth his next time at the plate. He attributed his many hitting achievements to this competitive ferocity, and he wasn't going to start taking a new approach with the record clearly in sight.

On September 6, while playing the Cubs in Chicago, Rose got two hits, leaving him just two shy of tying the record. With a left-hander pitching the next game, he didn't play. (Though a lifelong switch-hitter, Rose platooned that year with Tony Perez, facing only right-handers.) When righty Steve Patterson started the following game, Rose put himself in the lineup. He singled in the first inning and again in the fifth, tying Ty's 4,191. Of course, Reds fans wanted him to break the record, but they preferred he do it in Cincinnati, where the Reds would return the following day to start a 10-game home stand. As if obliging them, he failed to get a hit in his next two plate appearances.

After sitting out the first game of the home series with the San Diego Padres due to a left-handed starter, Rose returned to the lineup for the game on Tuesday, September 10, which drew 51,045 fans, most with cameras at the ready to capture the long-awaited moment. Rose disappointed them, getting no hits in four tries. The next night, facing right-hander Eric Show, he penciled in his own name in the second spot, his usual place in the batting order.

While it might seem that he was putting his personal goal above the needs of the team by making 501 plate appearances while playing first base, a power position to which he brought no power, Rose did produce a .395 OBP that season. Most teams would be happy with that number from the second spot in the batting order. And the game on September 11 drew another huge crowd, as 47,237 piled into Riverfront Stadium. Team owners probably weren't complaining.

All of those fans stood when Rose stepped to the plate in the bottom of the first inning. With the count two balls and one strike, Rose lined the next pitch to left field. In what is now a legendary radio call, broadcaster Joe Nuxhall shouted, "There it is!" as the ball bounced in front of Padres left fielder Carmelo Martinez. Rose raced around first base and looked ready to challenge the defender by breaking for second—as he had done literally thousands of times in his long career. He then trotted back to first base, where he slapped hands with coach

Tommy Helms. Reds players poured from the dugout to congratulate him and hoisted him up on their shoulders.

Cheering from the fans continued unabated for minutes, as Rose raised his helmet to the crowd while standing on first. Finally he took a deep breath and, as he has said many times, looked into the sky and saw his deceased father and Cobb himself looking down at him. Overcome with emotion, he put his head on Helms's shoulder and cried. His sons Ty and Pete Jr. were watching from the dugout. The Reds players urged young Pete to go to his dad. The two embraced, in what has become one of the most iconic moments in team history.

Despite the enormity of that moment, when the game continued, Rose remained in the lineup. In the third inning he walked and went to third on a single by Parker. He scored when left fielder Nick Esasky forced Parker at second base. Browning pitched well, holding the 1–0 lead as the Reds came to bat in the bottom of the seventh. With one out, Rose tripled, sending the crowd into yet another frenzy. Show walked Parker intentionally, and Esasky punched a long fly to center field, scoring Rose. The crowd roared as if watching a World Series game.

In the top of the ninth, Browning retired the first batter but surrendered a single to second baseman Jerry Royster. Still manning first base, Rose brought in lefty reliever John Franco to face right fielder Tony Gwynn, who flied out to center field. Closer Ted Power then took the mound to pitch to first baseman Steve Garvey. As if on cue, Garvey shot a ground ball to first base. Rose dove for the ball and from the turf flipped it to Power covering first for the final out. Once more, the crowd stood and cheered.

After the game, the team honored Rose in an on-field ceremony. Owner Marge Schott awarded him with a red Corvette bearing a special license plate number: PR4192. Rose had reached his record, and he had rekindled interest in the Reds. The dark days of his gambling scandal lay ahead, but on that night Cincinnati once again felt like capital of the baseball world.

| San Diego | 0 0 0 | 0 0 0 | 0 0 0 — 0 5 1 |
| Cincinnati | 0 0 1 | 0 0 0 | 1 0 x — 2 8 0 |

San Diego Padres

	AB	R	H	RBI
Templeton ss	4	0	0	0
Royster 2b	4	0	1	0
Gwynn rf	4	0	1	0
Garvey 1b	4	0	0	0
Martinez lf	3	0	0	0
McReynolds cf	3	0	1	0
Bochy c	3	0	1	0
Bevacqua 3b	3	0	1	0
Show p	2	0	0	0
Davis ph	1	0	0	0
Jackson p	0	0	0	0
Walter p	0	0	0	0
Totals	31	0	5	0

	IP	H	R	ER	BB	SO
Show L (9–10)	7.0	7	2	2	5	1
Jackson	0.1	1	0	0	1	0
Walter	0.2	0	0	0	0	2
Totals	8.0	8	2	2	6	3

Cincinnati Reds

	AB	R	H	RBI
Milner cf	5	0	0	0
Rose 1b	3	2	2	0
Parker rf	1	0	1	0
Esasky lf	3	0	0	2
Venable lf	0	0	0	0
Bell 3b	4	0	1	0
Concepcion ss	4	0	1	0
Diaz c	3	0	1	0
Redus pr	0	0	0	0
Van Gorder c	0	0	0	0
Oester 2b	3	0	1	0
Browning p	4	0	1	0
Franco p	0	0	0	0
Power p	0	0	0	0
Totals	30	2	8	2

	IP	H	R	ER	BB	SO
Browning W (16–9)	8.1	5	0	0	0	6
Franco	0.1	0	0	0	0	0
Power SV (20)	0.1	0	0	0	0	0
Totals	9.0	5	0	0	0	6

Time of game: 2:17.
Attendance: 47,237.

Big Red Sweeper

Through the first 100 games of the 1970 season, the Big Red Machine rolled right over the rest of the National League, winning 70 games. No team had an answer for Cincinnati's blend of power offense and power pitching. That is, until the Machine stalled somewhat, winning only 32 of the final 62 games.

What happened? Many fans and sportswriters blamed the midseason move from cozy Crosley Field to expansive Riverfront Stadium. The Reds hit 57 home runs in 36 games at Crosley and only 43 in 45 games at Riverfront.

While it's true that the farther fences sapped some of the team's power, the main reason the Reds suddenly started losing was injuries to the starting rotation. Longtime ace Jim Maloney ruptured his Achilles tendon in April and never won another major-league game. Rookie phenom Wayne Simpson, who compiled a 14–3 record and was the talk of the league, tore his rotator cuff on July 31 and missed the remainder of the year. For the rest of his career he won 22 games and lost 28, with a 4.87 ERA. Jim Merritt won his 20th game on August 26. Then he caught the injury bug and didn't win another game that season. After 1970, he sported a 6–26 record. Jim McGlothlin took 11 wins into the All-Star break, but after being drilled twice by line drives he won only two games the remainder of the year. Among their best pitchers, only Gary Nolan remained healthy and productive.

The great first half of the season allowed the Reds to take the NL West Division crown with a 102–60 record, but clearly they were limping into the postseason, where they met the Pittsburgh Pirates, champions of the NL East, in a best-of-five series to determine the pennant winner. Despite fielding competitive teams throughout the 1960s, the Reds hadn't won a pennant since

1961. Through the first months of 1970, they looked like a shoo-in to cop the flag. By October, many experts were picking the Pirates.

In Game One of the series, played in Pittsburgh, Nolan pitched nine shutout innings. So did Pirates starter Dock Ellis. But the Reds scored three runs in the 10th inning to win it. Reds center fielder Bobby Tolan scored all three Reds runs in Game Two to seal a 3–1 victory. The series moved to Cincinnati, with the Reds needing only one more win.

More than 40,000 fans took their seats on a Monday afternoon, hoping to witness a pennant-winning celebration at the end of the Game Three. With a depleted starting staff, Reds manager Sparky Anderson put Tony Cloninger on the mound, facing Bob Moose. After the Pirates scored a run in the first inning on two singles and two walks, the Big Red Machine answered right away with back-to-back home runs from third baseman Tony Perez and catcher (and National League Most Valuable Player) Johnny Bench, giving the Reds a 2–1 lead.

Cloninger struggled but kept the Pirates from scoring until the fifth inning, when left fielder Willie Stargell drove in center fielder Matty Aou. Satisfied that Cloninger had provided five innings, Anderson replaced him with 20-year-old Milt Wilcox, who had pitched only 22⅓ innings during the year. Wilcox, however, rose to the challenge. After surrendering a double and a walk to the first two batters he faced, he retired nine of the next 10, striking out five, and didn't allow a ball to leave the infield. With two out in the bottom of the eighth inning and no one on base, Anderson sent Ty Cline to the plate to hit for Wilcox, whose performance had electrified the crowd. The fans loudly booed the decision to take him out. With Wilcox pitching so well, why replace him in this situation?

Cline walked, bringing up the top of the order. Right fielder Pete Rose shot a liner into left field, moving Cline to second base. Pirates manager Danny Murtaugh brought in lefty reliever Joe Gibbon to replace the tiring Moose. The move might seem like an obvious choice with left-handed Tolan at the plate, but the Reds center fielder had hit .335 against left-handers that year. With the count no balls and two strikes, Tolan drove a ground ball into left field, and Cline took off for home. Stargell scooped it up and fired an accurate throw to the plate. Cline slid as catcher Manny Sanguillen landed on top of him. Umpire Paul Pryor yelled, "Safe!" The Reds had taken a 3–2 lead. Cline later told the press, "It was close. Very close. I got the back outside corner of the plate. Then he fell on top of me."

On the throw to the plate, Rose went to third. Murtaugh went to his top reliever, Dave Giusti, to face the dangerous Perez, who struck out. For the ninth, Anderson brought in his own bullpen ace, Wayne Granger, whose side-arm delivery had earned 35 saves that season by coaxing many a harmless grounder from National League hitters. And that's just what happened to the first two Pirate batters—pinch hitter Bob Robertson and Alou. But right fielder Roberto Clemente singled to right field to keep Pirates hopes alive. To dash those hopes, Anderson brought in 19-year-old fireballer Don Gullett. Speedy Johnny Jeter replaced Clemente on first base. When Stargell hit a grounder through the right side of the infield, Jeter dashed all the way to third.

With runners now on the corners, Gullett faced first baseman Al Oliver, a tough hitter. With composure far beyond his years, Gullett went to work. He threw an inside fastball that Oliver grounded to second baseman Tommy Helms, who ran toward first before tossing the ball to Lee May for the final out. Riverfront Stadium erupted. Fans who had paid for a game-ending mob scene on the field definitely got their money's worth as Reds players swarmed in celebration. They had weathered significant injuries to their staff and struggled to adapt to a new field, but in the end they'd reached their goal. They were champions of the National League. The Big Red Machine had rolled to its first pennant.

While the depleted pitching staff undermined the Machine's efforts to beat the Baltimore Orioles in the World Series, Cincinnati fans savored their status as league champions and looked forward to winning many more.

Pittsburgh	1	0	0	0	1	0	0	0	0	—	2	10 0
Cincinnati	2	0	0	0	0	0	0	1	x	—	3	5 0

Pittsburgh Pirates

	AB	R	H	RBI
Patek ss	3	0	0	0
Robertson ph	1	0	0	0
Alou cf	5	1	1	0
Clemente rf	5	1	2	0
Jeter pr	0	0	0	0
Stargell lf	4	0	3	1
Oliver 1b	5	0	2	1
Sanguillen c	4	0	0	0
Hebner 3b	2	0	2	0
Mazeroski 2b	2	0	0	0
Moose p	4	0	0	0
Gibbon p	0	0	0	0
Giusti p	0	0	0	0
Totals	35	2	10	2

	IP	H	R	ER	BB	SO
Moose L (0–1)	7.2	4	3	3	2	4
Gibbon	0.0	1	0	0	0	0
Giusti	0.1	0	0	0	0	1
Totals	8.0	5	3	3	2	5

Cincinnati Reds

	AB	R	H	RBI
Rose rf	4	0	1	0
Tolan cf	3	0	1	1
Perez 3b	4	1	1	1
Granger p	0	0	0	0
Gullett p	0	0	0	0
Bench c	3	1	2	1
May 1b	3	0	0	0
Carbo lf	3	0	0	0
Helms 2b	3	0	0	0
Woodward ss, 3b	3	0	0	0
Cloninger p	1	0	0	0
Bravo ph	1	0	0	0
Wilcox p	0	0	0	0
Cline ph	0	1	0	0
Concepcion ss	0	0	0	0
Totals	28	3	5	3

	IP	H	R	ER	BB	SO
Cloninger	5.0	7	2	2	4	1
Wilcox W (1–0)	3.0	1	0	0	2	5
Granger	0.2	1	0	0	0	0
Gullett SV (1)	0.1	1	0	0	0	0
Totals	9.0	10	2	2	6	6

Umpires: Paul Pryor, Doug Harvey, Bob Engel, Harry Wendelstedt, Stan
    Landes, Nick Colosi.
Time of game: 2:38.
Attendance: 40,538.

#7

RED STOCKINGS 45, GREAT WESTERNS 9
MAY 4, 1869

In the Very Beginning

Truth be told, the first official game of the first all-professional baseball team, the 1869 Cincinnati Red Stockings, wasn't all that much of a contest. The result was never in doubt, but as the beginning of professional sports in America, the game is historically significant for the legacy that it launched.

Baseball, then often called "townball," became popular in the New York City area in the years leading up to the Civil War. Brothers Harry and George Wright grew up playing cricket, the national sport of England, which used a bat and a ball, but, like many young men, they were smitten by this variation that included bases and different rules.

In 1865, right after the war, Harry moved to Cincinnati to run the Union Cricket Club and to help start the Cincinnati Base Ball Club. "Base ball" fever raged throughout the country by the late 1860s, though only on an amateur level. Leagues formed in major cities, especially in the East, and most small towns had at least one team. Crowds began showing up for the games, and newspapers began reporting the results. When enterprising organizers began charging money to watch, top players began selling their services, usually on a game-by-game basis. The National Association of Base Ball Players was formed as a loose governing body for the sport.

In 1868, businessmen Aaron Champion and John Joyce, members of the Cincinnati Base Ball Club, came up with the idea of forming an all-professional team that would travel to play the best eastern teams, many of which were paying some of their players. The Wright brothers were told to build the team, offering salaries to the best players they could find, to begin play in 1869. While the team might generate money, it mostly was seen as a potential marketing tool to promote Cincinnati and, with luck, attract investment in the city's businesses from wealthy easterners. A monthlong trip was planned for June, during which the experimental full-time team would play the best teams in cities such as Cleveland, Buffalo, Boston, New York, Philadelphia, Washington, DC, and Baltimore.

The Wrights were considered two of the most skilled "ballists" in the country, though Harry, at 34, was a bit past his prime. George, 12 years younger, was the star, batting first in the lineup and playing shortstop. The brothers had difficulty convincing eastern star players to come west and ended up settling for the top players in the area, many of whom had come from eastern cities to play for Harry the year before. Harry had convinced Asa Brainard, known for throwing the craftiest pitches, to move from Brooklyn to Cincinnati, and he was quickly given a contract to man the mound for the first pro team.

Only one Cincinnati native earned a contract—big first baseman Charlie Gould, who had played for the Wrights in 1868. Other than Gould, the players were generally small and quick. The game required speed, not power, as players slapped at underhanded pitches and focused on putting the ball in play. Fielders didn't wear gloves, leading to frequent errors. Players zipped around the bases, trying to create confusion among defenders, and runs were plentiful. Scores often climbed into the 40s and 50s.

Financing this experiment proved more challenging than anticipated. The backers not only faced the costs of salaries and travel, they had to pay for a place where the team could play. Baseball and cricket teams often used an area on the west side of town, roughly where the parking lot of Union Terminal is located today. The investors funded construction of a main grandstand, called the Grand Duchess, as well as two shelter areas running along the baselines. To help pay expenses, and to prepare the Red Stockings for their historic season, exhibition games were scheduled in late April against all-star amateur teams, called "picked nines." Any doubts about Harry's bunch were put to rest, as the Red Stockings won 25–14 and 50–7. They were ready to begin their season, the first official game, scheduled for May 4.

With an eye toward building interest before the June trip to the East, John Joyce scheduled games against the best amateur clubs in the southern Ohio-Indiana area—teams he felt confident the Red Stockings would whip. On Tuesday, May 4, the Red Stockings, wearing flashy white uniforms and flashier red socks, took the field at Union Grounds against the Great Westerns of Cincinnati. As author Stephen D. Guschov reports in his book *The Red Stockings of Cincinnati,* "Harry Wright's boys rode out to Union Grounds in a caravan of fancy, ribbon-adorned carriages, behind which followed hundreds of merry cranks, eager to see whether their boys could measure up to the first real competition of the season."

In brief: they did.

George Wright, in the first at bat in the first official game, cracked a home run, meaning he made a complete circuit of the bases. In that era, the ball didn't clear the outfield fences. Some fields didn't even have fences. The Red Stockings hit well in the opening inning, moving players across the plate; after three innings, they led the Great Westerns 7–4. Harry Wright pitched the opener. Perhaps he felt Asa Brainard's tricky arsenal of twists and curves wasn't needed against such modest competition. Brainard manned center field instead. In the fourth inning, the Red Stockings' bats came alive, scoring 15 runs, in part due to poor fielding by their opponent.

Right fielder Cal McVey, the youngest member of the team at 18, matched Wright with a home run of his own, as did Andy Leonard. When the dust finally settled at the Union Grounds, the Red Stockings won the game 45–9. After four more games in May, all victories, the team headed East to face much tougher competition.

To the delight of Cincinnatians and surprise of easterners, Harry's boys won every game, notching a 20–0 road trip. Newspapers throughout the country reported on this new type of team—salaried players whose jobs were to play baseball. When the team returned on July 1, a parade was held in their honor. As the season progressed, the Red Stockings proved to be invincible, even against the best eastern teams, who traveled to Cincinnati later in the summer, eager for a rematch. On November 6, the powerful New York Mutuals, previously considered the best team in the country, met the Red Stockings in the final game of the season. Behind George Wright's heroics, the Red Stockings won 17–8 to post a record of 57–0, the only undefeated season in the history of professional baseball. They were hailed as baseball's national champions.

The same players returned for the 1870 season, and proved to be just as difficult to defeat, though by then, other cities fielded teams made up mostly of salaried players. Cincinnati investors paid for player raises as well as for expansion of Union Grounds, where an upper deck was added.

On June 13, the Red Stockings won their 81st game in a row against the best teams in the country. Their success was attributed mostly to George Wright's exceptional abilities and Harry's strategic acumen. The team completed the season with a 67–6–1 record.

The expense of running the team, however, and the prospect of joining the National Association, the first professional baseball league, in 1871, was more than club president A. P. Bonte wanted to consider. Teams in big eastern cities began signing the best players to contracts larger than the Cincinnati club could afford. Things got ugly in salary disputes between Bonte and the

Wrights, who ended up taking their services, a few key players, and even their bright red stockings, to Boston. The birthplace of professional baseball was left without a team, though the claim of being the first city to field a professional team lives on even today.

[No box score was published.]

The Shot Heard 'round Reds Country

The Big Red Machine, reigning National League champions, collapsed in 1971. Center fielder Bobby Tolan ruptured his Achilles tendon and missed the entire season. The power-hitting lineup that had flourished in the cozy confines of Crosley Field struggled in the first full year playing in much larger Riverfront Stadium, winning just 79 games. The more distant fences and the Astroturf playing surface rewarded speed rather than power.

General Manager Bob Howsam addressed this need in the off-season. In a blockbuster deal, one of the most famous trades in team history, Howsam sent first baseman Lee May, second baseman Tommy Helms, and utility player Jimmy Stewart to the Houston Astros for second baseman Joe Morgan, third baseman Denis Menke, pitcher Jack Billingham, center fielder Cesar Geronimo, and reserve outfielder Ed Armbrister.

Reds fans now look back on the trade as the catalyst for the continued success of the Big Red Machine, but at the time many fans hated the deal. May and Helms were fan favorites who'd played key roles in winning the pennant in 1970. May's power—he hit 39 home runs in 1971 to lead the team—was a key driver of the Machine. Morgan was well regarded, a two-time all-star, but not seen as among the league's elite, and the others seemed like backups and roster-filler. Fans wondered what the front office was thinking. Was the Big Red Machine finished just as it was getting started?

Adding fuel to the ire of the fans, the 1972 season was delayed by a players' strike. When play began, the Reds got off to a terrible start, winning only eight of the first 21 games, seeming to prove the trade doubters right. But the team recovered, easily outdistancing the Astros to win the West Division title and setting up a showdown with the defending world champion Pittsburgh Pirates in the National League Championship Series.

The evenly matched teams split the first four games of the series, the Reds winning games Two and Four. The deciding Game Five was played on a Wednesday afternoon at Riverfront Stadium. Both teams had their aces on the mound—19-game-winner Steve Blass for the Pirates and 21-year-old phenom Don Gullett for the Reds. Blass had beaten the Reds in the opening game of the series, as Gullett surrendered five runs in six innings.

Hurt early in the season but dominant in the final months, Gullett posted a 9–10 record on the year with a 3.94 ERA. After his poor performance in the first game of the series, he was eager for redemption. Unfortunately, his struggles continued, as he gave up two runs in the second inning. The Reds scored in the third inning when Pete Rose doubled in shortstop Darrel Chaney. After the first two Pirates batters in the top of the fourth singled, Reds manager Sparky Anderson brought in reliever Pedro Borbon, who allowed one of the runs to score before setting down the Pirates.

Cesar Geronimo homered to lead off the bottom of the fifth inning, tightening the score to 3–2. The Reds had relied on their strong bullpen throughout the season, and once again the relievers came through. Tom Hall replaced Borbon, pitching three scoreless innings and allowing only one hit before giving way to Clay Carroll, who set down the Pirates in order in the ninth.

Blass, meanwhile, held the Reds scoreless until he was replaced in the eighth inning. An All-Star in 1972, Blass had won two games in the previous World Series, including the Game Seven. Just 30 years old, he inexplicably began struggling to throw strikes, ending his career in 1974. From then on, players who, for psychological reasons, lose their ability to accurately throw a baseball, are said to suffer from Steve Blass Disease.

Dave Guisti, one of the game's best relievers, took the mound to preserve the Pirates' one-run lead in the bottom of the ninth. Leading off for the Reds: catcher Johnny Bench, that year's National League Most Valuable Player. What followed was one of the greatest moments in Reds history. Reds announcer Al Michaels told listeners, "Hit in the air, to deep right field, back goes Clemente at the fence—she's gone! Johnny Bench, who hits almost every home run to left field has hit one to right and the game is tied."

First baseman Tony Perez followed Bench with a single to center field, and reserve outfielder George Foster entered the game as a pinch runner. Denis Menke then singled, moving Foster to second base. Bob Moose replaced the shaken Guisti to face Geronimo, who flied out to Roberto Clemente in right field. That catch would be the last putout in Clemente's legendary career. He was killed in a plane crash on December 31, 1972.

Testing one of the great right field arms in the game, Foster tagged and scampered to third base. Chaney popped out to shortstop Gene Alley. Anderson sent Hal McRae to pinch-hit for Carroll. Then, in one of the famous moments in team history, a moment that is captured in bronze at the Reds Hall of Fame, Moose threw a wild pitch, and Foster raced home to score the pennant-winning run. A season that had started with a controversial trade and a strike was capped for Reds fans by the team's second National League pennant in three years.

The Reds went on to lose the World Series in seven games to the Oakland Athletics. All four losses were by one run. There was no doubt that the retooled Big Red Machine was destined for better days ahead.

Pittsburgh	0	2	0	1	0	0	0	0	0	— 3	8	0
Cincinnati	0	0	1	0	1	0	0	0	2	— 4	7	1

Pittsburgh Pirates

	AB	R	H	RBI
Stennett lf	4	0	1	0
Oliver cf	3	0	0	0
Clemente rf	3	0	1	0
Stargell 1b	4	0	0	0
Robertson 1b	0	0	0	0
Sanguillen c	4	2	2	0
Hebner 3b	4	1	2	0
Cash 2b	4	0	2	2
Alley ss	4	0	0	0
Blass p	3	0	0	0
Hernandez p	0	0	0	0
Giusti p	0	0	0	0
Moose p	0	0	0	0
Totals	33	3	8	2

	IP	H	R	ER	BB	SO
Blass	7.1	4	2	2	2	4
Hernandez	0.2	0	0	0	0	1
Giusti L (0–1)	0.0	3	2	2	0	0
Moose	0.2	0	0	0	0	0
Totals	8.2	7	4	4	2	5

Cincinnati Reds

	AB	R	H	RBI
Rose lf	3	0	1	1
Morgan 2b	4	0	0	0
Tolan cf	4	0	0	0
Bench c	4	1	2	1
Perez 1b	4	0	1	0
Foster pr	0	1	0	0
Menke 3b	3	0	1	0
Geronimo rf	4	1	1	1
Chaney ss	4	1	1	0
Gullett p	0	0	0	0
Borbon p	0	0	0	0
Uhlaender ph	1	0	0	0
Hall p	0	0	0	0
Hague ph	0	0	0	0
Concepcion pr	0	0	0	0
Carroll p	0	0	0	0
McRae ph	0	0	0	0
Totals	31	4	7	3

	IP	H	R	ER	BB	SO
Gullett	3.0	6	3	3	0	2
Borbon	2.0	1	0	0	0	1
Hall	3.0	1	0	0	1	4
Carroll W (1–1)	1.0	0	0	0	0	0
Totals	9.0	8	3	3	1	7

Umpires: Augie Donatelli, John Kibler, Harry Wendelstedt, Ken Burkhart, Bill Williams, Doug Harvey.

Time of game: 2:19.

Attendance: 41,887.

#5

REDS 10, CHICAGO WHITE SOX 5
OCTOBER 9, 1919

Tainted Title

On a chilly, windy Chicago day in October 1919, Reds pitcher Hod Eller knew what he had to do—beat the White Sox in Game Eight of the World Series, which would give the Reds their first league championship since 1882 and their first world championship.

The Reds led the best-of-nine series four games to three but had lost the previous two games. They'd come into the series as underdogs, but had surprised the baseball world by winning four of the first five games. The experienced White Sox, however, had mounted a comeback. World champions in 1917, the White Sox weren't ready to quit yet.

In his third major-league season, 24-year-old Eller had hurled his shine ball to a 19–9 record and 2.39 ERA. He'd even thrown a no-hitter in May. A controversial pitch, the shine ball required rubbing one side of a ball to a smooth surface, while roughing up the other side. To aid the smoothing, a pitcher put a dab of paraffin wax on his uniform and rubbed the ball against it. The rough-smooth mix gave the ball unpredictable movement, making it very tough to hit. The key to success was controlling the pitch, as well as throwing it with enough velocity. Not many pitchers could do it successfully, but the few who mastered it were, at times, unhittable, leading an outcry to ban the pitch. The best shine baller in the majors was White Sox ace Eddie Cicotte, but Eller was not far behind. He felt confident that he'd beat the White Sox and the Reds would be, at last, world champions.

Doormats through much of the 1910s, the Reds rose to fourth in 1917 and third in 1918. By 1919, they were poised to win the National League pennant. Led by Hall of Fame center fielder Edd Roush, one of the most feared hitters in the game, third baseman Heinie Groh, and first baseman Jake Daubert, the team could score runs. But pitching was their strength. Youngsters Eller and Dutch Ruether dominated the league that season, while veteran Slim Sallee led the staff with 21 wins. With a 96–44 record, the best in the majors, the Reds took the league flag by a nine-game margin.

The White Sox won the American League pennant by 3½ games over the Cleveland Indians with an 88–52 record. Following their 1917 World Series championship, they suffered a terrible season, but had bounced back on the arms of Cicotte (who won 29 games that year) and Lefty Williams, as well as on the bats of outfielder Shoeless Joe Jackson and second baseman Eddie Collins.

When the series opened on October 1 at Redland Field in Cincinnati, the betting money favored the White Sox, in part because American League teams had won eight of the previous nine Fall Classics. It was clearly the stronger league. Why should this year be any different? And the White Sox were loaded with well-known stars who'd proven themselves in the postseason, while the Reds had not won a National League pennant since rejoining in 1890.

The Reds, however, lit up Cicotte in Game One, winning 9–1, and reeled off another three in a row. If the series had been the usual best-of-seven, it would have been over, but in hopes of recouping revenue lost in the shortened 1918 season (due to World War I), the series had been extended to best of nine. As the mighty South Siders lost game after game to the upstart Reds, rumors began to circulate that the fix was in. Gamblers swirled around baseball at the time, so much so that any oddball error or baserunning blunder could spark accusations. Before the season started, the Reds' own first baseman, Hal Chase, had been cleared of charges that he purposely helped lose some games in 1918. The Reds dealt him to the New York Giants, but his name would resurface in 1920 during the betting-conspiracy trial of Reds teammate Lee Magee. In retrospect, there is much evidence that players were consorting with, and being paid by, gamblers, while the teams and leagues looked the other way.

How the bet makers felt about Game Eight, of course, is unknown. While the White Sox had beaten the Reds two straight in Cincinnati, Eller on the mound boded well for his team. He'd tossed a three-hit shutout to win Game Five, besting Lefty Williams, whom he would face again in Game Eight that day. The White Sox clearly were now doing their best, even if they'd tanked for the gamblers in the first two games. In her book *Redlegs and Black Sox,* Susan Dellinger, the granddaughter of Roush, writes that her grandfather told her that Eller was approached the night before the game by gamblers offering him $10,000 to lose, which would set up a big final game. Eller, said Roush years later, told them he wasn't interested.

If Eller had wanted to blow the game, it wouldn't have been easy. The Reds scored four runs in the top of the first, sending Williams to the showers after retiring just one hitter. Back-to-back singles by Daubert and Groh, followed by back-to-back doubles from Roush and left fielder Pat Duncan, got things going for the Reds. Catcher Bill Rariden knocked in Duncan.

While Eller didn't dominate the White Sox as he'd done in Game Five, he kept them from scoring until Jackson's solo shot over the right field fence in the bottom of the third inning. After Greasy Neale knocked in shortstop Larry Kopf in the fifth inning, the Reds were well ahead at 6–1. In the sixth, they added three more runs on singles by Eller, Roush, and Duncan, a walk to second baseman Morrie Rath, and an error that allowed Daubert to reach base.

Leading 10–1 going into the bottom of the eighth, Eller started to wear out. Four hits and an error led to four runs for the White Sox. The 30,000 fans in the stands continued to roar, refusing to give up. They'd seen their team come from behind, and surely they would see it again. Throughout the series, White Sox manager Kid Gleason told reporters that the Reds had won by luck, not skill, and luck had a way of running out.

The White Sox mounted a final stand in the bottom of the ninth, and, with two out and runners on second and third, the great Jackson stepped to the plate. He amassed 12 hits in the series, a total that wouldn't be surpassed until 1964. His home run in the third inning was the best hit of the day off of Eller. If Jackson sent another one into the seats, the White Sox would creep to within two runs of a tie game. These thoughts likely occurred to Eller as he stood on the mound. Then he coaxed an easy ground ball from Jackson's bat to Rath at second. Rath fielded it and flipped to Daubert, giving the Reds their first world championship.

The Queen City went crazy. The euphoria lasted until September of the following year, when newspapers reported that an investigation was underway to prove that the series had been fixed. Eight White Sox players were put on trial; however, when their grand jury confessions mysteriously disappeared, they were acquitted in August 1921. In hopes of cleansing its tarnished reputation in the eyes of the fans, Major League Baseball banned the players for life.

For Hod Eller, the World Series victories were the high point of his career. The shine ball was banned in 1920, and he struggled to succeed without it. By 1922, he was out of the majors for good. Though the specific details of the fix have never fully come to light, the Reds' championship in 1919 remains tainted 100 years later.

| Cincinnati | 4 1 0 | 0 1 3 | 0 1 0 — 10 16 2 |
| Chicago | 0 0 1 | 0 0 0 | 0 4 0 — 5 10 1 |

Cincinnati Reds

	AB	R	H	RBI
Rath 2b	4	1	2	0
Daubert 1b	4	2	2	0
Groh 3b	6	2	2	0
Roush cf	5	2	3	4
Duncan lf	4	1	2	3
Kopf ss	3	1	1	0
Neale rf	3	0	1	1
Rariden c	5	0	2	2
Eller p	4	1	1	0
Totals	38	10	16	10

	IP	H	R	ER	BB	SO
Eller W (2–0)	9.0	10	5	4	1	6
Totals	9.0	10	5	4	1	6

Chicago White Sox

	AB	R	H	RBI
Leibold cf	5	0	1	0
Collins 2b	5	1	3	0
Weaver 3b	5	1	2	0
Jackson lf	5	2	2	3
Felsch rf	4	0	0	0
Gandil 1b	4	1	1	1
Risberg ss	3	0	0	0
Schalk c	4	0	1	0
Williams p	0	0	0	0
James p	2	0	0	0
Wilkinson p	1	0	0	0
Murphy ph	0	0	0	0
Totals	38	5	10	4

	IP	H	R	ER	BB	SO
Williams L (0–3)	0.1	4	4	4	0	0
James	4.2	8	4	3	3	2
Wilkinson	4.0	4	2	2	4	2
Totals	9.0	16	10	9	7	4

Umpires: HP—Dick Nallin (AL), 1B—Cy Rigler (NL), 2B—Jim Evans (AL), 3B—Ernie Quigley (NL).

Time of game: 2:27.

Attendance: 32,930.

#4

Sweep!

Hating the New York Yankees is a long and almost sacred tradition in Cincinnati.   It's probably fair to say that fans of most major-league teams share the sentiment, but Cincinnatians can point to the 1939 and 1961 World Series as particularly sore spots in their collective memory. A great Yankees team swept the Reds in 1939, when Reds catcher Ernie Lombardi took his famous "snooze" at home plate. In 1961, the Ragamuffin Reds managed only one victory against the Bronx Bombers. So when the Big Red Machine squared off against the American League champion Yankees in the 1976 World Series, this time it was, as the saying goes, personal.

That year all cylinders were firing on the Machine, as it rolled to a 102–60 record, taking the NL West Division title by a 10-game margin. It then rolled right over the East Division champion Philadelphia Phillies in a three-game sweep to win back-to-back pennants. With a mix of young players and veterans, speed and power, pitching, hitting, and fielding, the Reds really had no rival. The Great Eight had never been greater, led by Most Valuable Player Joe Morgan, and the mound crew stayed relatively healthy for a change. As the World Series got underway, starters Don Gullett, Gary Nolan, Jack Billingham, and Pat Zachry were all available.

The Yankees, however, had an MVP of their own in catcher Thurman Munson, who anchored a potent offense that featured slugging infielders Graig Nettles and Chris Chambliss and speedy outfielders Roy White and Mickey Rivers. Jim "Catfish" Hunter, the first player to sign a major-league free agent contract, topped an effective rotation, while Sparky Lyle was considered one of the game's best relievers. Led by feisty manager Billy Martin, the boys in pinstripes had grabbed the American League pennant.

Winning the World Series was no easy task for the Reds, but unlike the 1939 and 1961 National League champions, they were not a surprise upstart bunch that everybody figured would be kicked to the curb by the mighty Yankees. They were the reigning world champions and considered the better team. And they were determined to prove it when the series opened on October 16 in Cincinnati. Gullett surrendered just five hits in 7⅓ innings, as the Reds won 5–1. Too early yet to taste the sweet revenge, but Reds fans could smell it baking in the oven.

In Game Two, the Reds faced Hunter, who had beaten them twice in the 1972 series while pitching for the Oakland A's. Collecting 10 hits and four walks, the Reds bested him this time, winning 4–3. The two games in Cincinnati were the first in which a designated hitter was used in a National League ballpark, allowing manager Sparky Anderson to put hard-hitting reserve infielder Dan Driessen in the lineup.

When the teams moved to Yankee Stadium, the Big Red Machine continued to roll. Rookie of the Year Pat Zachry set down the Yanks, while the Reds battered Dock Ellis, knocking him out of the game in the fourth inning. With 13 hits, the Reds won 6–2, setting up a possible sweep in Game Four. Anderson picked Gary Nolan to start what could be the series-deciding game. Nolan led the rotation in wins (15) and innings (239⅓) that season. After years of arm issues, he'd been the workhorse. Martin chose 19-game winner Ed Figueroa to keep his team alive.

Determined to avoid a sweep, the Yankees took the lead in the bottom of the first inning, when Chambliss doubled to score Munson. The Reds responded in the fourth. Morgan opened the inning with a walk and then stole second base to put himself in scoring position for the big bats. Reds fans had seen the scenario unfold many times. "Little Joe," as he was fondly known, led the National League in on-base percentage (.444), walking 114 times. He also stole 60 bases and scored 113 runs.

Figueroa retired first baseman Tony Perez and then Driessen, but left fielder George Foster brought Morgan home with a single. Johnny Bench followed with a line shot over the left field wall, giving the Reds a 3–1 lead. Munson, however, was not ready to give up the fight. He and Bench were the premier catchers in the game, and the series gave them a rare opportunity to go head-to-head. Ferocious competitors, they made the most of it. Both played superb defense throughout the series. Bench, who would be chosen the series MVP, hit .533, including two home runs. Munson led the Yankees with a .529 average.

In the fifth inning, center fielder Mickey Rivers singled to right field. After White popped out to left, Munson came to the plate. Rivers stole second, and

Munson singled to center field to score him, tightening the Reds' lead to one run. It stayed right there until the top of the ninth. A tiring Figueroa walked Perez to start the inning, and then threw a wild pitch to Driessen, allowing Perez to take second base. After Driessen walked, Martin replaced his starter with Dick Tidrow. Foster launched a long fly to center field, where Rivers fielded it, but Perez moved to third. Bench then stepped in and smacked another home run, putting three more runs on the scoreboard. Center fielder Cesar Geronimo followed with a double, and shortstop Dave Concepcion doubled him in before Martin pulled Tidrow and put in Lyle, who got the final two outs.

Down 7–2 in the bottom of the ninth, the Yankees stared dejectedly from their dugout. Out of tricks, Martin sent pinch hitter Otto Velez to the plate to face Reds reliever Will McEnaney. Velez swung at strike three. Rivers then lined out to Rose at third base. White came to the plate, but fans were already filing out of Yankee Stadium. They'd seen enough. White knocked a can of corn into the outfield, where Foster grabbed it for the final out. The Reds had gotten their revenge—not only beating the Yankees but sweeping them, dominating them. The combined score of the four games was 22–8. The Reds were world champions once again.

Since the start of the league playoff system, no other team before or since has swept the postseason, a testament to the might of the Big Red Machine. After the final game, fans in Cincinnati flocked to Fountain Square to celebrate together. Soon enough they'd gather there again, braving a cold October day to salute their Reds, who had finally beaten the hated Yankees on the way to another world championship.

Cincinnati	0	0	0	3	0	0	0	0	4 — 7	9	2
New York	1	0	0	0	1	0	0	0	0 — 2	8	0

Cincinnati Reds

	AB	R	H	RBI
Rose 3b	5	0	1	0
Griffey rf	5	0	0	0
Morgan 2b	3	1	1	0
Perez 1b	3	1	0	0
Driessen dh	3	1	0	0
Foster lf	3	1	1	1
Bench c	4	2	2	5
Geronimo cf	4	1	2	0
Concepcion ss	3	0	2	1

	AB	R	H	RBI
Nolan p	0	0	0	0
McEnaney p	0	0	0	0
Totals	33	7	9	7

	IP	H	R	ER	BB	SO
Nolan W (1–0)	6.2	8	2	2	1	1
McEnaney SV (2)	2.1	0	0	0	1	1
Totals	9.0	8	2	2	2	2

New York Yankees

	AB	R	H	RBI
Rivers cf	5	1	1	0
White lf	5	0	0	0
Munson c	4	1	4	1
Chambliss 1b	4	0	1	1
May dh	3	0	0	0
Piniella ph, dh	1	0	0	0
Nettles 3b	3	0	2	0
Gamble rf	4	0	0	0
Randolph 2b	4	0	0	0
Stanley ss	1	0	0	0
Hendricks ph	1	0	0	0
Mason ss	0	0	0	0
Velez ph	1	0	0	0
Figueroa p	0	0	0	0
Tidrow p	0	0	0	0
Lyle p	0	0	0	0
Totals	36	2	8	2

	IP	H	R	ER	BB	SO
Figueroa L (0–1)	8.0	6	5	5	5	2
Tidrow	0.1	3	2	2	0	0
Lyle	0.2	0	0	0	0	0
Totals	9.0	9	7	7	5	2

Umpires: Bill Deegan (AL), Bruce Froemming (NL), Dave Phillips (AL), Lee Weyer (NL), Bill Williams (NL), Lou DiMuro (AL).

Time of game: 2:36.

Attendance: 56,700.

#3

REDS 2, OAKLAND ATHLETICS 1
OCTOBER 20, 1990

Wire to Wire

When the Reds met the Oakland A's in the 1972 World Series, they were picked to win it. The heavy-hitting Big Red Machine was expected to roll right over the A's. Didn't happen that way.

Oakland won the series four games to three due to superb pitching and timely, aggressive offense. When the franchises met again in 1990, the roles were reversed. The A's sported the big lumber, with a lineup that included the Bash Brothers (Mark McGwire and Jose Canseco) and Hall of Famer Ricky Henderson. They were heavily favored to beat the lighter-hitting Reds, who did boast superb pitching, with the likes of starters Jose Rijo, Danny Jackson, and Tom Browning backed by a bullpen trio known as the Nasty Boys—Randy Myers, Rob Dibble, and Norm Charlton.

The A's won 102 games that season, more than any team in the major leagues, to take their third straight American League pennant. They were reigning world champions, having swept the San Francisco Giants in the 1989 series. The Reds found themselves in the postseason due mostly to a fast start. After midseason they'd been little more than a .500 team. Led by fiery new manager Lou Piniella, the team played aggressively, always looking to take an extra base, and they played great defense. In their drive to the pennant, the Reds had gone wire to wire and had beaten a strong Pittsburgh team to make it to the World Series, but surely they'd offer little resistance to the awesome A's. At least that's what most media experts predicted.

And as most baseball fans of a certain age know, the experts were decidedly wrong. The series did end up being a lopsided affair, but not in the way everyone expected. Game One featured one of the most exhilarating moments in Reds history, when center fielder Eric Davis homered off A's ace Dave Stewart, one

205

of the most feared pitchers in the game, in the first inning. The home run sent a message: we're here to win. And they did win the opener, 7–0. In Game Two, the Reds came back to win with catcher Joe Oliver's clutch hit in the 10th inning to score Billy Bates. Game Three was a cakewalk, as the Reds scored seven runs in the third inning and coasted to an easy victory. Game Four would determine if the Reds could sweep the A's and win their first world championship since 1976.

Played in Oakland on a Saturday, the game featured a rematch of Game One starters Stewart and Rijo. The first inning didn't bode well for the Reds. Center fielder Billy Hatcher, who was hitting .750 in the series, took an inside fastball on his left hand. An inning later he left the game. In the bottom of the first inning, left fielder Eric Davis, after diving for a short fly ball off the bat of right fielder Willie McGee, landed hard on the grass, bruising a kidney. After the inning, he was rushed to a hospital for X-rays. Reds fans—and probably Reds players too—had to wonder if the team could win the game without two of their best hitters. And such serious injuries likely meant Hatcher and Davis were done for the series. Could the mighty A's stage a comeback against the crippled Reds?

With a 1–0 lead, Stewart faced replacement left fielder Glenn Braggs leading off the second inning. Although no match for All-Star Davis, Braggs was a solid hitter and one of the most physically powerful players in the game. While swinging at a high fastball—and missing—Braggs whipped the bat around so hard that it broke across his back. The moment has become legendary in team history, and it sent a message, like Davis's home run in Game One. The Reds were still strong, and they were here to win.

Struggling with his control early in the game, Rijo managed to keep the A's from scoring again. Stewart seemed to have little trouble shutting down the Reds, and Rijo started handling A's hitters just as easily. As the eighth inning began, both starters remained on the mound, and the score remained 1–0. The Reds needed to find a way to take the lead—not a simple task. When leading after five innings, the A's were 73–3 during the 1990 season. Coming back on them was, obviously, darn near impossible.

Shortstop Barry Larkin led off the eighth inning with a single to center field. Herm Winningham, who had replaced Hatcher, dropped down a bunt and beat the throw to first. Right fielder Paul O'Neill also bunted, hoping to move the runners. Stewart rushed from the mound and grabbed the ball but unleashed a bad throw, allowing O'Neill to reach first and load the bases.

Braggs then shot a grounder to shortstop Mike Gallego, who, realizing he couldn't nail the fleet Larkin at the plate, opted for the force out at second base. Larkin scored, and the Reds had tied the game. With Winningham on third base, designated hitter Hal Morris launched a deep fly to right field, where

McGee caught it but had no chance to get Winningham, who scored the go-ahead run. The Reds had come back to take a 2–1 lead.

Rijo set down the A's in order in the bottom of the inning. He'd retired 19 consecutive batters, not allowing a base runner since walking Ricky Henderson in the second inning. Stewart answered by retiring the Reds in order in the top of the ninth. The Reds needed just three more outs to finish a stunning sweep and become world champions.

Rijo, however, would have to face the heart of the A's batting order. First up: center fielder Dave Henderson, a tough hitter. Running on fumes at this point in the game, Rijo managed to punch out Henderson on a called third strike. Piniella then went to his bullpen, calling on Randy Myers to face Jose Canseco, batting for Harold Baines. Canseco had hit 37 home runs and knocked in 101 runs during the season. A's manager Tony LaRussa obviously hoped to tie the game with one swing. Instead, Canseco knocked a weak grounder to third baseman Chris Sabo, who threw to first for out no. 2. Third baseman Carney Lansford stepped into the box, Oakland's last hope. That hope fizzled when he popped up into foul territory, where first baseman Todd Benzinger caught the ball and immediately jumped into the air. The Reds were world champs.

Reds players dashed onto the field to relish the moment, while stunned Oakland fans slowly filed out of the stadium. The Reds had proven the experts wrong and, nearly 20 years later, avenged the loss in the 1972 series. In the locker room, champagne-soaked players celebrated. They praised their teammate Davis, who was recovering in the hospital. His home run in the first inning of Game One had set the tone of the series. Following his lead, the wire-to-wire Reds had gone all the way to the top.

| Cincinnati | 0 0 0 | 0 0 0 | 0 2 0 — 2 7 1 |
| Oakland | 1 0 0 | 0 0 0 | 0 0 0 — 1 2 1 |

Cincinnati Reds

	AB	R	H	RBI
Larkin ss	3	1	1	0
Hatcher cf	0	0	0	0
Winningham cf	3	1	2	0
O'Neill rf	3	0	0	0
Davis lf	0	0	0	0
Braggs ph, lf	3	0	0	1
Morris dh	3	0	0	0
Sabo 3b	4	0	3	0

	AB	R	H	RBI		
Benzinger 1b	4	0	0	0		
Oliver c	4	0	1	0		
Duncan 2b	4	0	0	0		
Rijo p	0	0	0	0		
Myers p	0	0	0	0		
Totals	31	2	7	2		

	IP	H	R	ER	BB	SO
Rijo W (2–0)	8.1	2	1	1	3	9
Myers SV (1)	0.2	0	0	0	0	0
Totals	9.0	0	0	0	0	0

Oakland Athletics

	AB	R	H	RBI		
Henderson R. lf	3	0	0	0		
McGee rf	4	1	1	0		
Henderson D. cf	4	0	0	0		
Baines dh	2	0	0	0		
Canseco ph, dh	1	0	0	0		
Lansford 3b	4	0	1	1		
Quirk c	3	0	0	0		
McGwire 1b	3	0	0	0		
Randolph 2b	3	0	0	0		
Gallego ss	1	0	0	0		
Hassey ph	1	0	0	0		
Bordick ss	0	0	0	0		
Stewart p	0	0	0	0		
Totals	29	1	2	1		

	IP	H	R	ER	BB	SO
Stewart L (0–2)	9.0	7	2	1	2	2
Totals	9.0	7	2	1	2	2

Umpires: Ted Hendry (AL), Randy Marsh (NL), Bruce Froemming (NL),
Frank Pulli (NL), Jim Quick (NL), Rocky Roe (AL).

Time of game: 2:48.

Attendance: 48,613.

#2

This Time There's No Denying

The Reds began the 1940 season as the defending National League champions. They'd been swept handily by the New York Yankees in the 1939 World Series, however, and the team still felt it had something to prove. Of the 10 major-league cities in that year, only Cincinnati lacked an undisputed world championship. Fairly or not, the 1919 team's victory will always be tainted by the infamous Black Sox gambling scandal. After a bleak decade of losing, the franchise also wanted to show the baseball world that their pennant had not been a fluke, that they were, indeed, the league's best team.

The core of the 1939 team remained intact, but the Reds did make some improvements. They added rookie outfielder Mike McCormick (no relation to All-Star first baseman Frank McCormick) and 36-year-old journeyman pitcher Jim Turner, as well as reliever Joe Beggs. In August, they acquired outfielder Jimmy Ripple to man left field, allowing McCormick to move to center. The star position players—catcher Ernie Lombardi, first baseman McCormick, right fielder Ival Goodman, and third baseman Billy Werber—all returned. And they were led once again by the dynamic pitching duo of Bucky Walters and Paul Derringer.

With such a strong cast, the Reds won 100 games in 1940, the first time a Reds team had reached the century mark, and handily took the National League flag, 12 games in front of second-place Brooklyn. The season was not without a significant loss, however. On August 3, backup catcher Willard Hershberger committed suicide while the team was in Boston. Manager Bill McKechnie rallied the team, dedicating the Reds' efforts to winning the pennant and the World Series for Hershberger. Coach Jimmy Wilson was activated to be the backup catcher.

The Detroit Tigers had a tough time winning the American League pennant, squeaking past Cleveland by one game with a 90–64 record. Led by future Hall of Famers Hank Greenberg and Charlie Gehringer, the Tigers had a potent lineup. Their veteran pitching staff included 21-game-winner Bobo Newsom and Schoolboy Rowe. The teams looked evenly matched, though the National League had not won a World Series since 1934, and many sportswriters expected that streak to continue.

Newsom beat the Reds in the first game of the series, only to learn that night that his father had died suddenly. The series developed into a seesaw battle, with the teams taking turns winning. After dropping the first game, the Reds won the second behind Bucky Walters, then lost the third game, won Game Four, lost the fifth game, and won the sixth as Walters hurled a shutout.

Game Seven would be the final showdown. Derringer faced Newsom at sold-out Crosley Field. Newsom had already beaten the Reds twice in the series, including a shutout in Game Five just two days before. Derringer had lost Game One, managing to last only 1⅓ innings, while giving up five runs. He redeemed himself in Game Four, throwing a five-hit complete-game victory. As fans settled into their seats, surely some realized that this game was as important as any in Reds history. A victory would finally bring to the city its first untainted world championship.

Derringer and Newsom got through the first two innings easily. In the top of the third, Tigers catcher Billy Sullivan led off with a single. Newsom sacrificed him to second base. After a popout and a walk, Gehringer grounded to Werber at third in what should have ended the inning, but Werber's wild throw allowed Sullivan to score, giving the Tigers a 1–0 lead. Reds fans must have wondered if one run was all Bobo needed.

If Dehringer had the same idea, he didn't show it. A big guy with an equally big personality, he helped give the Reds of that era a tough but fun-loving identity. He held the Tigers scoreless as the game progressed. By the bottom of the seventh, the score remained 1–0. Frank McCormick led off the inning with a double to left field. Ripple followed with a double to right. McCormick hesitated, unsure if the ball would be caught. By the time he started running, it wasn't clear if he could make it to home. But amid the din of screaming fans, shortstop Dick Bartell was unable to hear his teammates, so his relay throw went to second base. With no outs, the throw probably was the smart move. A throw to the plate might not have beaten McCormick and would have allowed the go-ahead run to reach third base. In his book *The Underrated Reds*, author Leo Bradley quotes Reds players saying just that.

Catcher Jimmy Wilson sacrificed Ripple to third, bringing up Lombardi, who had not started the game because of an ankle injury. Hoping to push another run in, McKechnie tapped the slugging Lombardi to pinch-hit for second baseman Eddie Joost. Newsom walked Lombardi intentionally. Shortstop Billy Myers then launched a long fly to deep center field. Reds fans jumped to their feet, hoping the ball would clear the fence, but it fell just short—and into Barney McCosky's glove. But Ripple tagged up and easily crossed the plate for the go-ahead run.

Neither team scored in the eighth, meaning that Derringer and the Reds were just three outs from the long-awaited world championship. He quickly induced two ground outs, bringing up pinch hitter (and future Hall of Famer) Earl Averill. At 38, Averill was at the end of his career, appearing mostly as a pinch hitter for the Tigers in 1940. He shot a grounder to second baseman Lonnie Frey, who tossed it to McCormick at first, and the Reds players and fans went wild. Despite featuring two tired pitchers, the game lasted just an hour and 47 minutes.

The city celebrated like never before. Thousands gathered at Fountain Square. A streetcar was pushed off its track. Downtown bars overflowed with fans toasting their world champions long into the night. McCormick would win the Most Valuable Player award that year, giving the Reds three in a row, following Lombardi in 1938 and Bucky Walters the next year. The future looked bright for the team, and the next couple of years did offer many wins, but no championships. Cincinnati would have to wait until 1975 to achieve another one.

Detroit	0	0	1	0	0	0	0	0	0 — 1	7	0
Cincinnati	0	0	0	0	0	0	2	0	x — 2	7	1

Detroit Tigers

	AB	R	H	RBI
Bartell ss	4	0	0	0
McCosky cf	3	0	0	0
Gehringer 2b	4	0	2	0
Greenberg lf	4	0	2	0
York 1b	4	0	0	0
Campbell rf	3	0	0	0
Higgins 3b	4	0	1	0
Sullivan c	3	1	1	0
Newsom p	2	0	1	0
Averill ph	1	0	0	0
Totals	32	1	7	0

	IP	H	R	ER	BB	SO
Newsom L (2–1)	8.0	7	2	2	1	6
Totals	8.0	7	2	2	1	6

Cincinnati Reds

	AB	R	H	RBI
Werber 3b	4	0	0	0
McCormick M. cf	4	0	2	0
Goodman rf	4	0	0	0
McCormick F. 1b	4	1	1	0
Ripple lf	3	1	1	1
Wilson c	2	0	2	0
Joost 2b	2	0	0	0
Lombardi ph	0	0	0	0
Frey pr, 2b	0	0	0	0
Myers ss	3	0	1	1
Derringer p	3	0	0	0
Totals	29	2	7	2

	IP	H	R	ER	BB	SO
Derringer W (2–1)	9.0	7	1	0	3	1
Totals	9.0	7	1	0	3	1

Umpires: HP—Lee Ballanfant (NL), 1B—Steve Basil (AL), 2B—Bill Klem (NL), 3B—Red Ormsby (AL).

Time of game: 1:47.

Attendance: 26,854.

#1

REDS 4, BOSTON RED SOX 3
OCTOBER 22, 1975

Champions at Last

Ask a knowledgeable baseball fan to name the best World Series, and the 1975 series between the Reds and the Boston Red Sox surely will be among those mentioned. It's often credited for revitalizing interest in the national pastime. Two great teams going head to head through seven very competitive contests. Five of the games were decided by one run; in four of the games, the winning run was scored in the winning team's final at bat.

After many years, the best remembered moment of the series remains Carlton Fisk's game-winning home run in the 12th inning of Game Six. That hit, and Fisk's "waving" it fair as he skipped down the first-base line, has been shown countless times on television. An iconic image we've all seen. *Sports Illustrated,* in their book titled *Baseball's Greatest,* chose the game as the greatest of all time. Younger fans might not even realize that the home run didn't win the series for Boston. It simply forced the series to a Game Seven. And for Reds fans, Game Seven is the one we must consider truly great. In fact, we have chosen it as the greatest game in team history.

Looking back on the Big Red Machine era, most fans only remember—or know about—the team's success. Today's tales of the team's greatness rarely note the frustration many fans felt at the time. By 1975, the Machine had lost two World Series—in 1970 and 1972. The first one was somewhat under-standable because the rotation was decimated by injuries, but the Reds had been favored to beat the Oakland A's in 1972 and fallen short. The next year the Reds were clearly the National League's best team, and yet they lost in the National League Championship Series to a New York Mets team that barely finished .500. In 1974, the Reds won 98 games, but lost the West Division title to the Los Angeles Dodgers. By 1975, the team was starting to age. Baseball fans and writers had begun to wonder openly if the Big Red Machine would be the greatest team never to win a world championship. Blowing a late lead to lose Game Six added even more pressure.

Given the Red Sox's thrilling comeback victory the night before, the fans that filled Fenway Park on the night of October 22 must have felt that the American Leaguers possessed the momentum. The Reds had blown a three-run lead in the eighth inning and lost. Surely there would be a carryover into Game Seven. Reds radio broadcaster Marty Brennaman later told *The Sporting News*, "[Manager] Sparky [Anderson] was convinced they weren't going to win it."

The starting pitchers were both lefties—Bill "Spaceman" Lee for the Red Sox and Don Gullett for the Reds—and both held the opposition scoreless for the first two innings. In the bottom of the third inning, first baseman Carl Yastrzemski singled to score left fielder Bernie Carbo, who had walked and then gone to third base on a single by second baseman Denny Doyle. Gullett walked Carlton Fisk intentionally, loading the bases, before striking out center fielder Fred Lynn. Then Gullett walked third baseman Rico Petrocelli, pushing Doyle across the plate. Then he walked right fielder Dwight Evans, pushing in Yaz. Gullett's control meltdown looked, to many fans, like a sign that the Reds were feeling the pressure of the Game Six defeat.

A single and a stolen base by Joe Morgan in the top of the fourth inning came to nothing, and when Lee led off in the bottom half, he hit a single into right field. Gullett threw a wild pitch that allowed Lee to take second base. He ended the inning standing right there, but Gullett still looked shaky to Reds fans, who were happy to see him stand down for pinch hitter Merv Rettenmund with two out in the fifth. They were less pleased when Rettenmund grounded into a double play to end the inning.

Jack Billingham, the senior member of the Reds rotation, took the mound. A long and lanky right-hander, "Cactus Jack" lacked dominant stuff, but seemed to find ways to win. He had been the team's most reliable pitcher since coming to Cincinnati as part of the November 1971 trade that brought Joe Morgan from the Houston Astros. In the fifth, Billingham walked two and allowed a single to Petrocelli, but kept Boston from scoring. Reds fans held their collective breath when Lee launched a fly to deep center field, but Cesar Geronimo caught it for the third out.

Pete Rose led off the sixth with a single to right field. After Morgan flied out, Bench grounded to shortstop Rick Burleson, who flipped the ball to Doyle at second base in what appeared to be an easy double play. But Rose slid hard into Doyle, who then threw the ball out of play, allowing Bench to make it to first safely. Minutes later he would score when Tony Perez jacked a "Spaceman"

Lee blooper pitch out of the park. Lee had used the pitch successfully on Perez earlier in the series, striking him out twice with it, but this time Perez timed his swing perfectly.

After Billingham set down the Sox in order in the bottom of the inning, the Reds came to bat looking to even the score. With one out, Lee walked Ken Griffey, and Red Sox manager Darrell Johnson called in reliever Roger Moret, who coaxed a weak popout from Geronimo. Ed Armbrister stepped up to pinch-hit for Billingham; during Armbrister's at bat, Griffey stole second base. Moret proceeded to walk Armbrister, bringing up Rose and the top of the order. Rose promptly popped a single into center field, scoring Griffey to tie the game at 3–3. When Moret walked Morgan to load the bases, he was replaced by Jim Willoughby. Bench popped out to Fisk to end the inning. While they'd missed the chance for a big rally, the Reds had tied the game.

Reliever Clay Carroll took the mound for the Reds. A ferocious competitor, Carroll, at 34, might have been past his physical prime, but he knew how to get outs. After walking right fielder Dwight Evans to open the inning, he induced a double play and then retired pinch hitter Cecil Cooper to preserve the tie. Jim Burton came in to face the Reds in the top of the ninth. He started out by walking Griffey, who moved to second base on Geronimo's sacrifice bunt. Griffey went to third when pinch hitter Dan Driessen grounded out to Doyle.

Pete Rose then worked a walk. It was the 17th time in his last 27 appearances in the World Series in which he reached base. Morgan followed by blooping a low-and-away pitch safely into center field, scoring Griffey. The Reds had come back to take a 4–3 lead.

Young Will McEnaney was charged with holding it. At 23, McEnaney was the baby of the bullpen, but had saved 15 games that season and made 70 appearances, posting a 2.47 ERA. A native of Springfield, Ohio, he'd grown up rooting for the Reds. Now he had the chance to earn the save that would give the Reds their first world championship in 35 years.

Johnson sent in Juan Beniquez to pinch-hit, but he flied harmlessly to Griffey in right. Bob Montgomery then pinch-hit for Doyle and grounded out to Concepcion at shortstop. With two out, the batter was, fittingly, Yastrzemski. The long-time "face of the franchise," Yaz offered Boston's final hope for another improbable comeback. But tonight was a different night, and this time there wouldn't be one. Instead, Yastrzemski lofted a lazy fly into center field, where Geronimo snagged it easily before leaping into the air.

Reds players mobbed each other on the field as Boston's faithful watched in silence. No one knew at the time that Game Six would live on in baseball history, or that this game, which determined the winner, would be overshadowed.

Reds players and fans, however, remember it well. After the defeats in the 1970 and 1972, the victory was especially sweet for the veteran players. The Big Red Machine finally could claim a world championship and truly be considered one of the greatest teams of all time.

Cincinnati	0 0 0	0 0 2	1 0 1	— 4 9 0
Boston	0 0 3	0 0 0	0 0 0	— 3 5 2

Cincinnati Reds

	AB	R	H	RBI
Rose 3b	4	0	2	1
Morgan 2b	4	0	2	1
Bench c	4	1	0	0
Perez 1b	5	1	1	2
Foster lf	4	0	1	0
Concepcion ss	4	0	1	0
Griffey rf	2	2	1	0
Geronimo cf	3	0	0	0
Gullett p	1	0	1	0
Rettenmund ph	1	0	0	0
Billingham p	0	0	0	0
Armbrister ph	0	0	0	0
Carroll p	0	0	0	0
Driessen ph	1	0	0	0
McEnaney p	0	0	0	0
Totals	33	4	9	4

	IP	H	R	ER	BB	SO
Gullett	4.0	4	3	3	5	5
Billingham	2.0	1	0	0	2	1
Carroll W (1–0)	2.0	0	0	0	1	1
McEnaney SV (1)	1.0	0	0	0	0	0
Totals	9.0	5	3	3	8	7

Boston Red Sox

	AB	R	H	RBI
Carbo lf	3	1	1	0
Miller lf	0	0	0	0
Beniquez ph	1	0	0	0
Doyle 2b	4	1	1	0
Montgomery ph	1	0	0	0
Yastrzemski 1b	5	1	1	1
Fisk c	3	0	0	0
Lynn cf	2	0	0	0
Petrocelli 3b	3	0	1	1
Evans rf	2	0	0	1
Burleson ss	3	0	0	0
Lee p	3	0	1	0
Moret p	0	0	0	0
Willoughby p	0	0	0	0
Cooper ph	1	0	0	0
Burton p	0	0	0	0
Cleveland p	0	0	0	0
Totals	31	3	5	3

	IP	H	R	ER	BB	SO
Lee	6.1	7	3	3	1	2
Moret	0.1	1	0	0	2	0
Willoughby	1.1	0	0	0	0	0
Burton L (0–1)	0.2	1	1	1	2	0
Cleveland	0.1	0	0	0	1	0
Totals	9.0	9	4	4	6	2

Umpires: Art Frantz (AL), Nick Colosi (NL), Larry Barnett (AL), Dick
  Stello (NL), Satch Davidson (NL), George Maloney (AL).
Time of game: 2:52.
Attendance: 35,205.

Bibliography

Fans of Reds history are lucky to have such a deep well of sources to consult for information about the team's 150-year legacy. Perhaps more than anyone, team historian Greg Rhodes deserves the most gratitude, having written a number of outstanding, well-researched books on Reds history. To write *Classic Reds*, we relied on the sources listed below. Direct quotations and specific references are noted within the text.

Websites

Baseball Almanac. http://www.baseball-almanac.com
Baseball Reference. https://www.baseball-reference.com
Society for American Baseball Research. https://sabr.org
Sports Illustrated. https://www.si.com/

Newspapers and Periodicals

The Cincinnati Enquirer
The Cincinnati Post
The Sporting Life
The Sporting News

Books

Allen, Lee. *The Cincinnati Reds.* 1948. Repr. Kent, OH: Kent State Univ. Press, 2006.

Bradley, Leo H. *The Underrated Reds: The Story of the 1939–1940 Cincinnati Reds, the Team's First Undisputed Championship.* Owensville, OH: Fried Publishing, 2009.

Brosnan, Jim. *Pennant Race.* New York: Harper and Brothers, 1962.

Browning, Tom, with Don Stupp. *Tales from the Reds Dugout: A Collection of the Greatest Reds Stories Ever Told.* Champaign, IL: Sports Publishing, 2006.

Collett, Ritter. *The Cincinnati Reds: A Pictorial History of Professional Baseball's Oldest Team.* Virginia Beach, VA: Jordan-Powers, 1976.

———. *Men of the Reds Machine: An Inside Look at Baseball's Team of the '70's.* Dayton, OH: Landfall Press, 1977.

Dellinger, Susan. *Red Legs and Black Sox: Edd Roush and the Untold Story of the 1919 World Series.* Cincinnati, OH: Emmis Books, 2006.

Erardi, John, and Joel Luckhaupt. *The Wire-to-Wire Reds: Sweet Lou, Nasty Boys, and the Wild Run to a World Championship.* Cincinnati, OH: Clerisy Press, 2010.

Guschov, Stephen D. *The Red Stockings of Cincinnati: Baseball's First All-Professional Team.* Jefferson, NC: McFarland, 1998.

Heffron, Joe, and Jack Heffron. *The Local Boys: Hometown Players for the Cincinnati Reds.* Birmingham, AL: Clerisy Press, 2014.

Neyer, Rob, and Eddie Epstein. *Baseball Dynasties: The Greatest Teams of All Time.* New York: W. W. Norton, 2000.

Rhodes, Greg. *Cincinnati Reds Hall of Fame Highlights.* Cincinnati, OH: Clerisy Press, 2007.

Rhodes, Greg, and John Erardi. *Cincinnati's Crosley Field: The Illustrated History of a Classic Ballpark.* Cincinnati, OH: Road West Publishing, 1995.

———. *The First Boys of Sumer: The 1869–1870 Cincinnati Red Stockings, Baseball's First Professional Team.* Cincinnati, OH: Road West Publishing, 1994.

Rhodes, Greg, and John Snyder. *Redleg Journal: Year by Year and Day by Day with the Cincinnati Reds Since 1866.* Cincinnati, OH: Road West Publishing, 2000.

Schmetzer, Mark J. *Before the Machine: The Story of the 1961 Pennant-Winning Cincinnati Reds.* Cincinnati, OH: Clerisy Press, 2011.

Schmetzer, Mark J., and Joe Jacobs. *The Comeback Kids: Cincinnati Reds—2010 Championship Season.* Cincinnati, OH: Clerisy Press, 2010.